The Solution of Social Problems

The Solution
of Social Problems
Five Perspectives

Second Edition

Edited by

MARTIN S. WEINBERG
EARL RUBINGTON
SUE KIEFER HAMMERSMITH

New York   Oxford
OXFORD UNIVERSITY PRESS
1981

Library of Congress Cataloging in Publication Data

Weinberg, Martin S   comp.
  The solution of social problems.

  Bibliography: p.
  1. Social problems—Addresses, essays, lectures.
I. Rubington, Earl, joint comp.   II. Hammersmith,
Sue Kiefer, joint comp.   III. Title.
HN18.W395 1981   361.1   80-14421
ISBN 0-19-502787-6

6 5 4 3 2

Printed in the United States of America.

Preface

The companion to this book, *The Study of Social Problems,* describes five perspectives sociologists have used in seeking to conceptualize and understand social problems.[1] In this book we go on to consider the implications of each perspective for the solution of social problems. In the text, we review the development and characteristics of the five perspectives and outline their implications for solving social problems. Each perspective is then illustrated by readings that describe proposed or attempted solutions to various social problems. These readings cover a wide assortment of problems of special interest to today's students—among them racism, sexism, poverty, drug addiction and alcoholism, delinquency, marihuana use, and homosexuality.

In this second edition of *The Solution of Social Problems,* the text has been completely rewritten and simplified with the undergraduate student in mind. The perspectives are illustrated by an updated set of readings. And the book has been shortened to facilitate its use as a supplementary text.

Bloomington	M.S.W.
Boston	E.R.
Indianapolis	S.K.H.
May 1980	

---

1. Earl Rubington and Martin S. Weinberg, *The Study of Social Problems: Five Perspectives,* 3rd edition (New York: Oxford University Press, 1981).

Contents

I / THE PROBLEM

1 / SOCIAL PROBLEMS AND THEIR SOLUTION

Social problems confront us everywhere. Pollution, poverty, crime, corruption, discrimination, drug abuse, inefficient government, inflation, delinquency—the list goes on and on. Of course, what is a problem to one group may be completely acceptable to another, and what some people see as a commendable effort to solve a social problem, others may see as presenting even bigger problems. Consider abortion, for example. Right-to-Life sympathizers see legal abortion as an abomination and cry out for a Constitutional amendment to outlaw abortion. Supporters of legalized abortion, on the other hand, think such an amendment would do more harm than good; they talk about unwanted births, child abuse, unsafe criminal abortions, birth defects, and overpopulation. In their view, then, the Right-to-Life "solution" would create more problems than it would solve.

Needless to say, trying to solve social problems is a very complex business. Even if critics do agree that something is a social problem, they are likely to have very different opinions about what should be done to solve it. And many times a solution is attempted, only to give rise to a whole new spate of problems.

As we noted in an earlier book, the field of sociology was originally developed in large part to understand and solve social problems.[1] Through the years, sociologists have developed several different ways of looking at social problems. These include different ways of identifying problems, of diagnosing their causes and consequences, and of formulating solutions to them. The different ways of approaching social problems are called *perspectives.* In

1. Earl Rubington and Martin S. Weinberg, *The Study of Social Problems: Five Perspectives* (New York: Oxford University Press, 1971).

this book, we review the five perspectives that have characterized most sociological work on social problems. We explore the type of solution that follows from each perspective, and we see assorted schemes of action that have been proposed or implemented in efforts to solve various social problems. First, though, we need to understand what is meant by the term *social problem.*

THE DEFINITION OF A SOCIAL PROBLEM

Most sociologists consider a social problem to be *an alleged situation that is incompatible with the values of a significant number of people who agree that action is needed to alter the situation.*[2] Let us consider this definition more closely.

An Alleged Situation.   The problematic situation is noticed, talked about, said to exist. Until this happens, the situation is not classified by most sociologists as a social problem. Consider the Watergate scandal, for example. As long as the web of domestic spying, abuse of power, and covering-up was unknown to the public, it was not classified as a social problem. Through newspaper exposés, the Congressional investigation, and the criminal prosecutions that followed in the Watergate case, however, the public gradually became informed of the situation. People began to talk about ongoing government corruption, abuse of power, and conspiracies. Once this happened, the situation escalated into a bona fide social problem.

Furthermore, if enough people think a problem exists, it can qualify as a social problem even if their shared belief is false. The witchcraft trials of Europe and New England attest to this point. The idea of witches may have been false, but the consequences of that idea were real enough![3] Since people believed witchcraft to be a problem requiring action, then we too consider it to have been a social problem for them—even though we view their belief in witchcraft as completely false.

---

2. Earl Rubington and Martin S. Weinberg, *The Study of Social Problems: Five Perspectives,* 3rd edition (New York: Oxford University Press, 1981).

3. In the widely quoted dictum of W. I. Thomas, "If men define situations as real, they are real in their consequences." W. I. Thomas and D. S. Thomas, *The Child in America; Behavior Problems and Programs* (New York: Knopf, 1928), p. 572.

Incompatible With Values. Situations come to be recognized as social problems because they are seen as threatening important values—e.g., moral standards, religious beliefs, or economic interests. Of course, different people have different values, and what is a social problem for one group may be perfectly all right with another group. Smoking serves as a good example. The antismoking faction consider it an affront to their freedom and health to have to breathe someone else's smoke, and they object to advertising that glorifies smoking and encourages young people to smoke. On the other hand, rumblings are heard about "smokers' rights," for example, to smoke on airplanes or to enjoy an after-dinner smoke in a restaurant. Moreover, cigarette producers view advertising restrictions as incompatible with our society's capitalistic values. Identifying a social problem, then, is often a complex matter and subject to considerable public debate.

A Significant Number of People. If a situation is considered a problem by only one or two people, it would not be classified as a social problem. But what is "a significant number"? There is no clear-cut answer because it is not just a matter of numbers. A good rule of thumb might be to consider a group or faction significant when they are able to make their presence felt by the rest of the society. In this regard, some people obviously are more "significant" than others. Adults, for example, are more significant than children in identifying social problems, and certain types of workers, such as journalists and politicians, are especially significant. As a rule, we would say that the people who are more significant in defining social problems are those who are organized or in leadership positions, and those who are economically, socially, or politically powerful.

Action is Needed. For something to emerge as a social problem, there must be a call for action—a demand that action be taken to improve the situation. If no one calls for action—if people are indifferent or believe the suffering to be inevitable—then most soclologists would not consider the situation to be a social problem, no matter how many people may be suffering. Discrimination against women, for example, emerged once more as a social problem when modern feminists organized, demanded change, and began to actively work for it. During the 1950s, by contrast, sexism was generally not considered as a social problem even though it was, objectively speaking, more pronounced than it is today.

SOLVING SOCIAL PROBLEMS

Identifying social problems and calling for action are quite different matters from actually designing and implementing programs to solve them. Calling attention to the problem, for example, can often be accomplished relatively quickly and easily. Trying to actually carry out a solution, by contrast, involves innumerable obstacles, delays, and frustrations, and demands immense dedication and perseverance. This is one reason why victims of the problem are sometimes the most effective allies in trying to solve it. They often understand the problem better than other people, and they have a level of commitment and dedication that is hard to come by among those who have never directly suffered from it. This is undoubtedly one of the reasons for the high success rates of self-help organizations such as Alcoholics Anonymous, Gamblers Anonymous, and Parents Anonymous (for parents who abuse their children).

Another important difference between defining a social problem and trying to solve it has to do with the difference between idealism and practicality. The definition of the problem is often couched in idealistic terms. The "threatened" values loom particularly large at this stage. Once people have agreed that indeed a particular situation is a problem, though, the concern with values and ideals is likely to subside as attention then turns to a possible solution. There is usually considerable conflict between what the *ideal* solution would be and what a *workable* solution may be. In addition, one may find important social forces working against efforts to correct the situation, even though everyone agrees the situation is a problem. It may become apparent that the solution involves costs as unacceptable as the original problem itself. Consider, for example, the current venereal disease epidemic. One proposed solution is to develop VD vaccines and then inoculate children as we now do for polio and whooping cough. This proposed solution was greeted with an outcry of public protest, however, as critics called it an outrageous affront to common decency and morality. Another example is found in the field of energy and pollution. Only a few years ago, industrial and power plants were encouraged to switch from coal to gas to cut down on air pollution. Yet, once the switch was made it became clear that the country faced gas and oil shortages, and plants were then urged to switch back to coal! In other words, eliminating the pollution problem by increased gas consumption may have been too great a price to pay.

Finally, the problem-defining and problem-solving stages may involve quite different personnel and machinery. Problems are often defined by journalists, religious leaders, or political or social activists. Once they have succeeded in calling attention to the problem and perhaps in initiating changes or programs aimed at solving the problem, there is a tendency for people in these roles to turn their attention to other problems and issues. After the slaves had been freed and given citizenship, for example, many former abolitionists turned their attention to stamping out polygamy among Utah's Mormons, to the evils of liquor, or to women's rights. Similarly, as the Vietnam War began to wane, many antiwar activists became active in the environmental movement. And for the journalist, there is always another story.

Who is left to continue dealing with the problem when the original leaders move on? Often the task falls to legislators, welfare agencies, or other parts of the government bureaucracy. In one sense this reflects the fact that problem-definition can be accomplished and finished, while problem-solving efforts must go on day after day, year after year. Because long-term programs, agencies, or organizations face unavoidable operational constraints, they may use procedures that help them operate smoothly but that do little to solve the problem they were designed to solve.

SOCIOLOGICAL PERSPECTIVES ON SOCIAL PROBLEMS

Perspectives are simply different ways of looking at things—in this case, different ways of viewing social problems. The same situation or event can be viewed from several perspectives, and often various groups have different or conflicting perspectives on the same social problem. Manufacturers, for example, view the problem of air pollution quite differently from people who live near industrial plants but do not directly profit from them. Similarly, unemployment is viewed quite differently by employers and laborers, and their solutions to the unemployment problem differ as well. As a rule, we can say that people's perspectives on social problems are tied to their political, economic, social, and ideological locations in the society.

Perspectives on social problems also vary historically. A given perspective may become quite popular at one point and then fade away with passing years, perhaps to be revived at a later date. Historical fluctuations are often linked with larger societal events (such as war) or with the ascending power of a particular group (such as feminists) in the society.

In the field of sociology, there have been five main perspectives on social problems: *social pathology, social disorganization, value conflict, deviant behavior,* and *labeling*. Each perspective defines the problem, what its causes and consequences are, and under what conditions it is likely to occur. In addition, each perspective suggests what actions should be taken to solve problems.

Definition.   Each perspective includes its own specialized definition of what is, in essence, the problem. The five perspectives focus on different aspects of the problematic situation and make different assumptions about the nature of people and society. Considering drug use, for example, one perspective might define the problem as reflecting "the moral decay of our society," while another might define it as simply too much "deviant behavior" on the part of individuals, and a third perspective might define the problem as lying not in the drug use itself but rather in the criminal sanctions that stigmatize drug users and alienate them from the rest of the society.

Causes.   Each perspective contains its own conceptual scheme for describing the immediate causes that precipitate social problems. In other words, different perspectives differ in where they lay the "blame" for social problems.

Conditions.   In addition to ideas about immediate causes of social problems, perspectives also contain notions about the underlying, background conditions out of which social problems are likely to arise and develop. These background conditions, which may be implicit or explicit in the perspective, are often tied to basic assumptions about human nature and social reality.

Consequences.   All five perspectives see social problems as harmful. They differ, however, in what they believe the harmful effects are and sometimes in whom or what they see as being hurt by the problem.

Solutions. Each perspective has a different approach to the solution of social problems. While some perspectives are more explicitly oriented toward reform than others, they all contain some notion about what a solution should accomplish and what actions might bring it about. Thus solutions are closely tied to how one defines the problem and what one sees as its major causes, conditions, and harmful effects. In keeping with their different conceptualizations of social problems, the solution suggested by one perspective often looks dramatically different from the solution suggested by another perspective, even though they may be directed toward the very same social problem. For this reason, some have complained that our problem is not too many social problems but too many attempted solutions!

It should be noted that not every possible solution necessarily reflects one of the five perspectives described in this book. Nonetheless, most of the solutions proposed by sociologists reflect one or a combination of these perspectives, as do many of the solutions advocated by politicians, writers, social activists, and others.

PLAN OF THE BOOK

Each of the following chapters presents a particular perspective on social problems.[4] We describe each perspective, review its historical development, and explore the type of solution it suggests. Selected readings illustrate how each perspective has been used in discussing a variety of social problems. The concluding chapter considers interrelationships among the perspectives and demonstrates how the perspectives are selected and in practice often intertwined in efforts to tackle the many problems facing our society.

---

4. Readers who wish to know more about the development and characteristics of the five perspectives should see Rubington and Weinberg, 1981, *op. cit.*

II / THE PERSPECTIVES

2 / SOCIAL PATHOLOGY

Social pathology is the oldest of the five perspectives on social problems. It developed in the late 1800s and enjoyed its heyday between 1900 and World War I. This was a time of great hope for social progress and advancement. People saw society changing all around them—often for the better—and several leaders of the day believed that a great new age was dawning in which human suffering could be overcome. While earlier generations had simply accepted many unfortunate situations as unavoidable, late nineteenth-century social reformers thought many of them could be stamped out. Humanitarianism and moral courage, they believed, were the keys to perfecting society and to curing the social problems of the day. Thus the social pathology perspective developed with a highly reformist bent, aimed primarily at practical solutions rather than advancing social theory or accumulating scientific data.

The social pathology perspective developed against a backdrop of evolutionary theory. In 1851 Charles Darwin had published his controversial *The Origin of Species,* which laid the foundations for the theory of biological evolution, and in the years that followed social theorists applied evolutionary theory to their theories of social development.[1] Thus they viewed civilization and institutions as evolving from primitive states to more complex, highly developed states.

1. At the forefront of this movement was the Englishman Herbert Spencer (1820–1903). Cf. Robert L. Carneiro (ed.), *The Evolution of Society: Selections from Herbert Spencer's Principles of Sociology* (Chicago: University of Chicago Press, 1967). In America, William Graham Sumner was instrumental in introducing and applying the concept of Social Darwinism. See Richard Hofstadter, *Social Darwinism in American Thought,* 2nd ed. (Boston: Beacon Press, 1955).

Related to the notion of social evolution is the organic analogy, by which theorists compared society to an organism.[2] Like organisms, this analogy suggests, societies are complex, differentiated masses. They can grow, evolve, and progress. On the other hand, they can get sick, suffer from unhealthy conditions, and perhaps even die. In the pathology perspective, the key concept is one of health versus illness, normal versus abnormal. Social problems interfere with the healthy functioning of the society, and the task of the social scientist is to diagnose and cure the resulting ailments.

The early social pathologists regarded the established order as healthy and normal. Most of them were native-born Americans who had been reared in small towns or rural areas, and many were ministers' sons. They took for granted that the values and lifestyle of rural America were "normal" and that anything deviating from that pattern was "abnormal." They were convinced it was necessary to sustain small-town virtues in the cities, and they believed that people need firm moral training to save them from destruction.

It was in this context that the early social scientists began to depict social problems as "sick" and in need of "treatment." They attributed social problems to sick individuals or to "social diseases" that were spreading through the society. Problems such as crime, delinquency, alcoholism, drug addiction, illegitimacy, and mental illness were viewed as social diseases that cause immeasurable suffering and pain. Often the early social pathologists denounced the poor living conditions and foreign moral codes of the immigrants. In other cases they addressed the lifestyles of deviant groups such as prostitutes or professional thieves. At its peak, this perspective is exemplified in the works of Charles Henderson and Samuel Smith.[3]

The early social pathologists noticed how social problems tended to occur more frequently among some segments of society than among others. Scholars of the day, for example, traced out family lines, noting that some families included more than their share of crime, alcoholism, prostitution, illegitimacy, and feeblemindedness, while other families tended to produce upstanding citizens for generation after generation. Rather than attributing this

---

2. Cf. Herbert Spencer, *The Principles of Sociology* (New York: Appleton, 1923 ed.), Vol. 1, pp. 447–62.

3. Charles Henderson, *Introduction to the Study of the Dependent, Defective, and Delinquent Classes and of Their Social Treatment* (Boston: D. C. Heath, 1909), and of Samuel Smith, *Social Pathology* (New York: Macmillan, 1911).

to mere differences in lifestyle, values, or economic circumstances, the early social pathologists saw deviance as a reflection of "bad blood" through which moral inferiority is passed on from parent to child.[4] Other scholars, noting that various forms of troublesome or criminal behavior seem to be more common in the lower classes, warned that through inbreeding these "inferior classes" pass their own deviant tendencies on generation after generation.[5] Leading criminologists diagnosed "born criminals" who could be easily identified by their physical characteristics; these "born criminals" were viewed as evolutionary throwbacks—atavisms—biologically inferior to "civilized" men.[6]

The early social pathologists felt that these sick or inferior individuals should be treated kindly, much as one would treat a sick child, rather than severely punished. And to prevent them from spreading their deviancies to others, many of these social pathologists favored removing them from the larger society or preventing them from reproducing.

Since the 1960s, the social pathology perspective has been resurrected. There are several important differences, however, between the approach of the early social pathologists and that of the modern social pathologists. First, instead of seeing the system as good and blaming social problems on sick individuals, the modern social pathologists tend to see individuals as mere victims of sick institutions or a sick society. The modern social pathologists see problems arising from social patterns or conditions that are inherently dangerous or destructive or that deny basic human needs. They focus, for instance, on the dehumanizing effects of such things as racism, sexism, mass society, or American imperialism. Some are concerned about the destructive potential of nuclear weaponry or the harmful effects of television violence. The degrading nature of our institutions (e.g., impersonal government bureaucracy) is the concern of others. And in recent years it has become popular to talk about our "sick society." See, for instance,

---

4. Cf. Richard L. Dugdale, *The Jukes: A Study in Crime, Pauperism, Disease, and Heredity,* 4th ed. (New York: Putnam, 1942); Henry H. Goddard, *The Kallikak Family: A Study in Heredity of Feeblemindedness* (New York: Macmillan, 1925).

5. Cf. Henry H. Goddard, *Heredity of Feeblemindedness* (Cold Springs Harbor, N.Y.: Eugenics Record Office Bulletin No. 1, 1911); Henderson *op. cit.*

6. Cf. Cesare Lombroso, *Crime, Its Causes and Remedies,* trans. H. P. Horton (Boston: Little, Brown, 1911); E. A. Hooton, *The American Criminal: An Anthropological Study* (Cambridge, Mass.: Harvard University Press, 1939).

the very influential writings of Erich Fromm, Herbert Marcuse, Charles Reich, or Philip Slater.[7]

Highly traditional and conventional in their assessment of what is healthy and what is pathological, the early social pathologists tended to agree with public opinion, for instance, that religion is good (hence, healthy) while a life of crime is bad (hence, pathological). But modern social pathologists question accepted customs and institutions, and this often leads them to attack as pathological the very things that more conventional people accept and respect.

The two groups also differ in the scope of the problems they address. The early social pathologists generally focused on individual deviations—e.g. alcoholism or mental illness. The modern social pathologists, by contrast, focus on problems of a larger scale—e.g., war, pollution, overpopulation, and poverty.

Whether attributing social problems to sick individuals or to a sick society, the social pathologists usually make highly moralistic, humanitarian judgments. They regard situations or people they approve of as healthy, normal, and good, and they tend to view those they disapprove of as inherently pathological or destructive. These judgments are frequently phrased in quasimedical language, as seen in their frequent use of words such as *abnormal, anomalies, cancer, growth, health, hypertrophy, illness, pathology, sick,* and *symptom.* And their humanitarian bent is reflected in terms like *alienation, anxiety, consciousness, dehumanization, depersonalization, feelings, human nature, humanism, love, need,* and *social consciousness.* Whether described in medical or humanitarian language, to social pathologists social problems consist ultimately of immoral behaviors, and their solution is viewed as a moral responsibility.

To social pathologists, social problems should be solved through moral reform. The early social pathologists believed the solution lay in the moral improvement of the individual "deviant" and the prevention of inherent moral defects in future generations. Often the efforts of the early social pathologists took the form of missionary work. In settlement houses, such as Chicago's Hull

7. Erich Fromm, *The Revolution of Hope* (New York: Harper & Row, 1968); Herbert Marcuse, *Eros and Civilization* (Boston: Beacon Press, 1955), *One-Dimensional Man* (Boston: Beacon Press, 1964), *An Essay on Liberation* (Boston: Beacon Press, 1969); Charles Reich, *The Greening of America* (New York: Random House, 1970); Philip Slater, *The Pursuit of Loneliness* (Boston: Beacon Press, 1970).

House, reformers made personal contact with so-called deviant individuals and tried to teach them middle-class morality and customs. In other cases, reform efforts were directed not toward curing the disease but toward preventing its spread. Reformers lobbied for special agencies, for example, to treat and house wayward or dependent youth and thus to save them from being "contaminated" by adult offenders. (At that time orphans and neglected youths often ended up in jail with hardened criminals, simply for lack of separate facilities.[8]) Many of the early social pathologists also endorsed the idea of selective breeding (eugenics) so that moral defects would not be passed on to future generations. "Tainted life blood," it was believed, was responsible for passing on vices such as drinking or prostitution and conditions like insanity and feeblemindedness as well.

As we have noted, modern social pathologists blame social problems not on "deviant" individuals but rather on the system—a sick society with dehumanizing institutions. Only by revamping the society and its various institutions, they believe, will social problems be solved. But where does one start? To begin with, people must be sensitized to the need for change. Then they must be introduced to a new way of thinking, a new set of values, and new modes of relating to one another. Through this kind of consciousness-raising presumably the whole system will begin to change and the problems will be alleviated.

The underlying thrust of these proposed solutions is the idea of *reform through moral education*. Dedicated to the belief that people have a great potential for good and convinced that their own actions would improve the lot of all people, the social pathologists advocate action to prevent pathological behaviors and to restore health to the social organism. They do not see their own moral standards as arbitrary, class-biased, or furthering the interests of one group over another. Rather, their standards are viewed, implicitly or explicitly, as deriving from human nature or natural law.

Regarding their belief in moral education, the social pathologists fight social problems primarily by trying to change people's ideas of what is right or desirable. Compliance to their moral standards will come voluntarily, the social pathologists assume, once people have been properly educated.

8. Anthony M. Platt, *The Child Savers: The Invention of Delinquency* (Chicago: University of Chicago Press, 1969).

CHARACTERISTICS OF THE SOCIAL PATHOLOGY PERSPECTIVE: A SUMMARY

From the social pathology perspective society is comparable to an organism, for which there is a normal, healthy state of existence. Social problems are viewed as deviations from this normal state and thus are viewed as "sick" and "abnormal," both for individuals and for the society. The central features of the social pathology perspective are as follows:

Definition. Social problems consist of conditions or people that violate a given set of moral expectations. Such situations or persons are viewed as sick or abnormal. The early social pathologists generally focused on individuals or groups whom they viewed as morally deficient, while modern social pathologists tend to talk about broadly based customs or institutions which they view as sick or immoral.

Causes. Social problems are caused, ultimately, by inadequate socialization. To the early social pathologists, social problems were caused by people who had not received proper moral training, or who were defective in their ability to learn middle-class morality. The modern social pathologists lay less blame on individuals and more blame on institutions that hinder humanistic consciousness.

Conditions. The background conditions that lay behind social problems include the phenomena of biological and social evolution. The early social pathologists believed that both morally deficient individuals and the immorality of modern urban life represent miscarriages of the evolutionary process. Modern social pathologists believe we have evolved social patterns and institutions that run contrary to basic human needs.

Consequences. Social pathologists portray social problems as resulting in unnecessary human suffering, waste, and disturbance. If left unchecked, these problems will spread and ultimately destroy the whole society. The early social pathologists tended to be optimists, believing that good would ultimately triumph over evil and the "healthiest" (the most moral) would survive. The modern social pathologists, by contrast, tend to paint a picture of doom. The most extreme portray social pathology as deeply rooted, spreading, and likely to dehumanize the entire population unless something is done very soon.

Solutions.   One solution to social problems lies in reform through moral education. Many of the early social pathologists urged that deviant individuals be taught middle-class morality and customs. Some who thought moral defects were inherited recommended a program of selective reproduction, or eugenics, to produce individuals who would be morally fit. Instead of focusing on the "deviant" individual, modern social pathologists usually urge large-scale reform of the society, with education of citizens about the issue in question and ultimately with changes in institutions.

AMERICAN CULTURE AT THE BREAKING POINT

Philip Slater

American culture, according to Slater, has become pathological, threatening human life and satisfaction. American technology produces an endless stream of inventions, but many of these only add to human misery and danger rather than enhancing health and happiness. The automobile, for example, has destroyed community life, military technology kills and maims, and pollution threatens to poison us. Government programs and regulations support systems of capitalism, imperialism, and militarism which decrease, rather than increase, human well-being. And a destructive competitiveness pervades the society. What is needed, according to Slater, is radical reform. First, people must be reeducated and their goals must be altered. Emphasis must be placed on cooperation, not competitiveness, and on social consciousness, not self-aggrandizement. Second, Slater urges a revision of existing institutions. Government programs should be redirected away from life-threatening programs (such as military production) and into life-enhancing programs (such as social services). At every step, new programs, systems, and inventions should be evaluated not in terms of how "efficient" or "progressive" they are but in terms of whether or not they will add to human well-being.

My main argument for rejecting the old [traditional] culture is that it has been unable to keep any of the promises that have sustained it for so long, and as it struggles more and more violently to maintain itself, *it is less and less able to hide its fundamental antipathy to human life and human satisfaction.*[*] It spends hundreds of billions of dollars to find

From Philip Slater, *The Pursuit of Loneliness: American Culture at the Breaking Point*, pp. 127–39, 141, 144. Copyright © 1970 by Philip E. Slater. Reprinted by permission of Beacon Press and Penguin Books, Ltd.

[*]Italics added.

ways of killing more efficiently, but almost nothing to enhance the joys of living. Against those who sought to humanize their physical environment in Berkeley the forces of "law and order" used a poison gas outlawed by the Geneva Conventions. The old culture is unable to stop killing people—deliberately in the case of those who oppose it, with bureaucratic indifference in the case of those who obey its dictates or consume its products trustingly. However familiar and comfortable it may seem, the old culture is threatening to kill us, like a trusted relative gone berserk so gradually that we are able to pretend to ourselves he has not changed.

But what can we cling to—what stability is there in our chaotic environment if we abandon the premises on which the old culture is based? To this I would answer that it is precisely these premises that have generated our chaotic environment. I recognize the desperate longing in America for stability, for some fixed reference point when all else is swirling about in endless flux. But to cling to old-culture premises is the act of a hopeless addict, who, when his increasingly expensive habit has destroyed everything else in his life, embraces his destroyer more fervently than ever. The radical change I am suggesting here is only the reinstatement of stability itself. It may appear highly unappealing, like all cold-turkey cures, but nothing else will stop the spiraling disruption to which our old-culture premises have brought us.

I am arguing, in other words, for a reversal of our old pattern of technological radicalism and social conservatism. Like most old-culture premises this is built upon a self-deception: we pretend that through it we actually achieve social stability—that technological change can be confined within its own sphere. Yet obviously this is not so. Technological instability creates social instability as well, and we lose both ways. Radical social change *has* occurred within the old culture, but unplanned and unheralded. The changes advocated by the new culture are changes that at least some people desire. The changes that have occurred under the old culture were desired by no one. They were not even foreseen. They just happened, and people tried to build a social structure around them; but it has always been a little like building sand castles in heavy surf and we have become a dangerously irritable people in the attempt. We have given technology carte blanche, much in the way Congress has always, in the past, given automatic approval to defense budgets, resulting in the most gigantic graft in history.

How long is it since anyone has said: "this is a pernicious invention, which will bring more misery than happiness to mankind"? Such comments occur only in horror and science-fiction films, and even there, in the face of the most calamitous outcomes that jaded and overtaxed brains can devise, the audience often feels a twinge of discomfort over the burning laboratory or the lost secret. Yet who would dare to defend even a small fraction of the technological innovations of the past century in terms of human satisfaction? The problem is that technology, industrialism, and capitalism have always been evaluated in their own terms. But it is absurd to evaluate capitalism in terms of the wealth it produces, or technology in terms of the inventions it generates, just as it would be absurd for a subway to evaluate its service in terms of the number of tokens it manufactured. We need to find ways of appraising these systems in terms of criteria that are truly independent of the systems themselves. *We need to develop a human-value index—a criterion that assesses the ultimate worth of an invention or a system or a product in terms of its total impact on human life,** in terms of ends rather than means. We would then evaluate the achievements of medicine not in terms of man-hours of prolonged (and often comatose) life, or the volume of drugs sold, but in terms of the overall increase (or decrease) in human beings feeling healthy. We would evaluate city planning and housing programs not in terms of the number of bodies incarcerated in a given location, or the number of millions given to contractors, but in terms of the extent to which people take joy in their surroundings. . . .

Lest I be accused of exaggeration, let me quote from a recent newspaper article: "How would you like to have your very own flying saucer? One that you could park in the garage, take off and land in your own driveway or office parking lot. . . . Within the next few years you may own and fly just such an unusual aircraft and consider it as common as driving the family automobile. . . ." The writer goes on to describe a newly invented vertical-takeoff aircraft which will cost no more to own and operate than a sports car and is just as easy to drive. After an enthusiastic description of the design of the craft he attributes its development to the inventor's "concern for the fate of the motorist," citing the inability of the highways and city streets to handle the increasing number of automobiles. The inventor claims that his saucer "will help solve some of the big city traffic problems"![1]

The inventor is so confident of the public's groveling submission to every technological command that he does not even bother to defend this outlandish statement. Indeed, it is clear that he does not believe it himself, since he brazenly predicts that every family in the future will own a car *and* a saucer. He even acknowledges rather flippantly that air traffic might become a difficulty, but suggests that "these are not his problems," since he is "only the inventor."[2] He goes on to note that his invention would be useful in military operations (such as machine-gun-

*Italics added.

ning oriental farmers and gassing students, functions now performed by the helicopter) and in spraying poisons on our crops.

How can we account for the lack of public resistance to this arrogance? Why does the consumer abjectly comply with every technological whim, to the point where the seller scarcely bothers to justify it, or does so with tongue in cheek? Is the man in the street so punchdrunk with technological propaganda that he can conceive of the saucer as a solution to *any* problem? How can he greet with anything but horror an invention that will blot out the sky, increase a noise level which is already intense to unbearable levels, pollute the air further, facilitate crime immeasurably, and cause hundreds of thousands of horrible accidents (translating our highway death toll to the saucer domain requires the addition of bystanders, walking about the city, sitting in their yards, sleeping in their beds, or strolling in the park) each year? Is the American public really so insane or obtuse as to relish the prospect of the sky being as filled with motorized vehicles as the ground is now? . . .

Furthermore, Americans are always hung over from some blow dealt them by their technological environment and are always looking for a fix—for some pleasurable escape from what technology has itself created. The automobile, for example, did more than anything else to destroy community life in America. It segmented the various parts of the community and scattered them about so that they became unfamiliar with one another. It isolated travelers and decoordinated the movement of people from one place to another. It isolated and shrank living units to the point where the skills involved in informal cooperation among large groups of people atrophied and were lost. As the community became a less and less satisfying and pleasurable place to be, people more and more took to their automobiles as an escape from it. This in turn crowded the roads more which generated more road-building which destroyed more communities, and so on.

The saucers will simply extend this process further. People will take to their saucers to escape the hell of a saucer-filled environment, and the more they do the more unbearable that hell will become. Each new invention is itself a refuge from the misery it creates—a new hero, a new heroin.

How far can it go? What new inventions will be offered the staggering American to help him blow up his life? Will he finally flee to outer space, leaving the nest he has so industriously fouled behind him forever? Can he really find some means to propel himself so fast that he will escape his own inventive destructiveness? Is the man in orbit— the true Nowhere Man, whirling about in his metal womb unable to encounter anyone or anything—the destiny of all Americans?

The old-culture American needs to reconsider his commitment to technological "progress." *If he fails to kick the habit he may retain his culture and lose his life.*° . . .

Some resistance comes from the old culture's dependence upon the substitutes and palliatives that its own pathology necessitates. "Without all these props, wires, crutches, and pills," its adherents ask, "how can I function? Without the 'extensions of man' I am not even a person. If you take away my gas mask, how can I breathe this polluted air? How will I get to the hospital without the automobile that has made me unfit to walk?" These questions are serious, since one cannot in fact live comfortably in our society without these props until radical changes have been made—*until the diseases that necessitate these palliatives have been cured.*° Transitions are always fraught with risk and discomfort and insecurity, but we do not enjoy the luxury of postponement. No matter how difficult it seems to engage in radical change when all is changing anyway, the risk must be taken.

Our servility toward technology, however, is no more dangerous than our exaggerated moral commitment to the "virtues" of striving and individual achievement. The mechanized disaster that surrounds us is in no small part a result of our having deluded ourselves that a motley scramble of people trying to get the better of one another is socially useful instead of something to be avoided at all costs. *It has taken us a long time to realize that seeking to surpass others might be pathological, and trying to enjoy and cooperate with others healthy, rather than the other way around.*°

The need to triumph over each other and the tendency to prostrate ourselves before technology are in fact closely related. . . .

The essentially ridiculous premises of a competitive society are masked not only by technology, but also by the complexity of our economic system and our ability to compartmentalize our thinking about it. . . .

Our refusal to recognize our common economic destiny leads to the myth that if we all overcharge each other we will be better off.

This self-delusion is even more extraordinary when we consider issues of health and safety. Why are executives living in cities indifferent to the air pollution caused by their own factories, since it is the air they and their families breathe? Or do they all live in exurbia? And what of oil company executives: have they given up ocean beaches as places of recreation? Do they all vacation at mountain lakes? Do automobile manufacturers share a secret gas mask for filtering carbon monoxide out of the air? Are the families of canning company executives immune to botulism? Those of farming tycoons immune to insecticides?

°Italics added.

These questions are not entirely facetious. To some extent wealth does purchase immunity from the effects of the crimes perpetrated to obtain it. But in many of the examples above the effects cannot be escaped even by those who caused them. When a tanker flushes its tanks at sea or an offshore well springs a leak the oil and tar will wash up on the most exclusive beach as well as the public one. The food or drug executive cannot tell his wife not to purchase his own product, since he knows his competitors probably share the same inadequate controls. We cannot understand the irresponsibility of corporations without recognizing that it includes and *assumes* a willingness on the part of corporate leaders to endanger themselves and their families for the short-run profit of the corporation. Men have always been able to subordinate human values to the mechanisms they create. They have the capacity to invest their libido in organizations that are then viewed as having independent life and superordinate worth. Man-as-thing (producer) can then enslave man-as-person (consumer), since his narcissism is most fully bound up in his "success" as a producer. What is overlooked, of course, is that the old-culture adherent's success as a producer may bring about his death as a consumer. Furthermore, since the Nuremberg and Eichmann trials there has been a gradual but increasing reluctance to allow individuals to hide behind the fiction of corporate responsibility.

One might object at this point that the preceding discussion places so much emphasis on individual motivation that it leaves us helpless to act. We cannot expect, after all, that everyone will arise one morning resolved simultaneously to act on different premises, and thus miraculously change the society. Competitive environments are difficult to modify, since whoever takes the first step is extremely likely to go under. "The system" is certainly a reality, no matter how much it is composed of fictions.

*An action program must thus consist of two parts: (1) a long-term thrust at altering motivation and (2) a short-term attempt to redirect existing institutions.** As the motivational underpinnings of the society change (and they are already changing) new institutions will emerge. But so long as the old institutions maintain their present form and thrust they will tend to overpower and corrupt the new ones. During the transitional period, then, those who seek peaceful and gradual change should work toward liberal reforms that shift the incentive *structure* as motivations in fact change. . . .

Let me give a concrete example of adjusting institutions to match motivational changes. It seems quite clear that a far smaller proportion of college graduates today are interested in careers of personal aggran-

*Italics added.

dizement, compared with twenty years ago. Far more want to devote themselves to social problems of one kind and another, or to helping individuals who are disadvantaged in some way. This is surely a beneficial shift in emphasis—we perhaps do not need as many people as we once did to enrich themselves at our expense, and we have no place to put the overpriced junk we already have. But our old-culture institutions continually place obstacles in the path of this shift. Those who seek to provide services are often prevented by established members of the professions—such as doctors, teachers, and social workers— since the principle behind any professional organization is (a) to restrict membership and (b) to provide minimum service at maximum cost. . . .

We need to reward everyone *except* the money-hungry—to reward those who are helping others rather than themselves. Actually, this could be done very easily by simply eliminating the entire absurd structure of deductions, exemptions, and allowances, and thus taxing the rich and avaricious instead of the poor and altruistic. This would have other advantages as well: discouraging overpopulation and home ownership, and saving millions of man-hours of senseless and unrewarding clerical labor.

Reforms in the kinds of priorities involved in the disbursement of federal funds would also help. At present, almost 80 percent of the federal budget is devoted to life-destroying activities, only about 10 percent to life-enhancing ones. The ending of the war should be the first item on everyone's agenda, but even without the war there is much to be done in the way of priority changes. At present most government spending subsidizes the rich: defense spending subsidizes war contractors, foreign aid subsidizes exporters, the farm program subsidizes rich farmers, highway and urban redevelopment programs subsidize building contractors, medical programs subsidize doctors and drug companies, and so on. Some programs, like the poverty program, subsidize middle-class service-oriented people to some extent, and this is helpful. It is probably impossible to subsidize the poor themselves with existing techniques—such a profound reversal of pattern requires a more radical approach, like the negative income tax or guaranteed employment.

It must be made clear that we are not trying to make money-grubbers out of those who are not, but rather to restore money to its rightful place as a medium of exchange—to reduce the role of money as an instrument of vanity. . . .

Such a profound transformation is not likely to occur soon. Yet it is interesting that it is precisely the reversal of the incentive structure that is most feared by critics of such plans as the negative income tax. Why would people want to work and strive, they ask, if they could get all they wanted to eat without it? Why would they be willing to sell out their friends, sacrifice family ties, cheat and swindle themselves and everyone else, and disregard social problems and needs, if in fact they could obtain goods and services without doing these things? "They would have to be sick," we hear someone say, and this is the correct answer. Only the sick would do it—those who today when they have a million dollars keep striving for more. *But the non-sick would be free from the obligation to behave as if they were sick—an obligation our society presently enjoins.* It would not be made so difficult, if these proposals were carried out, for Americans to be motivated by something other than greed. People engaged in helping others, in making communities viable, in making the environment more attractive, would be able to live more comfortably if they wished. Some people would of course do nothing at all but amuse themselves, like the idle rich, and this seems to disturb people: "subsidized idleness," they call it, as if thus to discredit it. Yet I personally would far rather pay people *not* to make nerve gas than pay them to make it; pay them *not* to pollute the environment than pay them to do it; pay them *not* to inundate us with instant junk than pay them to do it; pay them *not* to swindle us than pay them to do it; pay them *not* to kill peasants than pay them to do it; pay them *not* to be dictators than pay them to do it; pay them *not* to replace communities with highways than pay them to do it, and so on. One thing must be said for idleness: it keeps people from doing the Devil's work. The great villains of history were busy men, since great crimes and slaughters require great industry and dedication.

Those skilled in social and political action can probably devise many more profound programs for defusing the perverse incentive structure our society now enjoys, but the foregoing will at least serve to exemplify the point I wish to make. As a general rule it can be said that every institution, every program in our society should be examined to determine whether it encourages social consciousness or personal aggrandizement.

Let us now turn to the question of long-range modifications in motivation. For no matter how much we try to eliminate scarcity assumptions from the incentive structures of our institutions, they will continue to reemerge if we do not devote some attention to reforming the psychic structures that our family patterns generate in children. . . .

It is difficult . . . not to repeat patterns that are as deeply rooted in primary emotional experiences as these are, particularly when one is unprepared. The new parents may not be as absorbed in material possessions and occupational self-aggrandizement as their own parents were. They may channel their parental vanity into different spheres, pushing their children to be brilliant artists, thinkers, and performers. But the hard narcissistic core on which the old culture was based will not be dissolved until the parent-child relationship itself is de-intensified, and this is precisely where the younger generation is likely to be most inadequate. . . .

Breaking the pattern means establishing communities in which (a) children are not socialized exclusively by their parents, (b) parents have lives of their own and do not live vicariously through their children, hence (c) life is lived for the present, not the future, and hence (d) middle-aged and elderly people participate in the community. This constellation of traits forms a coherent unit, as does its opposite. . . .

Given general recognition by old-culture adherents of the necessity for change, and equally general commitment to it, there is no particular reason why the United States could not become the center of the most beautiful, benign, and exciting culture the world has ever known. We have always been big, and have done things in big ways; having lately become in many ways the worst of societies we could just as easily become the best. No society, after all, has ever solved the problems that now confront us. Potentiality has always been our most attractive characteristic, which is one reason why we have always been so reluctant to commit ourselves to finally realizing it. But perhaps the time has come to make that commitment—to abandon our adolescent dreams of omnipotentiality and demonstrate that we actually *can* create a palatable society. . . .

Notes

1. Alvin Smith, *Boston Sunday Globe*, January 5, 1969.
2. One is reminded of Tom Lehrer's brilliant song about the rocket scientist:

> "Once they are up who cares where they come down:
> That's not my department," says Werner Von Braun.

The Nuremberg and Eichmann trials were attempts to reverse the general rule that those who kill or make wretched a single person are severely punished, while those (heads of state, inventors, weapons manufacturers) who are responsible for the death, mutilation, or general wretchedness of thousands or millions are generally rewarded with fame, riches, and prizes. The old culture's rules speak very clearly: if you are going to rob, rob big; if you are going to kill, kill big.

INTIMATE BEHAVIOR

Desmond Morris

The human animal is by nature a species of simple tribal hunters, living in small groups in which the individual is surrounded by familiar, loving, intimate relationships. Modern urbanites, however, live in unnaturally enlarged and overcrowded conditions. In such an environment, people become increasingly distrustful and alienated, and their contacts become increasingly impersonal and inhibited. We have become especially inhibited, Morris claims, about touching one another, casually and nonsexually, and in so doing we have come to deny a basic human need for physical contact. Carrying over into our family relationships, Morris claims, such inhibition generates emotional insecurity and interferes with effective parenting. Searching for a solution to this emotional insecurity, many people in recent years have turned to the encounter group movement, which legitimates touching and expressing. Ultimately, however, the solution will have to involve more pervasive reeducation that will include both a shift in public opinion and a relaxation of informal customs prohibiting touching behavior. In this way, people will enjoy more fully the bonds of intimacy and the fulfillment of their basic human needs.

We are born into an intimate relationship of close bodily contact with our mothers. As we grow, we strike out into the world and explore, returning from time to time to the protection and security of the maternal embrace. At last we break free and stand alone in the adult world. Soon we start to seek a new bond and return again to a condition of intimacy with a lover who becomes a mate. Once again we have a secure base from which to continue our explorations.

If, at any stage in this sequence, we are poorly served by our intimate relationships, we find it hard to deal with the pressures of life. We solve the problem by searching for substitutes for intimacy. We indulge in social activities that conveniently provide us with the missing body contacts, or we use a pet animal as a stand-in for a human partner. Inanimate objects are enlisted to play the vacant role of the intimate companion, and we are even driven to the extreme of becoming intimate with our own bodies, caressing and hugging ourselves as if we were two people.

These alternatives to true intimacy may, of course, be used as pleasant additions to our tactile lives, but for many they become sadly necessary replacements. The solution seems obvious enough. If there is such a strong demand for intimate contact on the part of the typical human adult, then he must relax his guard and open himself more easily to the friendly approaches of others. He must ignore the rules that say, "Keep yourself to yourself, keep your distance, don't touch, don't let go, and never show your feelings." Unfortunately, there are several powerful factors working against this simple solution. Most important of these is the *unnaturally enlarged and overcrowded society** in which he lives. He is surrounded by strangers and semi-strangers whom he cannot trust, and there are so many of them that he cannot possibly establish emotional bonds with more than a minute fraction of them. With the rest, he must restrict his intimacies to a minimum. Since they are so close to him physically, as he moves about in his day-to-day affairs, this requires an *unnatural degree of restraint.** If he becomes good at it, he is likely to become increasingly inhibited in *all* his intimacies, even those with his loved ones.

In this body-remote, anti-intimate condition the modern urbanite is in danger of becoming a bad parent. If he applies his contact restraint to his offspring during the first years of their life, then he may cause irreversible damage to their ability to form strong bonds of attachment later on. If, in seeking justification for his inhibited parental behaviour, he (or she) can find some official blessing for such restraint, then it will, of course, help to ease the parental conscience. Unhappily, such blessings have occasionally been forthcoming and have contributed harmfully to the growth of personal relationships within the family.

One example of this type of advice is so extreme that it deserves special mention. The Watsonian method of child-rearing, named after its perpetrator, an eminent American psychologist, was widely followed earlier in this century. In order to get the full flavour of his advice to parents, it is worth quoting him at some length. Here are some of the things he said:

> Mothers just don't know, when they kiss their children and pick them up and rock them, caress them and jiggle them upon their knee, that they are slowly building up a human being totally unable to cope with the

*Italics added.

world it must later live in. . . . There is a sensible way of treating children. Treat them as though they were young adults. . . . Never hug of kiss them, never let them sit on your lap. If you must, kiss them once on the forehead when they say goodnight. . . . Can't a mother train herself to substitute a kindly word, a smile, in all of her dealings with the child, for the kiss and the hug, the pickup and the coddling? . . . If you haven't a nurse and cannot leave the child, put it out in the backyard a large part of the day. Build a fence around the yard so that you are sure no harm can come to it. Do this from the time it is born. . . . If your heart is too tender and you must watch the child, make yourself a peephole so that you can see it without being seen, or use a periscope. . . . Finally, learn not to talk in endearing and coddling terms.

Since this was described as treating a child like a young adult, the obvious implication is that the typical Watsonian adults never kiss or hug one another either, and spend their time viewing one another through metaphorical peepholes. This is, of course, precisely what we are all driven to do with the *strangers* who surround us in our daily lives, but to find such conduct seriously recommended as the correct procedure between parents and their babies is, to say the least, remarkable.

The Watsonian approach to child-rearing was based on the behaviourist view, to quote him again, that in man "There are no instincts. We build in at an early age everything that is later to appear . . . there is nothing from within to develop." It therefore followed that to produce a well-disciplined adult it was necessary to start with a well-disciplined baby. If the process was delayed, then "bad habits" might start to form which would be difficult to eradicate later.

This attitude, based on a totally false premise concerning the natural development of human behaviour in infancy and childhood, would merely be a grotesque historical curiosity were it not for the fact that it is still occasionally encountered at the present day. But because the doctrine lingers on, it requires closer examination. The main reason for its persistence is that it is, in a way, self-perpetuating. If a tiny baby is treated in this unnatural manner, it becomes basically insecure. Its high demand for bodily intimacy is repeatedly frustrated and punished. Its crying goes unheeded. But it adapts, it learns—there is no choice. It becomes trained and it grows. The only snag is that it will find it hard ever to trust anyone again, in its entire life. Because its urge to love and be loved was blocked at such a primary stage, the mechanism of loving will be permanently damaged. Because its relationship with its parents was carried on like a business deal, all its later personal involvements will proceed along similar lines. It will not even enjoy the advantage of being able to behave like a cold automaton, because it will still feel the basic biological urge to love welling inside it, but will be unable to find a way of letting it out. Like a withered limb that could not be fully amputated, it will go on aching. If, for conventional reasons, such an individual then marries and produces offspring, the latter will stand a high chance of being treated in the same way, since true parental loving will now, in its turn, have become virtually impossible. This is borne out by experiments with monkeys. If an infant monkey is reared without loving intimacies with its mother, it later becomes a bad parent. . . .

All this could have been avoided if only the baby had been treated as a baby in the first place, instead of a "young adult." During the first years of life, an infant requires total love, nothing less. It is not "trying to get the better of you," but it does need the best of you. If the mother is unstressed, and has not herself been warped in infancy, she will have a natural urge to give her best, which is why, of course, the disciplinarian has to repeatedly warn mothers against giving in to those tender "weaknesses" that "tug at their heart-strings," to use a favourite Watsonian phrase. If the mother *is* under pressure, as a result of our modern way of life, it will not be so easy; but even so, without an artificially imposed regime, it is still not impossible to come close enough to the ideal to produce a happy and well-loved baby.

Far from growing into a "spoilt child," such an infant will then be able to mature into an increasingly independent individual, remaining loving, but with no inhibitions about investigating the exciting world around it. The early months gave it the assurance that there is a truly safe and secure base from which to venture forth and explore. . . . Experiments with monkeys bear this out. The infant of a loving monkey mother readily moves off to play and test the environment. The offspring of a non-loving mother is shy and nervous. This is the exact opposite of the Watsonian prediction, which expects that an "excess" of early loving, in the intimate, bodily sense, will make for a soft, dependent creature in later years. The lie to this can even be seen by the time the human child has reached the third year of life. The infant that was lavished with love during its first two years already begins to show its paces, launching out into the world with great, if unsteady, vigour. If it falls flat on its face it is not more, but less, likely to cry. The infant that was less loved and more disciplined as a tiny baby is already less adventurous, less curious about what it sees, and less inclined to start making the first fumbling attempts at independent action.

In other words, once a totally loving relationship has been established in the first two years of life, the infant can readily move on to the next stage in its development. As it grows, however, its headlong rush to explore the world *will*, at this later phase, require some discipline from the parents. What was wrong at the baby stage now becomes right. The Watsonian distaste for the doting, over-protective parents of *older* children has some justification, but the irony is that where protection of this type occurs to excess, it is probably a reaction against the damage caused by earlier Watsonian baby-training. The child that was a fully loved baby is less likely to provoke such behaviour.

During later life the adult who, as a baby, formed a strong bond of attachment with its parents in the primary phase to total love, will also be better equipped to make a strong sexual bond of attachment as a young adult and, from this new "safe base," continue to explore and lead an active, outgoing, social life. It is true that, in the stage before an adult bond of attachment has formed, he or she will be much more sexually exploratory as well. All exploring will have been accentuated, and the sexual sphere will be no exception. But if the individual's early life has been allowed to pass naturally from stage to stage, then the sexual explorations will soon lead to pair-formation and the growth of a powerful emotional bond, with a full return to the extensive body intimacies typical of the loving baby phase.

Young adults who establish new family units and enjoy uninhibited intimacies within them will be in a much better position to face the harsh, impersonal world outside. Being in a "bond-ful," rather than a bond-starved, condition, they will be able to approach each type of social encounter in its own terms and not make inappropriate, bond-hungry demands in situations which, inevitably, will so often require emotional restraint.

One aspect of family life that cannot be overlooked is the need for privacy. It is necessary to have private space in order to enjoy intimate contacts to the full. Severe overcrowding in the home makes it difficult to develop any kind of personal relationship except a violent one. Bumping into one another is not the same as performing a loving embrace. Forced intimacy becomes anti-intimate in the true sense, so that, paradoxically, we need more space to give body contact greater meaning. Tight architectual planning that ignores this fact creates unavoidable emotional tension. For personal body intimacy cannot be a permanent condition, like the persistent impersonal crowding of the urban world outside the home. The human need for close bodily contact is spasmodic, intermittent, and only requires occasional expression. To cramp the home-space is to convert the loving touch into a suffocating body proximity. If this seems obvious enough, then it is hard to understand the lack of attention that has been given to private home-space by the planners of recent years.

In painting this picture of the "intimate young adults," I may have given the impression that, if only they can acquire an adequate private home-space, have a loving infancy behind them, and have formed strong new bonds of attachment to one another, then all will be well. Sadly, this is not the case. The crowded modern world can still encroach on their relationship and inhibit their intimacies. There are two powerful social attitudes that may influence them. The first is the one that uses the word "infantile" as an insult. Extensive body intimacies are criticized as regressive, soft or babyish. This is something that can easily deter a potentially loving young adult. The suggestion that to be too intimate constitutes a threat to his independent spirit, summed up in such sayings as "the strongest man is the man who stands alone," begins to make an impact. Needless to say, there is no evidence that for an adult to indulge in body contacts typical of the infant stage of life necessarily means he will find his independence impaired at other times. If anything, the contrary is the case. The soothing and calming effects of gentle intimacies leave the individual freer and better equipped emotionally to deal with the more remote, impersonal moments of life. They do not soften him, as has so often been claimed; they strengthen him, as they do with the loved child who explores more readily.

The second social attitude that tends to inhibit intimacies is the one which says that bodily contact implies sexual interest. This error has been the cause of much of the intimacy restraint that has been needlessly applied in the past. There is nothing implicitly sexual about the intimacies between parent and child. Parental love and infantile love are not sexual love, nor need the love between two men, two women, or even between a particular man and a particular woman be sexual. Love is love—an emotional bond of attachment—and whether sexual feelings enter into it or not is a secondary matter. In recent times we have somehow come to overstress the sexual element in all such bonds. If a strong, primarily non-sexual bond exists, but with minor sexual feelings accompanying it, the latter are automatically seized upon and enlarged out of all proportion in our thinking. The result has been a massive inhibition of our non-sexual body intimacies, and this has applied to relationships with our parents and offspring (beware, Oedipus!), our siblings (beware, incest!), our close same-sex friends (beware, homosexuality!), our close opposite-sex friends (beware, adultery!), and our many casual friends (beware, promiscuity!). All of this is understandable, but totally unnecessary. What it indicates is that in our true sexual relationships we are, perhaps, not enjoying a sufficiently erotically exhausting degree of body intimacy. If our pair-bond sexual intimacies were intensive and extensive enough, then there should be none left over to invade the other types of bond relationships, and we could all relax and enjoy them more than we seem to dare to do at present. If we remain sexually inhibited or frustrated with our mates, then of course the situation is quite different.

The general restraint that is applied to non-sexual body contacts in modern life has led to some curious anomalies. For example, recent

American studies have revealed that in certain instances women are driven to use random sex simply for the purpose of being held in someone's arms. When questioned closely, the women admitted that this was sometimes their sole purpose in offering themselves sexually to a man, there being no other way in which they could satisfy their craving for a close embrace. This illustrates with pathetic clarity the distinction between sexual and non-sexual intimacy. Here there is no question of body intimacy leading to sex, but of sex leading to body intimacy, and this complete reversal leaves no doubt about the separation between the two.

These, then, are some of the hazards facing the modern intimate adult. To complete this survey of intimate human behaviour, it remains to ask what signs of change there are in the attitudes of contemporary society.

At the infant level, thanks to much painstaking work by child psychologists, a greatly improved approach to the problems of child-rearing is being developed. A much better understanding now exists of the nature of parent/offspring attachments, and of the essential role that warm loving takes in the production of a healthy growing child. The rigid, ruthless disciplines of yesterday are on the wane. However, in our more overcrowded urban centres, the ugly phenomenon of the "battered baby syndrome" remains with us to remind us that we still have a long way to go.

At the level of the older child, constant gradual reforms are taking place in educational methods, and more sensitive appreciation is growing of the need for social as well as technical education. The demands for technological learning are, however, heavier than ever, and there is still a danger that the average schoolchild will be better trained to cope with facts than with people.

Amongst young adults, the problem of handling social encounters seems, happily, to be solving itself. It is doubtful whether there has ever before been a period of such openness and frankness in dealing with the intricacies of personal interaction. Much of the criticism of the conduct of young adults, on the part of the older generation, stems from a heavily disguised envy. It remains to be seen, however, how well the new-found freedom of expression, sexual honesty and disinhibited intimacies of present-day youth survive the passage of time and approaching parenthood. The increasingly impersonal stresses of later adult life may yet take their toll.

Amongst older adults there is clearly a growing concern about the survival of resolved personal life inside the ever-expanding urban communities. As public stress encroaches more and more on private living, a mounting alarm can be felt concerning the nature of the modern human condition. In personal relationships, the world *"aliena-tion"** is constantly heard, as the *heavy suits of emotional armour,** put on for social battle in the streets and offices, become increasingly difficult to remove at night.

In North America, the sounds of a new rebellion against this situation can now be heard. A new movement is afoot, and it provides an eloquent proof of the burning need that exists in our modern society for a revision of our ideas concerning body contact and intimacy. Known in general terms as "Encounter Group Therapy," it has appeared only in the last decade, beginning largely in California and spreading rapidly to many centres in the United States and Canada. Referred to in American slang as "Bod Biz" (for "show business" read "body business"), it goes under a number of official titles, such as "Transpersonal Psychology," "Multiple Psychotherapy" and "Social Dynamics."

The principal common factor is the bringing together of a group of adults for sessions lasting from roughly one day to one week, in which they indulge in a wide variety of personal and group interactions. Although some of these are largely verbal, many are non-verbal and concentrate instead on body contacts, ritual touchings, mutual massage, and games. The aim is to break down the facade of civilized adult conduct, and to remind people that they "do not *have* bodies; they *are* bodies."

The essential feature of these courses is that inhibited adults are encouraged to play like children again. The avant-garde scientific atmosphere licenses them to behave in an infantile manner without embarrassment or fear of ridicule. They rub, stroke and tap one another's bodies; they carry one another around in their arms and anoint one another with oil; they play child-like games and they expose themselves naked to one another, sometimes literally, but usually metaphorically. . . .

The organizers of these courses refer to them as "therapy for normal people." The visitors are not patients; they are group members. They go there because they are urgently seeking some way of finding a return to intimacy. If it is sad to think that modern, civilized adults should need official sanction to touch one another's bodies, then it is at least reassuring that they are sufficiently aware that something has gone wrong to actively do something about it. Many of the people who have been through such sessions repeatedly return for more, since they find themselves loosening up emotionally and unwinding in the course of the ritual body contacts. They report a sense of release and a

*Italics added.

growing feeling of warmth in connection with their personal interactions at home.

Is this a valuable new social movement, a passing fad, or a dangerous, new, drugless addiction? With dozens of new centres opening up every month, expert opinions are varied. Some psychologists and psychiatrists vigorously support the encounter-group phenomenon, others do not. One argues that group members "don't improve—they just get a maintenance dose of intimacy." If this is true, then even so, the courses may at least see certain individuals through a difficult phase in their social lives. This puts group attendance at the intimacy level of going dancing, or going to bed with a cold and being comforted there, but there is nothing wrong with that. It merely adds one more string to the bow of a person seeking a "licensed to touch" context. Other criticisms, however, are more severe. "The techniques that are supposed to foster real intimacy sometimes destroy it," says one. A theologist, no doubt sensing a new form of serious competition, comments that all that people learn in encounter groups is "new ways to be impersonal—a new bag of tricks, new ways to be hostile and yet appear friendly." . . .

The more severe criticism that the group sessions actually do serious harm has yet to be proved. "Instant intimacy," as it has been called, does, however, have its hazards for the returning devotee when he steps back, fully or partially "reawakened," into his old environment. He has been changed, but his home companions have not, and there is a danger that he may make insufficient allowance for this difference. The problem is essentially one of competing relationships. If an individual visits an encounter group, has himself massaged and stroked by total strangers, plays intimate games with them, and indulges in a wide variety of body contacts, then he is doing more with them than he will have been doing with his true "intimates" in his home setting. (If he is not, then he had no problem in the first place.) If—as will inevitably happen—he later describes his experiences in glowing detail, he is automatically going to arouse feelings of jealousy. Why was he prepared to act like that at the encounter centre, when he was so remote and untouching at home? The answer, of course, was the official, scientific sanction for such acts in the special atmosphere of the centre, but that is no comfort to his "real life" intimates. Where couples attend intimacy sessions together, the problem is greatly reduced, but the "back home" situation still requires careful handling.

Some have argued that the most distasteful aspect of the encounter groups is the way in which they are converting something which should be an unconscious part of everyday life into a self-conscious, highly organized, professional pursuit, with the act of intimacy in danger of becoming an end in itself, rather than as one of the basic means by which we can intuitively help ourselves to face the outside world.

Despite all these understandable fears and criticisms, it would be wrong to scorn this intriguing new trend. Essentially, its leaders have seen an increasing and damaging shift towards impersonality in our personal relationships and have done their best to reverse this process. . . . If the movement spreads and grows to a point where it becomes a matter of common knowledge, then, even for the nonenthusiasts, it will exist as a constant reminder that something is wrong with the way in which we are using—or, rather, not using—our bodies. If it does no more than make us aware of this, it will be serving its purpose. . . . [A] comparison with psycho-analysis is relevant. Only a small proportion of the general population have ever been directly involved in analysis, and yet the basic idea that our deepest, darkest thoughts are not shameful or abnormal, but are probably shared by most others, has permeated healthily throughout our culture. In part, it is responsible for the more honest and frank approach to mutual personal problems in young adults today. If the encounter-group movement can provide the same indirect release for our inhibited feelings concerning intimate bodily contact, then it will ultimately have proved to have made a valuable social contribution.

The human animal is a social species, capable of loving and greatly in need of being loved. A simple tribal hunter by evolution, he finds himself now in a bewilderingly inflated communal world. Hemmed in on all sides, he defensively turns in on himself. In his emotional retreat, he starts to shut off even those who are nearest and dearest to him, until he finds himself alone in a dense crowd. Unable to reach out for emotional support, he becomes tense and strained and possibly, in the end, violent. Lost for comfort, he turns to harmless substitutes for love that ask no questions. But loving is a two-way process, and in the end the substitutes are not enough. In this condition, if he does not find true intimacy—even if it is only with one single person—he will suffer. Driven to armour himself against attack and betrayal, he may have arrived at a state in which all contact seems repellent, where to touch or to be touched means to hurt or be hurt. *This, in a sense, has become one of the greatest ailments of our time, a major social disease of modern society that we would do well to cure before it is too late.** If the danger remains unheeded, then—like poisonous chemicals in our food—it may increase from generation to generation until the damage has gone beyond repair.

In a way, our ingenious adaptability can be our social undoing. We are capable of living and surviving in such appallingly unnatural

*Italics added.

conditions that, instead of calling a halt and returning to a saner system, we adjust and struggle on. In our crowded urban world, we have battled on in this way, further and further from a state of loving, personal intimacy, until the cracks have begun to show. Then, sucking our metaphorical thumbs and mouthing sophisticated philosophies to convince ourselves that all is well, we try to sit it out. We laugh at educated adults who pay large sums to go and play childish games of touch and hug in scientific institutes, and we fail to see the signs. How much easier it would all be if we could accept the fact that tender loving is not a weakly thing, only for infants and young lovers, if we could release our feelings, and indulge ourselves in an occasional, and magical, return to intimacy.

BEYOND MASCULINITY

Warren Farrell

Farrell argues that traditional sex roles are dehumanizing not only for women but for men as well. Men, for example, are reared to be emotionally inhibited—unable to express their emotions and afraid to acknowledge feelings of vulnerability, dependency, or intimacy. And just as women are treated as sex objects, men are viewed as "success objects." How can the negative effects of sex roles be overcome? According to Farrell, we must reject traditional notions of masculinity and the masculine value system and seek changes in our education and other institutions. Through consciousness-raising, men can learn a new set of values that are neither "masculine" nor "feminine" but simply human. Farrell urges changes in both work roles and family roles to allow more flexibility and sharing of family and financial responsibilities. And he suggests steps that could be taken to ensure nonsexist childrearing for the next generation.

The masculine value system is a series of characteristics and behaviors which men more than women in our society are *socialized* to adopt, especially outside of the home environment. Men are not born

From *The Liberated Man*, by Warren Farrell. Copyright © 1974 by Warren Farrell. Reprinted by permission of Random House, Inc.

with masculine values. They are taught them by both men and women. But one lesson derived from the teaching is that it is more permissible for a man to lead and dominate than a woman. Since the dominant group in a society generally has its values adopted by the majority, masculine values have become the society's values in the public sphere. As they become society's most rewarded values, it is easy for both men and women to assume that masculine values (and therefore most men) are superior to traditionally feminine values (and therefore most women). Many women, therefore, who seek equality seek it on men's terms, or by adopting masculine values, such as by becoming an aggressive salesman. The woman questions neither the function of aggression nor the assumption that she is a sales*man*. . . .

What are some of these masculine (now societal) values which we assume to be superior to traditional feminine values?

- a good talker and articulator *rather than a good listener*
- logic *as opposed to emotion*
- visible conflict and adventure *rather than behind-the-scenes incremental growth*
- self-confidence *in place of humility*
- quick decision-making *rather than thoughtful pondering*
- charisma and dynamism *more than long-term credibility*
- an active striving for power *rather than a general desire to achieve even if power does not accompany the achievement*
- politics or business as an end in itself *rather than a human concern as an end*
- a hard, tough and aggressive approach *instead of a soft, persuasive approach*
- a responsiveness to concrete results and to external and tangible rewards (money, trophies, votes) *rather than less concrete, more internal satisfactions, as the rewards of learning, of communicating, or of a good family life*
- sexuality *rather than sensuality*

There are some characteristics associated with men, such as sexual conquest and stoicism, which are not considered superior to feminine characteristics, but are still developed by men as a consequence of the other expectations of masculinity. . . . The masculine characteristics above are valued by both men and women as most worthy of adoption in the "real world"—defined by society as the world outside the home. Women might display these characteristics, such as quick decision-making, in the world inside the home, but it is seldom assumed they can transfer them to the "real world."

The assumption that the masculine values are superior encourages the liberation of women to be narrowly interpreted as women coming "up to" masculine values. Women, for example, can put "Dr." on their résumé and gain society's respect; men cannot put "1972–74 I took care of children" and earn respect. (When I asked a group of employers how they would react to a man with a such a résumé, the first response was, "Oh, he must be a fag!") Despite the assumption of the superiority of the masculine value system, in almost all cases some balance between or combination of the masculine and feminine value systems is usually most desirable. . . .

When I refer to something as "masculine" or "feminine," I am referring to the socialization of men or women as it exists, which is impossible to outline here. At an early age boys see models of men who seek material success, physical and psychological strength, leadership, invulnerability; who suppress their fear, control their emotions; who are pragmatic, know all the answers, never seek help, are tough and independent; who have a substantial degree of power, ambition, and physical and sexual aggression; who have control in sexual relations and in all relations, initiate sexual relations, make decisions, can get what they want when they want it; who generally want to be on top, be a protector, earn more than—and in general to be better than— (preferably a man; if not, then a woman). If John Wayne—the Moses of masculinity—were to hand down "The Ten Commandments of Masculinity," they might look like this:

Ten Commandments of Masculinity

1. Thou shalt not cry or expose other feelings of emotion, fear, weakness, sympathy, empathy or involvement before thy neighbor.
2. Thou shalt not be vulnerable, but honor and respect the "logical," "practical" or "intellectual"—as thou define them.
3. Thou shalt not listen, except to find fault.
4. Thou shalt condescend to women in the smallest and biggest of ways.
5. Thou shalt control thy wife's body, and all its relations, occasionally permitting it on top.
6. Thou shalt have no other egos before thee.
7. Thou shalt have no other breadwinners before thee.
8. Thou shalt not be responsible for housework—before anybody.
9. Thou shalt honor and obey the straight and narrow pathway to success: job specialization.
10. Thou shalt have an answer to all problems at all times.

And above all: Thou shalt not read *The Liberated Man* or commit other forms of introspection.

The woman's socialization encourages domesticity, nurturance, dependency, modesty, coyness, deviousness, warmth, emotionality, illogicality, the ability to be sensually and sexually arousing (while simultaneously properly inhibited and submissive), fearfulness, the need for protection, tenderness, fragility, displays of affection and "sugar and spice and everything nice" (meaning: something extra to be added to the real substance). These traits are off-limits for the male. . . .

The stereotype of masculinity that a given culture accepts is imposed upon a boy from the day he is born. Goldberg and Lewis, who conducted one of the very few studies of six-month-old-infants, found that infant girls are touched by their mothers much more than infant boys.[1] Mothers breast-fed girls significantly more than boys[2] and vocalized to girls significantly more than boys.[3]

The importance of these findings can be seen just seven months later. Goldberg and Lewis found that "the more physical contact the mother made with a boy at six months, the more he touched the mother at 13 months."[4] In a similar vein, "when the children were six months old, mothers touched, talked to, and handled their daughters more than their sons, and when they were 13 months old, girls touched and talked to their mothers more than boys did."[5] *Boys are unconsciously taught to be emotionally constipated.* The self-fulfilling prophecy of stereotyped masculinity is flourishing by the time a child is thirteen months old. . . .

Men's liberation means breaking down stereotyped roles so that men can gain the freedom to change places with women, or switch jobs or even just resist on their jobs without risking the entire family income. The ability to resist can be an important part of creating a sense of self. For me, resisting traditional ways of teaching at Rutgers University was an important part of helping me discover my own creativity. Psychologically, though, I found myself freer to resist (and therefore be creative) the more losing my job did not mean losing the entire family income. This meant devoting supportive hours to my attaché's* career. Ironically, that supportiveness of *her* freed me to develop a sense of myself. . . .

MASCULINITY AS EMOTIONAL CONSTIPATION

Males in bureaucracies reinforce each other's tendency toward specialization and protect each other's safe bastion of expertise. As they specialize and protect, their personalities adapt. Max Weber's description of the development of bureaucracy is striking for its similarity to the male personality: "Its specific nature . . . develops the more perfectly the more bureaucracy is 'dehumanized,' the more completely it succeeds in eliminating from official business, love, hatred, and all purely personal, unrational and emotional elements which escape cal-

*An attaché is a person with whom one has a deep emotional attachment.

culation."[6] *In this atmosphere, men cannot help but be either emotionally incompetent* (unable to handle emotions expressed by others) *or emotionally constipated* (unable to express their own emotions) *or both.*[7]* His emotional constipation leaves no outlet for his stomach but ulcers. One wonders if there is such a thing as a liberated top executive, or does the trip through the bureaucracy maim them all? . . .

If the emotionally constipated man acknowledges that he has emotions, he certainly cannot *show* them. A cardinal tenet of the masculine mystique is that a man must not cry. When confronted with this edict, many men say, "If a man wants to express himself crying or what have you, no one's stopping him." It is not easy to find a man who has tested this proposition in public. The overt liberalism expressed toward crying is like the overt liberalism once expressed by northern whites toward integration: People were free to do it until they did it.

A friend explained to me that he broke down and cried in front of a colleague at the office after some personal tragedies and office frustrations. He explained, "The news of my crying was all over the office in an hour. At first no one said anything. They just sort of looked. They couldn't handle the situation by talking about it. Before this only girls had cried. One of the guys did joke, 'Hear you and Sally been crying lately, eh?' I guess that was a jibe at my masculinity, but the 'knowing silence' of the others indicated the same doubts. What really hurt was that two years later, when I was doing very well and being considered for a promotion, it was brought up again. My manager was looking over my evaluations, read a paragraph to himself and said, 'What do you think about that crying incident?' You can bet that was the last time I let myself cry."

One of the conditions men will gain from breaking down sex roles is not only the freedom to cry, but ultimately a change in the environment which will encourage men to cry when they feel the need. One of the incidents revealed in a consciousness-raising group was related by a man who had recently had a highway accident. The man, Larry, and his friend, Joyce, were in Larry's car which Joyce was driving. She wasn't used to the steering mechanism and the car swerved into the onrushing traffic in the opposite direction. A number of cars swerved around them and a Trailways bus skidded to a stop a few inches before their car. After a moment, the people in the bus piled out to help them. The women went up to Joyce. They took her aside, asked her if she was upset, and created the conditions which encouraged her to cry and obtain the needed relief by crying. The men approached Larry, who was also totally shaken and said, "Wow, that was a close one, man—are

*Italics added.

you sure you're okay? How's the car?" For the next five minutes they discussed the problems with the steering mechanism and its possible connection to other mechanical difficulties. When Larry and Joyce returned to the car, they were both aware of the tremendous tension Larry still had pent up within him, as well as the relief from the tension which Joyce felt. Yet on the surface, Joyce had been the one who appeared to be emotionally upset. By allowing Joyce to appear weak, society allowed her to gain internal strength, while Larry suffered the consequences of surface strength.

DEPENDENCY CONSTIPATION

A man's emotional constipation is supplemented by his dependency constipation. The job and leadership striver thinks of himself as independent, but the very characteristics which make him appear independent—his success, money and status among peers—are the things on which he is dependent: success, money and peer-group approval. His dependence on success may lead to assertiveness at work, but it saps his energy to the point of his being passive with his family. He refuses to admit his dependence because his identity is attached to everything on which he is dependent. The vicious cycle makes dependency constipation an important topic for consciousness-raising groups.

 . . . Some men cannot let their attachés drive without feeling uncomfortable; others have difficulty even asking for driving directions until it is absolutely proved they are lost. Still others will avoid doctors until it is proved they are sick. Psychotherapy provokes the worst cases of dependency constipation. To see a psychiatrist is to admit not only weakness, but mental weakness, the kind unrecognized by "real men." To enter a consciousness-raising group is even harder for some men, since it entails a trusting of equals, a partial dependency on and opening up before the type of men before whom one is normally especially closed. For this reason consciousness-raising and psychotherapy are usually good preparation for each other. It is this freedom to change and to examine oneself, growing out of a willingness to be vulnerable on a number of levels, that is an important dimension of the liberated man.

Denial of dependency and emotions leads to silence and the creation of a male mystique. Silence seems to contradict the description of the male as a striver and dominant interrupter, but men employ silence in special situations—those requiring the expression of emotional and dependency needs. Silence is an obvious by-product of the striver's need to maintain an image of success, omniscience and invulnerability. . . .

MASCULINITY UNCONFINED AND UNCONSTIPATED

It will take a new social pressure to define masculinity as seeking internal self-improvement goals with the freedom to express dependency and emotions, and the development of a broader sense of sexuality. But it is only that attitude which will allow for a balancing of financial success and human success. Men's liberation, however, will meet some of the same resistance which greeted women's liberation at the beginning and which women's liberation is still facing. The persons who need it the most have most internalized their role and are most afraid to question it.

Some men use women as an excuse not to change—"My wife likes me the way I am." Women who place all the blame for their not growing on men are guilty of the same escape mechanism, but the excuse is not nearly as valid for men. Women's liberation has advanced far beyond men's liberation. Liberated women who have questioned their own limited roles invariably find it easier to question the limited roles of men. Even the traditional woman has a much more open view of what she would like men to be than men have of women. Studies of the ideal wife a man would choose indicate that only 31 percent desire women who are courageous, forceful, independent, deliberate, daring, rugged and sharp-witted.[8] The woman's image of the ideal man, though, is one who should have many "feminine" as well as "masculine" qualities.[9] In the mixed consciousness groups it often comes as a surprise to men to find the women willing to forgo many of his stereotyped masculine qualities for some of the more human of the so-called feminine qualities. . . .

THE FAMILY REDEFINED

. . . [A] new type of family, where the mother and father constantly have role choices opened to them, where the images for children are options for children, lays the foundation for true equality. The solution does not mean making the woman into a man or the man into a househusband, but rather for the man and the woman to share the responsibility for both breadwinning and family involvement.

Studies of families with creative children find that in these families the father interacts both "strongly and positively with the child, and the mother also interacts strongly but is sometimes ambivalent in her maternal feelings."[10] Actual observers of the children describe their characteristics as both masculine and feminine, but "not characterized by markedly effeminate manner or appearance . . . They showed an openness to their feelings and emotions, a sensitive awareness of self and others, and wide-ranging interests, many of which are regarded [as] feminine in our culture."[11]

Developing a liberated man does not mean substituting new pressures for the old. Showing an openness to feelings does not mean a pressure to always express feelings as a mark of manhood. Once we establish a norm for masculinity, men will strive to prove they are not abnormal.

Will the absence of an enforced model to strive toward make a person insecure? In practice, having no enforced model helps a person feel secure in whatever he chooses rather than feel secure only if the model is achieved. *Insecurity comes from a conflict between the search for a self and society's (or one's family's) expectations of what one should be. . . .*

[CHILD-CARE]

With the exception of the family, child-care centers have perhaps the most potential for either forming or eliminating sex-role channeling. By the time children reach early elementary school age they are imitating their parents and exhibiting the sex-differentiated behavior seen all around them.[12] By the age of five, the children view the mother's role as housekeeping and caring for children and the father's role as related to earning a living.[13] When they see their parents performing each other's function they interpret it as "helping" the other parent.[14] The child-care center—especially if it admits children at the age of six months, as is the custom in Sweden—can be an important factor in eradicating the thousands of models which channel children into limited perceptions of themselves. . . .

The most simple form of child-care arrangement is to get enough parents together to pool resources to take care of children. In almost any given geographical area there are usually dozens of mothers who would like to make some arrangements for child care but who do not because "There are no centers around here." Despite their experience with children, they don't consider starting their own center. The first step in starting a simple child-care arrangement, however, is simply to advertise a few weeks in succession in a number of the local papers, companies, supermarkets, and NOW newsletters. The ad should indicate the desire to get parents together who are interested in child care that doesn't reinforce sex-role stereotypes. The second step is to get a book on family day care. . . .

An important third step is getting the men involved. Despite the initial difficulty, ultimately this will mean that enough persons will be involved to enable each individual's commitment to be small enough to maintain a full-time job while also participating in child care. For example, participation by ten couples[15] means each person must take only one day per month off from work; involvement of the men also has the obvious advantage of breaking down the sex-role models of only mothers taking care of the children.

A center with approximately fifteen children should have two supervisors. If twenty parents are involved, they can hire either a professional person or one of the parents to supervise overall arrangements and be a full-time supervisor at the center. The second supervisor is drawn from the parents on a rotating basis, so, as already mentioned, each one might contribute one day per month. Taking off one day per month may not seem feasible without giving up vacation days. However, companies without their own centers may be amenable to working out either reimbursement for child care or a "parent leave." A parent leave is a policy in which employees who have children five years or under can take off one day per month without losing pay. It is a method by which the company can contribute to child care without having to invest in its own center. Employers reluctant to do this at the outset may be more amenable to it when they are presented with the possibility of losing good employees completely, retraining the employees and dealing with high absentee rates. . . .

If the parents wish to keep the child-care arrangements simple and inexpensive, they can use the home of the parent who is taking the day off from work to be the co-supervisor rather than rent space for a permanent center. Although this arrangement will require the center to operate informally, and technically without legal sanction due to licensing needs, it offers the children different home settings, and enables each child to solidify his or her identity as the other children see where he lives. The warmth and involvement of the parents provides a stability which balances the diversified home settings. The parent supervisor can be responsible for planning special activities, even an outing or trip for that one day in the month for which s/he is responsible. The enthusiasm of a parent involved only one day per month will doubtless be higher than that of a person who returns to the same job and same place every day. For the children each day is a new surprise. Yet the children have the continuity of the one professional full-time supervisor.

The advantages of such an arrangement are its low cost, informality, and lack of red tape in planning. The disadvantages are its dependence on a competent and flexible organizer to organize the parents, and on a cooperative group of committed parents whose philosophies are not radically divergent. In an informal arrangement creative flexibility is essential. For example, sliding scales might be developed to accommodate parents with more than one child or those who cannot take off under any circumstances, for families who cannot make their home available or for those who can supply extra time or facilities. . . .

Child-care centers, though, can reinforce sex roles as thoroughly as the normal family arrangement if precautions are not taken.[16] Many recent child-care manuals still speak in terms which assume the teaching staff are women. This is particularly harmful to the large percentage of children who presently attend child-care centers that come from fatherless homes and from homes receiving welfare under Aid to Families of Dependent Children (AFDC), in which over 80 percent of the children come from fatherless homes.[17] Male teachers are especially helpful for the dependency problems developing among the boys.[18] *The crucial element in the involvement of men, though, is not only the male per se, but the involvement of men who are trained not to reinforce all the stereotyped masculine traits such as aggression and insensitivity.* The crucial factor in the involvement of such men is the supportiveness of *women* colleagues. If the women make the men feel like "sissies," the men usually withdraw (just one more connection between women's and men's liberation). Sweden has found it necessary to undertake extensive teacher reeducation so sex roles are not unconsciously taught by habitual acts such as giving dolls only to girls, or not encouraging girls to be involved in active sports, or pitting boys against girls in certain activities. Experimental programs in Sweden encourage men to enter the child-care and preschool nursing fields as a career. For a transitional period men are allowed to enter with less preservice qualifications, to compensate for past discrimination against them.[19] . . .

. . . Paternity leaves are fundamental to the sharing of responsibility for child care. Ultimately the terms "paternity" and "maternity" leaves should be replaced with "parent leaves." Court cases for parent leaves, such as the suit against the New York City Board of Education, must be encouraged. Industry must be pressured into making a "one day per month plan" available for parents who wish to take off one day per month for two or three years at neighborhood-formed child-care center, as discussed above. Legislation must also establish guidelines or even graduated quotas for the hiring of men in child-care centers.

Education. Until recently the only pressures brought on the publishing industry about sex roles were to bring about changes in the image of women in children's books by showing women "making it" in industry, politics or the professions. While the production of books with titles like "Women Who Work" must be continued, a men's movement must pressure publishers to produce children's books with titles like "Men Who Care," with pictures of men in the home, men cooking, expressing emotion, wanting sympathy, crying, admitting they are wrong, and especially asking for help and being dependent (even on a woman). Most importantly, men must be pictured loving children and staying home with them occasionally out of choice, rather than in the blue strait jackets of a policeman or businessman (and the accompanying authority symbols of attaché case or gun). The Masculine Mystique Task Force of NOW organized just such a demonstration on August 26, 1973, in New York City. It was the first major "action" of a men's liberation movement focusing on the injustices to men resulting from traditional sex roles.

Demonstrations before toy departments might encourage a broader range of dolls for boys—not just G.I. Joes—to prepare men for father-hood; and an end to separate male and female areas in toy departments with Mighty Mike Astro trains, guns and tanks for boys, while dolls and Susie Homemaker sets are the fare of the girl's department.

A national effort must be made to involve men as elementary school teachers, nurses and guidance counselors. This implies pressure on colleges to undertake special campaigns to attract men to prepare in these fields. In colleges the R.O.T.C. and war research as well as money used for football or wrestling teams should be questioned from a masculine mystique perspective. Courses in sex roles and men's liberation might be financed instead as a way of expanding the feminist studies curriculum.

American educators often complain, "We open our home eco-nomics courses to men and no one shows up. What can we do?" Sweden has found that schools must do more than open up courses; they must actively counteract the biases of the mass media and environment by undertaking *critical* analysis and discussion.[20] This critical analysis is incorporated into *every* subject, from geography to home economics, civics, and biology. Commenting on some of the concrete curriculum changes actually made in his school, a school principal noted: "It turned out that differences of achievement between pupils didn't have anything at all to do with sex. The boys often sewed their own athletic uniforms. Many knit jersey gloves and mufflers. The girls learned to use tools that were brand-new to them. They sawed and planed, hammered nails and glued things together."[21] . . .

Image and Aggression. The image of war, crime and violence as exciting, and the corollary excitement attributed to men who enter war, solve and even commit crimes, are perpetuated daily by tele-vision, radio, and papers.

The six volumes of the U.S. Surgeon General's report of Television and Social Behavior made it repeatedly apparent that publicizing violence leads to imitation of violence. Specifically, crimes in newspapers should be listed similarly to obituaries—mostly in small print in the back pages of the paper with an occasional one listed on the front page, not because of the amount of blood spilled but because of its implications for society.

Reporters should be freed from chasing crimes and enabled to do research on conditions which are likely to lead to crimes. Masculine values, as we have seen, are conflict, power and external action rather than human cooperation, careful background work (except to investigate or create conflict), and internal values. The media reinforces and encourages these values. The pressure to change the media, though, will have to include the most careful strategizing, since demonstrations play right into their hands as a form of conflict and violence, and nonviolence allows them to dismiss efforts to force change. Among the methods which are both effective and have a minimal chance of backfiring are lawsuits, research . . . , and alternate radio and television stations (e.g., the WBAI and Pacifica radio stations and cable TV stations).

Notes

1. Susan Goldberg, and Michael Lewis, "Play Behavior in the Year-Old Infant: Early Sex Differences," *Child Development*, Vol. 40, No. 1 (March 1969), p. 29. See also Sylvia Brody, *Patterns of Mothering* (New York: International Universities Press, Inc., 1956), p. 356. The data for the article by Goldberg and Lewis is drawn from children of parents from all classes but limited to Caucasian families.

2. Breast-feeding is important not for its own sake, but as a form of intimacy, as is any warm human contact important to a child.

3. Goldberg and Lewis, *op. cit.*, p. 29.

4. *Ibid.*

5. *Ibid.*

6. Max Weber, *Essays in Sociology*, translated by H. H. Gerth and C. W. Mills (New York: Oxford University Press, 1946), p. 214.

7. See Louis J. Cutrona, Jr., "What Goes on Inside a Men's Liberation Rap Group," *Glamour*, August 1971.

8. John P. Kee and Alex C. Sherriffs, "Men's and Women's Beliefs, Ideals, and Self-Concepts" in Jerome Seidman, *The Adolescent: A Book of Readings* (New York: Holt, Rinehart & Winston, 1960).

9. *Ibid.*

10. Torrance, *Guiding Creative Talent* (Englewood Cliffs, N.J.: Prentice-Hall, 1962), p. 78.

11. D. W. MacKinnon, "What Do We Mean by Talent and How Do We Test for It?" *The Search for Talent* (New York: College Entrance Examination Board, 1960), pp. 20–29, cited in Torrance, *ibid.*, p. 68.

12. Edith H. Grotberg (ed.), *Day Care: Resources for Decisions* (Washington, D.C.: Office of Economic Opportunity, Office of Planning, Research, and Evaluation, June 1971), p. 121.

13. R. E. Hartley, "Children's Concepts of Male and Female Roles," *Merrill-Palmer Quarterly*, Vol. 6 (1966), pp. 83–91.

14. Mott, 1954, cited in Grotberg, *op. cit.* p. 121.

15. "Couples" is used only as a convenience. Persons divorced or absolutely unable to take off any time from work can usually pay extra money into the center to pay someone who would like to work at the center in a paid position.

16. Grotberg, *op. cit.*, p. 122.

17. *Ibid.*, p. 64.

18. *Ibid.*, p. 122.

19. Ingrid Frederiksson, "Sex Roles and Education in Sweden," *N.Y.U. Education Quarterly*, Vol. 3, No. 2, Winter 1972, p. 20.

20. Lgr 69. Läroplan för grundskolan. Stockholm: Svenska Utbildnings-förlaget Liber AB, 1969, cited in Frederiksson, *op. cit.*, p. 22.

21. Birger Wiklund, Mya slöjden bra för vänskapen mellan projkar och flickor, "PM Pedagogiska meddelanden froän Skolöverstyrelsen" (Stockholm o, 7, 1970), cited in Frederiksson, *op. cit.*, p. 21.

Selected References

Chilman, Catherine S., *Growing Up Poor,* Washington, D.C.: U.S. Government Printing Office, 1966.
The traditional social pathology perspective is still popular among social workers—as illustrated in the way this book conceptualizes the poor and proposes to solve the poverty problem.

Fromm, Erich, *The Revolution of Hope: Toward a Humanized Technology,* New York: Harper & Row, 1968.
Fromm believes that modern technology, bureaucracy, and consumption patterns have produced a state of pathology, with numerous symptoms of people's unfulfilled needs. He advocates a solution through introspection, education, and the replacement of market values with humanistic ones.

Green, Arnold W., *Social Problems: Arena of Conflict,* New York: McGraw-Hill, 1975.
Green discusses humanitarianism and massive educational programs as important elements in the solution of social problems.

Lauer, Robert, *Social Problems,* Dubuque, Iowa: Wm. C. Brown, 1976.

Lauer examines a variety of social problems and calls on the reader to "rise above our personal pains, frustrations, and aspirations, and recognize that we are a part of humanity, and that all too many of our fellow human beings are oppressed by problems that demand . . . concern. . . ." Part of Lauer's program involves educating people to the fallacies of conservative thinking.

Moran, Richard, "Medicine and Crime: The Search for the Born Criminal and the Medical Control of Criminality," in Peter Conrad and Joseph W. Schneider (eds.), *Deviance and Medicalization: From Badness to Sickness,* St. Louis: C. V. Mosby, 1980, pp. 215–40.

Moran surveys the work of some of the main thinkers in the "born criminal" tradition (Cesare Lombroso, J. Lange, E. A. Hooton, and William H. Sheldon) and shows how medical explanations of crime give rise to attempts at medical or biological intervention to prevent crime or to "treat" the criminal. Moran also discusses some modern-day versions of this approach in attempting to either control or prevent crime—such as screening people for chromosomal aberration (e.g., the XYY syndrome), and use of psychosurgery or behavior modification to "rehabilitate" criminals.

Platt, Anthony M., *The Child Savers: The Invention of Delinquency,* Chicago: The University of Chicago Press, 1969.

Alarmed by the treatment of delinquent and dependent youth at the turn of the century, women employing a social pathology perspective fought for the creation of special juvenile courts and special correctional institutions (reformatories) for troubled youths. In so doing, they created a new concept—that of juvenile delinquency.

Rosenberg, Bernard, Israel Gerver, and F. William Howton, *Mass Society in Crisis: Social Problems and Social Pathology,* 2nd ed., New York: Macmillan, 1971.

This book illustrates the modern social pathology perspective. The fourth part of the book, which deals with solutions to social problems, illustrates how problems may be diagnosed from one perspective but treated from other perspectives.

Yablonsky, Lewis, *Robopaths,* Indianapolis: Bobbs-Merrill, 1972.

According to Yablonsky, people with no sympathy or compassion for others suffer from what he calls "robopathology." One aspect of this includes the tendency to treat others as objects rather than as human beings. Successful treatment of the disorder, Yablonsky argues, can take place in humanizing groups such as Synanon or psychodrama groups in which robopaths can rediscover their common humanity.

Yochelson, Leon, and Stanton E. Samenow, *The Criminal Personality, Volume I: A Profile for Change* and *Volume II: The Change Process,* New York: Jason Aronson, 1977.

Yochelson and Samenow argue that criminals are fundamentally different from noncriminals; they have a "criminal personality" and different ways of thinking. Based on a sample of patients in an institution for the criminally insane, Yochelson and Samenow contrast these patients' thought processes with ordinary people's and, in Volume II, outline a program for changing the "criminal personality" and rehabilitating the criminal.

Questions for Discussion

1. Farrell describes traditional sex roles as dehumanizing for men as well as for women. Do you agree? How would you evaluate Farrell's proposed solutions?

2. Why does Slater consider our traditional notions of competitiveness and ambition to be "sick"? How would you evaluate his proposed solutions? Can you see why Slater's proposals represent a form of moral reeducation?

3. To what extent are the problems discussed by Farrell, Morris, and Slater related to one another? Do you see any connections between their proposed solutions? Do you think people are moving in the directions these writers advocate? How so, or why not?

4. How do you evaluate the social pathology perspective and the type of solutions it suggests? Can you identify a contemporary problem (other than those discussed in the readings) to which you think the social pathology perspective applies. What steps would you propose, from a social pathology perspective, to alleviate this problem?

3 / SOCIAL DISORGANIZATION

After World War I, the social pathology perspective was gradually supplanted by another approach—the social disorganization perspective. This second perspective arose at a time when the urban-industrial age was bringing great changes to American society. The population shifted from rural areas to rapidly growing cities. The economy changed from agriculture to industry. And waves of immigration from Europe and the Orient brought thousands of foreigners—often jobless and indigent—to American shores. Numerous problems accompanied these changes—e.g., poverty for the immigrants, overcrowded housing, pollution. In addition, immigrant families sometimes found it hard to maintain control over their youngsters in an alien environment, and they found that some customs acceptable at home were not accepted in America. At the same time, life became more complex for native-born Americans as well. The swelling cities and a changing economy, for example, made life complicated and unpredictable. More and more, it seemed that social problems arose not just from a few aberrant individuals but from the nature of the society itself. As America became visibly more complex and diversified, it became apparent that the old concept of the "social organism" was too simple. Likewise, the concept of social problems as "social illnesses" caused by a few "sick" individuals no longer seemed adequate.

Concomitant with these changes in American society were changes in the status of sociology as a discipline—changes that would add to the thrust for forging a new perspective. At this time sociology was becoming more established as a distinct discipline.[1] No longer did it seem adequate to borrow metaphors and concepts from the field of medicine. Thus sociologists began to develop their

1. Cf. Roscoe C. Hinkle, Jr. and Gisela J. Hinkle, *The Development of Modern Sociology: Its Nature and Growth in the United States* (New York: Doubleday, 1954).

own distinct set of concepts for analyzing the social world around them.[2] Rather than comparing society to an organism, these early sociologists defined society as a huge, complex system whose various parts must all be coordinated if it is to continue functioning smoothly. The concept of *social organization* was developed to refer to this coordination and regulation, and it continues to be one of the key concepts in sociology. Central to the concept of social organization is the notion of *social rules.* Rules provide coordination between the various parts of the society and regulate the behavior of individuals. With the concepts of social organization and social rules, sociology now had its own distinctively sociological subject matter, its own concepts, and its own way of depicting reality.

These early sociologists also came to see that the concepts of social rules and social organization could be used to understand social problems. Increasingly, they began to view social problems as the result of *social disorganization*—situations that lack adequate rules. Two early pioneers in this perspective, W. I. Thomas and Florian Znaniecki, defined social disorganization as "a decrease of the influence of existing social rules of behavior upon individual members of the group."[3]

In applying the concepts of social disorganization to social problems, such problems were no longer seen as primarily a moral issue. They were blamed not on the moral defects of individuals, or even the moral character of the society, but rather on the inadequacy of the social rules themselves and a resulting lack of coordination or control. For the individual, these writers observed, social disorganization produces stress, which in turn can give rise to various forms of personal disorganization. Crime, juvenile delinquency, mental illness, and alcoholism, for instance, have been regarded in this light. To these early sociologists, city life seemed particularly weak in social organization. Moreover, some areas of the city were seen as more disorganized than others—e.g., the transitional areas of warehouses, marginal businesses, and housing for transients. In these areas, they believed, social problems abounded because social controls were especially weak.[4]

2. Emile Durkheim, *The Rules of Sociological Method*, trans. Sarah Solovay & John Mueller (Chicago: University of Chicago Press, 1938).

3. W. I. Thomas and Florian Znaniecki, *The Polish Peasant in Europe and America* (Boston: Richard G. Badger, 1918), Vol. 4, p. 2.

4. See, for example, Robert E. L. Faris and H. Warren Dunham, *Mental Disorders in Urban Areas: An Ecological Study of Schizophrenia and Other Psychoses* (Chicago: University of Chicago Press, 1939); Clifford R. Shaw and Henry D. McKay, *Juvenile Delinquency and Urban Areas* (Chicago: University of Chicago Press, 1942).

As time went on, sociologists began to conceptualize three different types of social disorganization. First is the concept of *normlessness*. When there simply are no clear rules to govern a situation it is said to be in a state of normlessness. Examples of normlessness can often be found during natural disasters, civil disorders, or unprecedented types of crises such as the first airplane hijackings and political kidnappings. Without rules to guide them, people may simply stand by and not take any action. Or, lacking coordination, they may take ineffective action. Still others may take the attitude that "anything goes" and turn to looting or violence.

A second type of social disorganization is called *culture conflict*. In culture conflict there are plenty of rules to follow, but the rules are mutually contradictory. Thus conformity to one set of rules automatically means violating another set. Immigrant groups often face this situation when the rules they brought with them from their homeland do not agree with the predominant rules in their new locale, and ethnic groups (such as the American Indians) may face this situation if their ethnic culture provides rules that contradict those of the dominant culture. One early study, for example, blamed culture conflict for the high rates of alcoholism, crime, juvenile delinquency, mental illness, and suicide among Polish immigrants.[5] Sociologists also saw culture conflict resulting from rapid changes in American society. In this case, traditional rules conflict with modern rules, and people are left frustrated and confused.

A third type of social disorganization is called *breakdown*. In this case, conformity to the rules fails to bring the expected rewards or proves punishing instead; thus the rules break down and become ineffective. A rookie policeman, for example, may come out of the police academy with a certain set of rules. Yet on the job he may discover that these rules are ineffective, inefficient, and not rewarded by the police department anyway. Thus the academy-learned rules may lose their ability to regulate this policeman's behavior. When the breakdown of rules occurs on a larger scale, the result can be a loss of coordination and effectiveness by whole organizations or governments.

What produces social disorganization? Social change seems to be the basic culprit, including changes in technology (e.g., automation), demography (e.g., immigration, overpopulation), and culture (e.g., social movements, changing popular values). Such changes

5. Thomas and Znaniecki, *op. cit.*

require continual adjustments in the system. One early sociologist, William Ogburn, noticed that technology often changes faster than ideas and customs, and he introduced the concept of *culture lag* to describe this phenomenon.[6] While technology races ahead, he suggested, ideas and customs lag behind and eventually become completely out of phase with the technology. Another important sociologist, Charles H. Cooley, discussed the fact that people's behaviors tend to become less regulated and coordinated as traditions break down, again giving rise to a host of social problems.[7]

The vocabulary used in connection with the social disorganization perspective often refers to types of change (*social change, cultural change, demographic change, technological change*), to the speed of change (*accelerating change, abrupt change, disaster, rapid change, rate of change*), or to the inconsistent rate of change in different parts of the society (*lag, cultural lag*). Other terms reflect the concern with social coordination—e.g., *complexity, consistency, control, coordination, disintegration, disorder, integration, malfunction,* and *malintegration.* And the effects of social disorganization on the individual are often described as a sense of *confusion, disorientation, meaninglessness, normlessness, unpredictability,* and *personal disorganization.*

Few contemporary textbooks are titled *Social Disorganization.* In fact, the notion receives only passing mention in most textbooks on social problems. Yet the types of phenomena highlighted by the social disorganization perspective seem to be receiving increasing attention (overpopulation, ineffective bureaucracies, and famine amid plenty are only a few examples), and the key concepts of this approach continue in many circles to organize thinking about social problems.

To solve social problems, the social disorganization perspective suggests, one must restore consistency between the various parts of the system and between ideas and actions as well. This is accomplished through *more adequate social rules.* By implementing social rules that are explicit, workable, and consistent, the system can be readjusted and the behaviors of individuals can be guided. The particular form this may take depends on the particular type of social disorganization that gave rise to the problem in the first place.

6. William F. Ogburn, *Social Change with Respect to Culture and Original Nature* (New York: B. W. Huebsch, 1922), pp. 199–280.
7. Charles Horton Cooley, *Social Organization: A Study of the Larger Mind* (New York: Scribner's, 1909).

Problems resulting from normlessness can be solved by constructing a clear set of rules to govern the problem situation. After natural disasters such as floods or tornadoes, for example, communities may draw up a set of emergency procedures to follow the next time such an event occurs. Such procedures can help the community to meet the crisis and carry out relief operations. Similarly, effective guidelines can help maintain order by controlling looting and panic. Thus, while the natural disaster may be unavoidable, at least the amount of disorder, loss, and suffering resulting from it can be lessened.

Culture conflict often results from rapid change. One remedy to problems involving culture conflict is to control the rate of change. A few cities have passed ordinances designed to limit the growth of the city (e.g., by limiting the number of new residents who can move into the city) and thus to preserve a particular quality of life.

Another solution to problems of culture conflict is to address the elements of the culture that are at odds. For example, immigrants can band together and set up rules for deciding what aspects of the host culture to integrate with their own. In this fashion, they can assimilate into the host culture while still maintaining their ethnic identity and pride.[8]

Problems resulting from a breakdown of rules appear to be solvable, at least theoretically, by centralization, communication, and feedback. Confusion and inefficiency resulting from a jumble of government bureaucracies, for example, could be alleviated by centralizing the various agencies and by coordinating their activities. Communication would enable them to make mutual adjustments in their operations, and feedback would allow them to make adjustments to better meet the needs of their clients. Whether resulting from normlessness, culture conflict, or breakdown, then, the solution to social problems is to devise and enforce rules for better coordination and control.

CHARACTERISTICS OF THE SOCIAL DISORGANIZATION PERSPECTIVE: A SUMMARY

Society is a complex, dynamic social system whose parts are coordinated and regulated by social rules. When events change one part

8. See, for example, Puerto Rican Forum, *A Study in Poverty Conditions in the New York Puerto Rican Community* (New York: Puerto Rican Forum, 1964).

of the system, there is corresponding need for adjustment in other parts as well. Social disorganization refers ultimately to a lack of adjustment, or poor adjustment, between the parts. The major elements of this perspective are as follows:

Definition.   Social problems are the effects of social disorganization. In turn, social disorganization reflects a failure of social rules.

Causes.   Social problems are usually due to social change that causes the various parts of the social system to get out of phase with one another. Existing rules become inadequate and no longer regulate people's relations and behaviors.

Conditions.   Modern technology, increasingly complex institutions, movements of people, demographic changes, cultural diversity and change—all these form the context within which social disorganization is likely to occur. In many instances the complexity of modern life itself forms the backdrop for problems of social disorganization.

Consequences.   For the individual, social disorganization produces stress, which in turn can produce a variety of problems such as mental illness or alcoholism. For the social system, social disorganization may become so disruptive that the whole system eventually breaks down. Most often, though, the system continues despite the disorganization—continuing to "bungle along" with a great deal of confusion, inefficiency, and "slack." (Government bureaucracies often seem to exemplify this result.)

Solutions.   Adequate social rules to govern the situation must be instigated and reinforced. Such rules should be explicit, workable, and consistent. They should provide guidelines for individuals, and they should coordinate various parts of the system. In addition, the rules should be reevaluated and readjusted from time to time.

PROBLEMS IN POPULATION POLICY

Kingsley Davis

Current population policies provide an example of social disorganiza-
tion. They are inconsistent and therefore ineffective. They provide the
technological means for effective contraception, but they leave unad-
dressed the more important question of how many children a couple
wants to have. Thus, since most societies are notably pro-family and
pro-children, such policies are bound to fail. The goal of zero population
growth cannot be attained, Davis suggests, until governments adopt a
more coordinated and comprehensive strategy. This would include not
only making contraception available but also broad changes in the
social system—namely, the "selective restructuring of the family in
relation to the rest of society." There must be a change in women's
roles, less emphasis on the family institution, and greater rewards for
women outside the family (e.g., in education and in the workplace). In
this way, Davis argues, societies could be reorganized in such a way as
to make effective population control more likely.

THE NATURE OF CURRENT POLICIES

With more than 30 nations now trying or planning to reduce population
growth and with numerous private and international organizations
helping, the degree of unanimity as to the kind of measures needed is
impressive. The consensus can be summed up in the phrase "family
planning." . . .

As is well known, "family planning" is a euphemism for contraception. The family-planning approach to population limitation, therefore, concentrates on providing new and efficient contraceptives
on a national basis through mass programs under public health
auspices. . . .

From Kingsley Davis, "Population Policy: Will Current Programs Succeed?" *Science 158*
(10 Nov. 1967), pp. 730–39. Copyright © 1967 by American Association for the Advancement of Science. Reprinted by permission of author and publisher.

Goals.   Curiously, it is hard to find in the population-policy movement any explicit discussion of long-range goals. By implication the policies seem to promise a great deal. This is shown by the use of expressions like *population control* and *population planning.* . . . It is also shown by the characteristic style of reasoning. Expositions of current policy usually start off by lamenting the speed and the consequences of runaway population growth. This growth, it is then stated, must be curbed—by pursuing a vigorous family-planning program. That family planning can solve the problem of population growth seems to be taken as self-evident. . . .

When the terms *population control* and *population planning* are used, as they frequently are, as synonyms for current family-planning programs, they are misleading. Technically, they would mean deliberate influence over all attributes of a population, including its age-sex structure, geographical distribution, racial composition, genetic quality, and total size. No government attempts such full control. By tacit understanding, current population policies are concerned with only the *growth* and *size* of populations. These attributes, however, result from the death rate and migration as well as from the birth rate; their control would require deliberate influence over the factors giving rise to all three determinants. Actually, current policies labeled population control do not deal with mortality and migration, but deal only with the birth input. This is why another term, *fertility control,* is frequently used to describe current policies. But, as I show below, family planning (and hence current policy) does not undertake to influence most of the determinants of human reproduction. Thus the programs should not be referred to as population control or planning, because they do not attempt to influence the factors responsible for the attributes of human populations, taken generally; nor should they be called fertility control, because they do not try to affect most of the determinants of reproductive performance. . . .

The actual programs seem to be aiming simply to achieve a reduction in the birth rate. . . . The Pakistan plan adopted in 1966 aims to reduce the birth rate from 50 to 40 per thousand by 1970; the Indian plan aims to reduce the rate from 40 to 25 "as soon as possible"; and the Korean aim is to cut population growth from 2.9 to 1.2 percent by 1980. A significant feature of such stated aims is the rapid population growth they would permit. Under conditions of modern mortality, a crude birth rate of 25 to 30 per thousand will represent such a multiplication of people as to make use of the term *population control* ironic. A rate of increase of 1.2 percent per year would allow South Korea's already dense population to double in less than 60 years. . . .

Most discussions of the population crisis lead logically to zero population growth as the ultimate goal, because *any* growth rate, if continued, will eventually use up the earth. Yet hardly ever do arguments for population policy consider such a goal, and current policies do not dream of it. Why not? The answer is evidently that *zero population growth is unacceptable to most nations and to most religious and ethnic communities.*[*] To argue for this goal would be to alienate possible support for action programs.

Turning to the actual measures taken, we see that the very use of family planning as the means for implementing population policy poses serious but unacknowledged limits on the intended reduction in fertility. The family-planning movement, clearly devoted to the improvement and dissemination of contraceptive devices, states again and again that its purpose is that of enabling couples to have the number of children they want. "The opportunity to decide the number and spacing of children is a basic human right," say the 12 heads of state in the United Nations declaration. . . .

Logically, it does not make sense to use *family* planning to provide *national* population control or planning. The "planning" in family planning is that of each separate couple. The only control they exercise is control over the size of *their* family. . . . There is no reason to expect that the millions of decisions about family size made by couples in their own interest will automatically control population for the benefit of society. . . .

Actually, the family-planning movement does not pursue even the limited goals it professes. It does not fully empower couples to have only the number of offspring they want because it either condemns or disregards certain tabooed but nevertheless effective means to this goal. One of its tenets is that "there shall be freedom of choice of method so that individuals can choose in accordance with the dictates of their consciences," but in practice this amounts to limiting the individual's choice, because the "conscience" dictating the method is usually not his but that of religious and governmental officials. Moreover, not every individual may choose: even the so-called recommended methods are ordinarily not offered to single women, or not all offered to women professing a given religious faith.

Thus, despite its emphasis on technology, current policy does not utilize all available means of contraception, much less all birth-control measures. . . . A greater limitation on means is the exclusive emphasis on contraception itself. Induced abortion, for example, is one of the surest means of controlling reproduction, and one that has been proved capable of reducing birth rates rapidly. . . . Yet this method is rejected in nearly all national and international population-control programs. . . .

[*]Italics added.

The questions of sterilization and unnatural forms of sexual inter-course usually meet with similar silent treatment or disapproval, al-though nobody doubts the effectiveness of these measures in avoiding conception. . . .

On the side of goals, then, we see that a family-planning orientation limits the aims of current population policy. Despite reference to "population control" and "fertility control," which presumably mean determination of demographic results by and for the nation as a whole, the movement gives control only to couples, and does this only if they use "respectable" contraceptives.

The Neglect of Motivation. By sanctifying the doctrine that each woman should have the number of children she wants, and by assuming that if she has only that number this will automatically curb population growth to the necessary degree, the leaders of current policies escape the necessity of asking why women desire so many children and how this desire can be influenced. Instead, they claim that satisfactory motivation is shown by the popular desire (shown by opinion surveys in all countries) to have the means of family limitation, and that therefore the problem is one of inventing and distributing the best possible contra-ceptive devices. Overlooked is the fact that a desire for availability of contraceptives is compatible with *high* fertility.

Given the best of means, there remain the questions of how many children couples want and of whether this is the requisite number from the standpoint of population size. That it is not is indicated by continued rapid population growth in industrial countries, and by the very surveys showing that people want contraception—for these show, too, that people also want numerous children.

The family planners do not ignore motivation. They are forever talking about "attitudes" and "needs." But they pose the issue in terms of the "acceptance" of birth control devices. At the most naive level, they assume that lack of acceptance is a function of the contraceptive device itself. This reduces the motive problem to a technological question. The task of population control then becomes simply the invention of a device that *will* be acceptable. The plastic IUD is acclaimed because, once in place, it does not depend on repeated *acceptance* by the woman, and thus is "solves" the problem of motiva-tion.

But suppose a woman does not want to use *any* contraceptive until after she has had four children. This is the type of question that is seldom raised in the family-planning literature. In that literature, wanting a specific number of children is taken as complete motivation, for it implies a wish to control the size of one's family. The problem woman, from the standpoint of family planners, is the one who wants "as many as come," or "as many as God sends." Her attitude is construed as due to ignorance and "cultural values," and the policy deemed necessary to change it is "education." No compulsion can be used, because the movement is committed to free choice. . . . The effort is considered successful when the woman decides she wants only a certain number of children and uses an effective contraceptive.

In viewing negative attitudes toward birth control as due to ignorance, apathy, and outworn tradition, and "mass-communication" as the solution to the motivation problem, family planners tend to ignore the power and complexity of social life. If it were admitted that the creation and care of new human beings is socially motivated, like other forms of behavior, by being a part of the system of rewards and punishments that is built into human relationships, and thus is bound up with the individual's economic and personal interests, it would be apparent that *the social structure and economy must be changed before a deliberate reduction in the birth rate can be achieved.* As it is, reliance on family planning allows people to feel that "something is being done about the population problem" without the need for painful social changes.

Designation of population control as a medical or public health task leads to a similar evasion. This categorization assures popular support because it puts population policy in the hands of respected medical personnel, but by the same token it gives responsibility for leadership to people who think in terms of clinics and patients, of pills and IUD's, and who bring to the handling of economic and social phenomena a self-confident naiveté. The study of social organization is a technical field; an action program based on intuition is no more apt to succeed in the control of human beings than it is in the area of bacterial or viral control. Moreover, *to alter a social system, by deliberate policy, so as to regulate births in accord with the demands of the collective welfare would require political power, and this is not likely to inhere in public health officials, nurses, midwives, and social workers. To entrust population policy to them is "to take action," but not dangerous "effective action."* . . .

. . . By implying that the only need is the invention and distribution of effective contraceptive devices, they allay fears, on the part of religious and governmental officials, that fundamental changes in social organization are contemplated. Changes basic enough to affect motivation for having children would be changes in the structure of the family, in the position of women, and in the sexual mores. Far from proposing such radicalism, spokesmen for family planning frequently state their purpose as "protection" of the family—that is, closer observ-

*Italics added.

ance of family norms. In addition, by concentrating on *new* and *scientific* contraceptives, the movement escapes taboos attached to old ones (the Pope will hardly authorize the condom, but may sanction the pill). . . .

We thus see that the inadequacy of current population policies with respect to motivation is inherent in their overwhelmingly family-planning character. Since family planning is by definition private planning, it eschews any societal control over motivation. . . . Unacquainted for the most part with technical economics, sociology, and demography, [family planners] tend honestly and instinctively to believe that something they vaguely call population control can be achieved by making better contraceptives available.

The Evidence of Ineffectiveness. If this characterization is accurate, we can conclude that current programs will not enable a government to control population size. In countries where couples have numerous offspring that they do not want, such programs may possibly accelerate a birth-rate decline that would occur anyway, but the conditions that cause births to be wanted or unwanted are beyond the control of family planning, hence beyond the control of any nation which relies on family planning alone as its population policy.

This conclusion is confirmed by demographic facts. . . . [T]he widespread use of family planning in industrial countries has not given their governments control over the birth rate. In backward countries today, taken as a whole, birth rates are rising, not falling; in those with population policies, there is no indication that the government is controlling the rate of reproduction. The main "successes" cited in the well-publicized policy literature are cases where a large number of contraceptives have been distributed or where the program has been accompanied by some decline in the birth rate. Popular enthusiasm for family planning is found mainly in the cities, or in advanced countries such as Japan and Taiwan, where the people would adopt contraception in any case, program or no program. It is difficult to prove that present population policies have even speeded up a lowering of the birth rate (the least that could have been expected), much less that they have provided national "fertility control." . . .

NEW DIRECTIONS IN POPULATION POLICY

In thinking about other approaches, one can start with known facts. In the past, all surviving societies had institutional incentives for marriage, procreation, and child care which were powerful enough to keep the birth rate equal to or in excess of a high death rate. . . .

If excessive population growth is to be prevented, the obvious requirement is somehow to impose restraints on the family. However, because family roles are reinforced by society's system of rewards, punishments, sentiments, and norms, any proposal to demote the family is viewed as a threat by conservatives and liberals alike, and certainly by people with enough social responsibility to work for population control. One is charged with trying to "abolish" the family, but what is required is *selective restructuring of the family in relation to the rest of society.* *

The lines of such restructuring are suggested by two existing limitations on fertility. (1) Nearly all societies succeed in drastically discouraging reproduction among unmarried women. (2) Advanced societies unintentionally reduce reproduction among married women when conditions worsen in such a way as to penalize childbearing more severely than it was penalized before. In both cases the causes are motivational and economic rather than technological.

It follows that population-control policy can de-emphasize the family in two ways: (1) by keeping present controls over illegitimate childbirth yet making the most of factors that lead people to postpone or avoid marriage, and (2) by instituting conditions that motivate those who do marry to keep their families small.

Postponement of Marriage. Since the female reproductive span is short and generally more fecund in its first than in its second half, postponement of marriage to ages beyond 20 tends biologically to reduce births. Sociologically, it gives women time to get a better education, acquire interests unrelated to the family, and develop a cautious attitude toward pregnancy. Individuals who have not married by the time they are in their late twenties often do not marry at all. For these reasons, for the world as a whole, the average age at marriage for women is negatively associated with the birth rate: a rising age at marriage is a frequent cause of declining fertility during the middle phase of the demographic transition; and, in the late phase, the "baby boom" is usually associated with a return to younger marriages.

. . . In agrarian societies, postponement of marriage (when postponement occurs) is apparently caused by difficulties in meeting the economic prerequisites for matrimony, as stipulated by custom and opinion. In industrial societies it is caused by housing shortages, unemployment, the requirement for overseas military service, high costs of education, and inadequacy of consumer services. Since almost no research has been devoted to the subject, it is difficult to assess the relative weight of the factors that govern the age at marriage.

*Italics added.

Encouraging Limitation of Births within Marriage. As a means of encouraging the limitation of reproduction within marriage, as well as postponement of marriage, a greater rewarding of nonfamilial than of familial roles would probably help. A simple way of accomplishing this would be to allow economic advantages to accrue to the single as opposed to the married individual, and to the small as opposed to the large family. For instance, the government could pay people to permit themselves to be sterilized; all costs of abortion could be paid by the government; a substantial fee could be charged for a marriage license; a "child-tax" could be levied; and there could be a requirement that illegitimate pregnancies be aborted. Less sensationally, governments could simply reverse some existing policies that encourage childbearing. They could, for example, cease taxing single persons more than married ones; stop giving parents special tax exemptions; abandon income-tax policy that discriminates against couples when the wife works; reduce paid maternity leaves; reduce family allowances; stop awarding public housing on the basis of family size; stop granting fellowships and other educational aids (including special allowances for wives and children) to married students; cease outlawing abortions and sterilizations; and relax rules that allow use of harmless contraceptives only with medical permission. Some of these policy reversals would be beneficial in other than demographic respects and some would be harmful unless special precautions were taken. . . .

A closely related method of deemphasizing the family would be modification of the complementarity of the roles of men and women. Men are now able to participate in the wider world yet enjoy the satisfaction of having several children because the housework and childcare fall mainly on their wives. Women are impelled to seek this role by their idealized view of marriage and motherhood and by either the scarcity of alternative roles or the difficulty of combining them with family roles. To change this situation women could be required to work outside the home, or compelled by circumstances to do so. If, at the same time, women were paid as well as men and given equal educational and occupational opportunities, and if social life were organized around the place of work rather than around the home or neighborhood, many women would develop interests that would compete with family interests. . . .

THE DILEMMA OF POPULATION POLICY

It should now be apparent why, despite strong anxiety over runaway population growth, the actual programs purporting to control it are limited to family planning and are therefore ineffective. (1) The goal of zero, or even slight, population growth is one that nations and groups find difficult to accept. (2) The measures that would be required to implement such a goal, though not so revolutionary as a Brave New World or a Communist Utopia, nevertheless tend to offend most people reared in existing societies. As a consequence, the goal of so-called population control is implicit and vague; the method is only family planning. . . .

The things that make family planning acceptable are the very things that make it ineffective for population control. By stressing the right of parents to have the number of children they want, it evades the basic question of population policy, which is how to give societies the number of children they need. By offering only the means for *couples* to control fertility, it neglects the means for societies to do so.

Because of the predominantly pro-family character of existing societies, individual interest ordinarily leads to the production of enough offspring to constitute rapid population growth under conditions of low mortality. Childless or single-child homes are considered indicative of personal failure, whereas having three to five living children gives a family a sense of continuity and substantiality.

. . . Hardships that seem particularly conducive to deliberate lowering of the birth rate are (in managed economies) scarcity of housing and other consumer goods despite full employment, and required high participation of women in the labor force, or (in freer economies) a great deal of unemployment and economic insecurity. When conditions are good, any nation tends to have a growing population.

It follows that, in countries where contraception is used, a realistic proposal for a government policy of lowering the birth rate reads like a catalogue of horrors: squeeze consumers through taxation and inflation; make housing very scarce by limiting construction; force wives and mothers to work outside the home to offset the inadequacy of male wages, yet provide few child-care facilities; encourge migration to the city by paying low wages in the country and providing few rural jobs; increase congestion in the cities by starving the transit system; increase personal insecurity by encouraging conditions that produce unemployment and by haphazard political arrests. No government will institute such hardships simply for the purpose of controlling population growth. *Clearly, therefore, the task of contemporary population policy is to develop attractive substitutes for family interests, so as to avoid having to turn to hardship as a corrective.*

*Italics added.

POST-BUREAUCRATIC LEADERSHIP

Warren G. Bennis

Technological developments and vast social change are producing social disorganization. Bureaucracy has become outmoded, and bureaucratic leadership is no longer an adequate way to make decisions and formulate policies. In this reading, Bennis suggests an alternative form of leadership. Above all, social organizations must be regarded as dynamic systems in an ever-changing environment. Data-gathering and feedback would be continual features of social organization, providing a basis for constant adaptation to changing conditions. And decision-making would be carried out not by a single authority figure within an organization but by collegial teams. In this way, Bennis claims, organizations will be better able to adapt to changing circumstances and to deliberately and effectively accomplish their goals.

In an . . . [earlier article] I forecast that in the next 25 to 50 years we would participate in the end of bureaucracy as we know it and in the rise of new social systems better suited to the 20th century demands of industrialization. The prediction was based on the evolutionary principle that every age develops an organizational form appropriate to its genius, and that *the prevailing form today**—the pyramidal, centralized, functionally specialized, impersonal mechanism known as *bureaucracy—was out of joint with contemporary realities.**

This breakdown of a venerable form of organization so appropriate to 19th century conditions is caused, I argued, by a number of factors, but chiefly the following four: *1) rapid and unexpected change; 2) growth in size beyond what is necessary** for the work being done (for example, inflation caused by bureaucratic overhead and tight controls, impersonality caused by sprawls, outmoded rules, and organizational

From Warren G. Bennis, "Post-Bureaucratic Leadership," *Transaction 6*, No. 9., pp. 44–49, 61. Copyright © 1969 by Transaction, Inc.

*Italics added.

rigidities); 3) *complexity of modern technology,** in which integration between activities and persons of very diverse, highly specialized competence is required; 4) *a change in managerial values** toward more . . . democratic practices.

Organizations of the future, I predicted, will have some unique characteristics. They will be adaptive, rapidly changing *temporary systems,* organized around problems-to-be-solved by groups of relative strangers with diverse professional skills. The groups . . . will evolve in response to problems rather than to programmed expectations. People will be evaluated, not in a rigid vertical hierarchy according to rank and status, but flexibly, according to competence. Organizational charts will consist of project groups rather than stratified functional groups, as is now the case. Adaptive, problem-solving, temporary systems of diverse specialists, linked together by coordinating executives in an organic flux—this is the organizational form that will gradually replace bureaucracy.

Ironically, the bold future I had predicted is now routine and can be observed wherever the most interesting and advanced practices exist. Most of these trends are visible and have been surfacing for years in the aerospace, construction, drug, and consulting industries as well as professional and research and development organizations, which only shows that the distant future now has a way of arriving before the forecast is fully comprehended.

A question left unanswered, however, has to do with leadership. How would these new organizations be managed? . . . Do the behavioral sciences provide any suggestions? How can these complex, ever-changing, free-form, kaleidoscopic patterns be coordinated.? Of course there can be no definitive answers, but unless we can understand the leadership requirements for organizations of the future, we shall inevitably back blindly into it rather than cope with it effectively.

. . . For the moment, . . . I want to quickly review some of the key situational features likely to confront the leader of the future.

The overarching feature is change itself, its accelerating rate and its power to transform. The phrase "the only constant is change" has reached the point of a cliché, which at once anesthetizes us to its pain and stimulates grotesque fantasies about a Brave New World with no place in the sun for us. Change is the "godhead" term for our age as it has not been for any other. One has only to recall that the British Parliament was debating in the last part of the 19th century whether to close up the Royal Patent Office, as it was felt that all significant inventions had already been discovered.

But what are the most salient changes affecting human organization,

*Italics added.

the ones with most relevance to their governance? Foremost is the changing nature of our institutions. In 1947, employment stood at approximately 58 million and now is at about 72 million. According to V. K. Fuchs, "Virtually all of this increase occurred in industries that provide services, for example, banks, hospitals, retail stores, and schools." This nation has become the only country to employ more people in services than in production of tangible goods. The growth industries today, if we can call them that, are education, health, welfare, and other professional institutions. The problem facing organizations is no longer manufacturing—it is the management of large-scale sociotechnical systems and the strategic deployment of high-grade professional talent.

There are other important correlates and consequences of change. For example, the working population will be younger, smarter, and more mobile. Half of our country's population is under 25, and one out of every three persons is 15 years of age or younger. More people are going to college; over half go to college in certain urban areas. The United States Postal Department reports that one out of every five families changes its address every year.

Most of these changes compel us to look beyond bureaucracy for newer models of organizations that have the capability to cope with contemporary conditions. The general direction of these changes— toward more service and professional organizations, toward more educated, younger, and mobile employees, toward more diverse, complex, science-based systems, toward a more turbulent and uncertain environment—forces us to consider new styles of leadership. Leading the enterprise of the future becomes a significant social process, requiring as much, if not more, managerial than substantive competence. Robert McNamara is a case in point. Before he came to Washington, he was considered for three Cabinet positions: Defense, State, and Treasury. His "only" recommendation was that he was a superior administrator. Chris Argyris has concluded that success or failure in the United States Department of State depends as much or more on one's interpersonal and managerial competence as one's substantive knowledge of "diplomacy." It can also be said that leadership of modern organizations depends on new forms of knowledge and skills not necessarily related to the primary task of the organization. In short, the pivotal function in the leader's role has changed away from a sole concern with the substantive to an emphasis on the interpersonal and organizational processes. . . .

One striking index of the rapidity of change—for me, the single, most dramatic index—is the shrinking interval between the time of a discovery and its commercial application. Before World War I, the lag between invention and utilization was 33 years, between World War I and World War II, it was 17 years. After World War II, the interval decreased to about nine years, and if the future can be extrapolated on the basis of the past, by 1970 it will be around five to six years. The transistor was discovered in 1948, and by 1960, 95 percent of all the important equipment and over 50 percent of *all* electronic equipment utilized them in place of conventional vacuum tubes. The first industrial application of computers was as recent as 1956.

Modern organizations, even more than individuals, are acutely vulnerable to the problem of responding flexibly and appropriately to new information. *Symptoms of maladaptive responses, at the extremes, are a guarded, frozen, rigidity that denies the presence or avoids the recognition of changes . . . ; or, at the opposite extreme, an overly receptive, susceptible gullibility to change resulting in [an] unreliable faddism.* It is obvious that there are times when openness to change is appropriate and other times when it may be disastrous. Organizations, in fact, should reward people who act as counterchange agents to create forces against the seduction of novelty for its own sake. . . .

The modern organizations we speak of are composed of [people] who love independence as fiercely as the ancient Greeks; but it is also obvious that they resist what every Athenian, as a matter of course, gave time and effort for: "building and lifting up the common life."

Thucydides has Pericles saying:

> We are a free democracy. . . . We do not allow absorption in our own affairs to interfere with participation in the city's. We regard men who hold aloof from public affairs as useless; nevertheless we yield to none in independence of spirit and complete self-reliance.

A modern version of the same problem (which the Greeks couldn't solve either, despite the lofty prose) has been stated by the president of a large university:

> The problem with this institution is that too few people understand or care about the overall goals. Typically they see the world through their own myopic departmental glasses; i.e., too constricted and biased. What we need more of are professional staff who can wear not only their own school departmental "hat" but the overall university hat.

Specialism, by definition, implies a peculiar slant, a skewed vision of reality. McLuhan tells a good joke on this subject. A tailor went to Rome and managed to get an audience with his Holiness. Upon his return, a friend asked him, "What did the Pope look like?" The tailor answered, "A 41 regular."

Having heard variations of this theme over the years, a number of faculty and administrators, who thought they could "wear the overall university hat" formed what later came to be known as "the HATS group." They came from a variety of departments and hierarchical levels and represented a rough microcosm of the entire university. The

*Italics added.

HATS group has continued to meet over the past several years and has played an important role in influencing university policy.

There are a number of functions that leadership can perform in addition to developing HATS groups. First, it can identify and support those persons who are "linking pins," individuals with a psychological and intellectual affinity for a number of languages and cultures. Secondly, it can work at the places where the different disciplines and organizations come together (for example, setting up new interdisciplinary programs), in order to create more intergroup give and take.

The third important function for leadership is developing and shaping identity. Organizations, not only the academic disciplines, require philosophers, individuals who can provide articulation between seemingly inimical interests, and who can break down the pseudospecies, transcend vested interests, regional ties, and professional biases. . . .

The challenge for the leader is to develop a climate of inquiry and enough psychological and employment security for continual reassessment and renewal. This task is connected with the leader's ability to collect valid data, feed it back to the appropriate individuals, and develop action planning on the basis of the data. This three-step "action-research" model sounds deceptively simple. In fact, it is difficult. Quite often, the important data cannot be collected by the leader for many obvious reasons. Even when the data are known, there are many organizational short circuits and "dithering devices" that distort and prevent the data from getting to the right places at the right time. And even when data-gathering and feedback are satisfactorily completed, organizational inhibitions may not lead to implementation.

In response to the need for systematic data collection, many organizations are setting up "Institutional Research" centers that act as basic fact-gathering agencies. In some cases, they become an arm of policy-making. Mostly, they see as their prime responsibility the collection and analysis of data that bear on the effectiveness with which the organization achieves its goals.

Fact-gathering, by itself, is rarely sufficient to change attitudes and beliefs and to overcome . . . resistance to change. Individuals have an awesome capacity to "selectively inattend" to facts that may in their eyes threaten their self-esteem. Facts and reason may be the least potent forms of influence that man possesses.

Some progressive organizations are setting up organizational development departments that attempt to reduce the "implementation gap" between information and new ideas and action. These OD departments become the center for the entire strategic side of the organization, including not only long-run planning, but plans for gaining participation and commitment to the plans. This last step is the most crucial for the guarantee of successful implementation.

In addition to substantive competence and comprehension of both social and technical systems, the new leader will have to possess interpersonal skills, not the least of which is the ability to defer his own immediate desires and gratifications in order to cultivate the talents of others. Let us examine some of the ways leadership can successfully cope with the new organizational patterns.

UNDERSTANDING THE "SOCIAL TERRITORY"

"You gotta know the territory," sang "Professor" Harold Hill to his fellow salesmen in *The Music Man*. The "social territory" encompasses the complex and dynamic interaction of individuals, roles, groups, organizational and cultural systems. Organizations are, of course, legal, political, technical, and economic systems. For our purposes, we will focus on the social system.

Analytic tools, drawn primarily from social psychology and sociology, are available to aid in the understanding of the social territory. But we need more than such tools to augment and implement these understandings. Leadership is as much craft as science. The main instrument or "tool" for the leader-as-a-craftsman is *himself* and how creatively he can use his own personality. . . . Understanding the social territory and how one influences it is related to the "action-research" model of leadership mentioned earlier: 1) collect data, 2) feed it back to appropriate sources, and 3) action-planning. The "hang-up" in most organizations is that people tend to distort and suppress data for fear of real or fancied retaliation. (Samuel Goldwyn, a notorious martinet, called his top staff together after a particularly bad box-office flop and said: "Look, you guys, I want you to tell me exactly what's wrong with this operation and my leadership—even if it means losing your job!")

THE CONCEPT OF "SYSTEM-INTERVENTION"

Another aspect of the social territory that has key significance for leadership is the idea of *system*. At least two decades of research have been making this point unsuccessfully. Research has shown that productivity can be modified by what the group thinks important, that training effects fade out and deteriorate if they do not fit the goals of the social system, that group cohesiveness is a powerful motivator, that conflict between units is a major problem in organizations, that individuals take many of their cues and derive a good deal of their satisfaction from their primary work group, that identification with the small work group turns out to be the only stable predictor of productivity, and so on.

The fact that this evidence is so often cited and rarely acted upon leads one to infer that there is [something] . . . that makes us locate problems in faulty individuals rather than in malfunctioning social systems. What this . . . is based upon is not altogether clear. But individuals, living amidst complex and subtle organizational conditions, do tend to oversimplify and distort complex realities so that people rather than conditions embody the problem. This tendency toward personalization can be observed in many situations. In international affairs, we blame our troubles with France on deGaulle, or talk sometimes as though we believe that replacing Diem, or Khanh, or Ky will solve our problems with the Saigon government. Other illustrations can be seen when members of organizations take on familial nicknames, such as "Dad," "Big Brother," "Man," "Mother Hen," "Dutch Uncle," etc. We can see it in distorted polarizations such as the "good guy" leader who is too trusting, and his "hatchet man" assistant who is really to blame. These grotesques seem to bear such little resemblance to the actual people that one has to ask what psychological needs are being served by this complex labeling and stereotyping. . . .

If management insists on personalizing problems that arise from systems, serious repercussions must result. In the new organizations—where roles will be constantly changing and ambiguous, where changes in one subsystem will clearly affect other subsystems, where diverse activities have to be coordinated and integrated, where individuals work simultaneously in many different jobs and groups—a system viewpoint must be developed. Just as psychotherapists find it difficult to treat a "problem child" without treating the entire family, it will be more difficult to influence individual behavior without working with his particular subsystem. The leader will be compelled to intervene at the system level if the intervention is to last and serve its purpose.

NEW SYSTEMS FOR THE FUTURE

Alvin Toffler

Problems of social organization, Toffler suggests, are not limited to bureaucratic organizations. In fact, change has become so fast and massive that it pervades the whole society—producing social disorganization and feelings of bewilderment and stress. Toffler uses the term "future shock" to refer to this phenomenon. In essence, he claims, the future is already upon us, and we lack effective means of dealing with it. No longer is there a sense of control over where we are going, and efforts to exert control merely end in a proliferation of ineffective, uncoordinated programs only vaguely related to the ends they are supposed to serve. To gain control and reduce the sense of normless- ness, Toffler advocates a new system of societal decision-making. The steps he outlines include the organization of what he calls "imaginetic centers," utopianism, and institutes for scientific futurism—all intended to generate a rich flow of ideas about possible futures. Through "antici- patory democracy," these visions and relevant data could then be used to consciously set goals and make decisions about the future. Change could thus be comprehended, organized, and controlled rather than being a major source of disorganization and disorientation.

Can one live in a society that is out of control? That is the question posed for us by the concept of future shock. For that is the situation we find ourselves in. If it were technology alone that had broken loose, our problems would be serious enough. The deadly fact is, however, that many other social processes have also begun to run free, oscillating wildly, resisting our best efforts to guide them.

Urbanization, ethnic conflict, migration, population, crime—a thousand examples spring to mind of fields in which our efforts to shape change seem increasingly inept and futile. Some of these are strongly related to the breakaway of technology; others partially independent of it. The uneven, rocketing rates of change, the shifts and jerks in direction, compel us to ask whether the techno-societies, even comparatively small ones like Sweden and Belgium, have grown too complex, too fast to manage?

How can we prevent mass future shock, selectively adjusting the tempos of change, raising or lowering levels of stimulation, when governments—including those with the best intentions—seem unable even to point change in the right direction?

Thus a leading American urbanologist writes with unconcealed disgust: "At a cost of more than three billion dollars, the Urban Renewal Agency has succeeded in materially reducing the supply of low cost housing in American cities." Similar debacles could be cited in a dozen fields. Why do welfare programs today often cripple rather than help their clients? Why do college students, supposedly a pam- pered elite, riot and rebel? Why do expressways add to traffic conges- tion rather than reduce it? In short, why do so many well-intentioned liberal programs turn rancid so rapidly, producing side effects that cancel our their central effects? No wonder Raymond Fletcher, a frustrated Member of Parliament in Britain, recently complained: "Society's gone random!"

If random means a literal absence of pattern, he is, of course, overstating the case. But if random means that the outcomes of social policy have become erratic and hard to predict, he is right on target. Here, then, is the political meaning of future shock. For just as individual future shock results from an inability to keep pace with the rate of change, governments, too, suffer from a kind of collective future shock—a breakdown of their decisional processes.

With chilling clarity, Sir Geoffrey Vickers, the eminent British social scientist, has identified the issues: "The rate of change increases at an accelerating speed, without a corresponding acceleration in the rate at which further responses can be made; and this brings us nearer the threshold beyond which control is lost." . . .

TIME HORIZONS

Technocrats suffer from myopia. Their instinct is to think about immediate returns, immediate consequences. They are premature members of the now generation.

If a region needs electricity, they reach for a power plant. The fact that such a plant might sharply alter labor patterns, that within a decade it might throw men out of work, force large-scale retraining of workers, and swell the social welfare costs of a nearby city—such considerations are too remote in time to concern them. The fact that the plant could trigger devastating ecological consequences a generation later simply does not register in their time frame.

In a world of accelerant change, next year is nearer to us than next month was in a more leisurely era. This radically altered fact of life must be internalized by decision-makers in industry, government and elsewhere. Their time horizons must be extended.

To plan for a more distant future does not mean to tie oneself to dogmatic programs. Plans can be tentative, fluid, subject to continual revision. Yet flexibility need not mean shortsightedness. To transcend technocracy, our social time horizons must reach decades, even generations, into the future. . . .

We are . . . witnessing a perfectly extraordinary thrust toward more scientific appraisal of future probabilities, a ferment likely, in itself, to have a powerful impact on the future. It would be foolish to oversell the ability of science, as yet, to forecast complex events accurately. Yet the danger today is not that we will overestimate our ability; the real danger is that we will under-utilize it. For even when our still-primitive attempts at scientific forecasting turn out to be grossly in error, the very effort helps us identify key variables in change, it helps clarify goals, and it forces more careful evaluation of policy alternatives. In these ways, if no others, probing the future pays off in the present.

Anticipating *probable* futures, however, is only part of what needs doing if we are to shift the planner's time horizon and infuse the entire society with a greater sense of tomorrow. For we must also vastly widen our conception of *possible** futures. To the rigorous discipline of science, we must add the flaming imagination of art.

Today as never before we need a multiplicity of visions, dreams and prophecies—images of potential tomorrows. Before we can rationally decide which alternative pathways to choose, which cultural styles to pursue, we must first ascertain which are possible. Conjecture, speculation and the visionary view thus become as coldly practical a necessity as feet-on-the-floor "realism" was in an earlier time.

This is why some of the world's biggest and most tough-minded corporations, once the living embodiment of presentism, today hire intuitive futurists, science fiction writers and visionaries as consultants. . . .

Corporations must not remain the only agencies with access to such services. Local government, schools, voluntary associations and others also need to examine their potential futures imaginatively. One way to help them do so would be to establish in each community "imaginetic centers" devoted to technically assisted brainstorming. These would be places where people noted for creative imagination, rather than technical expertise, are brought together to examine present crises, to anticipate future crises, and to speculate freely, even playfully, about possible futures.

What, for example, are the possible futures of urban transportation? Traffic is a problem involving space. How might the city of tomorrow cope with the movement of men and objects through space? To speculate about this question, an imaginetic center might enlist artists, sculptors, dancers, furniture designers, parking lot attendants, and a variety of other people who, in one way or another, manipulate space imaginatively. Such people, assembled under the right circumstances, would inevitably come up with ideas of which the technocratic city planners, the highway engineers and transit authorities have never dreamed.

Musicians, people who live near airports, jack-hammer men and subway conductors might well imagine new ways to organize, mask or suppress noise. Groups of young people might be invited to ransack their minds for previously unexamined approaches to urban sanitation,

*Italics added.

crowding, ethnic conflict, care of the aged, or a thousand other present and future problems. . . .

The rushing stream of wild, unorthodox, eccentric or merely color-ful ideas generated in these sanctuaries of social imagination must, after they have been expressed, be subjected to merciless screening. Only a tiny fraction of them will survive this filtering process. These few, however, could be of the utmost importance in calling attention to new possibilities that might otherwise escape notice. . . .

While imaginetic centers concentrate on partial images of tomorrow, defining possible futures for a single industry, an organization, a city or its subsystems, however, we also need sweeping, visionary ideas about the society as a whole. Multiplying our images of possible futures is important; but these images need to be organized, crystallized into structured form. In the past, utopian literature did this for us. It played a practical, crucial role in ordering men's dreams about alternative futures. Today we suffer for lack of utopian ideas around which to organize competing images of possible futures.

Most traditional utopias picture simple and static societies—i.e., societies that have nothing in common with super-industrialism. B. F. Skinner's *Walden Two,* the model for several existing experimental communes, depicts a pre-industrial way of life—small, close to the earth, built on farming and handcraft. Even those two brilliant anti-utopias, *Brave New World* and *1984,* now seem oversimple. Both describe societies based on high technology and low complexity: the machines are sophisticated but the social and cultural relationships are fixed and deliberately simplified.

Today we need powerful new utopian and anti-utopian concepts that look forward to super industrialism, rather than backward to simpler societies. These concepts, however, can no longer be produced in the old way. First, no book, by itself, is adequate to describe a super-industrial future in emotionally compelling terms. . . . Second, it may now be too difficult for any individual writer, no matter how gifted, to describe a convincingly complex future. We need, therefore, a revolu-tion in the production of utopias: collaborative utopianism. We need to construct "utopia factories."

One way might be to assemble a small group of top social scientists—an economist, a sociologist, an anthropologist, and so on—asking them to work together, even live together, long enough to hammer out among themselves a set of well-defined values on which they believe a truly super-industrial utopian society might be based.

Each member of the team might then attempt to describe in non-fiction form a sector of an imagined society built on these values. What would its family structure be like? Its economy, laws, religion, sexual practices, youth culture, music, art, its sense of time, its degree of differentiation, its psychological problems? By working together and ironing out inconsistencies, where possible, a comprehensive and adequately complex picture might be drawn of a seamless, temporary form of super-industrialism. . . .

Meanwhile, other groups could be at work on counter-utopias. While Utopia A might stress materialist, success-oriented values, Utopia B might base itself on sensual, hedonistic values, C on the primacy of aesthetic values, D on individualism, E on collectivism, and so forth. Ultimately, a stream of books, plays, films and television programs would flow from this collaboration between art, social science and futurism, thereby educating large numbers of people about the costs and benefits of the various proposed utopias.

Finally, if social imagination is in short supply, we are even more lacking in people willing to subject utopian ideas to systematic test. More and more young people, in their dissatisfaction with industrialism, are experimenting with their own lives, forming utopian communities, trying new social arrangements, from group marriage to living-learning communes. Today, as in the past, the weight of established society comes down hard on the visionary who attempts to practice, as well as merely preach. Rather than ostracizing utopians, we should take advantage of their willingness to experiment, encouraging them with money and tolerance, if not respect.

Most of today's "intentional communities" or utopian colonies, however, reveal a powerful preference for the past. These may be of value to the individuals in them, but the society as a whole would be better served by utopian experiments based on super- rather than pre-industrial forms. Instead of a communal farm, why not a computer software company whose program writers live and work communally? Why not an education technology company whose members pool their money and merge their families? Instead of raising radishes or crafting sandals, why not an oceanographic research installation organized along utopian lines? Why not a group medical practice that takes advantage of the latest medical technology but whose members accept modest pay and pool their profits to run a completely new-style medical school? Why not recruit living groups to try out the proposals of the utopia factories?

In short, we can use utopianism as a tool rather than an escape, if we base our experiments on the technology and society of tomorrow rather than that of the past. And once done, why not the most rigorous, scientific analysis of the results? The findings could be priceless, were they to save us from mistakes or lead us toward more workable organizational forms for industry, education, family life or politics. . . .

Indeed, with these as a background, we must consciously begin to multiply the scientific future-sensing organs of society. Scientific futurist institutes must be spotted like nodes in a loose network throughout the entire governmental structure in the techno-societies, so that in every department, local or national, some staff devotes itself systematically to scanning the probable long-term future in its assigned field. Futurists should be attached to every political party, university, corporation, professional association, trade union and student organization.

We need to train thousands of young people in the perspectives and techniques of scientific futurism, inviting them to share in the exciting venture of mapping probable futures. We also need national agencies to provide technical assistance to local communities in creating their own futurist groups. And we need a similar center, perhaps jointly funded by American and European foundations, to help incipient futurist centers in Asia, Africa, and Latin America.

We are in a race between rising levels of uncertainty produced by the acceleration of change, and the need for reasonably accurate images of what at any instant is the most probable future. The generation of reliable images of the most probable future thus becomes a matter of the highest national, indeed, international urgency.

As the globe is itself dotted with future-sensors, we might consider creating a great international institute, a world futures data bank. Such an institute, staffed with top caliber men and women from all the sciences and social sciences, would take as its purpose the collection and systematic integration of predictive reports generated by scholars and imaginative thinkers in all the intellectual disciplines all over the world.

Of course, those working in such an institute would know that they could never create a single, static diagram of the future. Instead, the product of their effort would be a constantly changing geography of the future, a continually re-created overarching image based on the best predictive work available. . . .

Only when decision-makers are armed with better forecasts of future events, when by successive approximation we increase the accuracy of forecast, will our attempts to manage change improve perceptibly. For reasonably accurate assumptions about the future are a precondition for understanding the potential consequences of our own actions. And without such understanding, the management of change is impossible. . . .

ANTICIPATORY DEMOCRACY

In the end, however, social futurism must cut even deeper. For technocrats suffer from more than econothink and myopia; they suffer, too, from the virus of elitism. To capture control of change, we shall, therefore, require a final, even more radical breakaway from technocratic tradition: we shall need a revolution in the very way we formulate our social goals. . . .

Intermittently, a change-dazed government will try to define its goals publicly. Instinctively, it establishes a commission. In 1960 President Eisenhower pressed into service, among others, a general, a judge, a couple of industrialists, a few college presidents, and a labor leader to "develop a broad outline of coordinated national policies and programs" and to "set up a series of goals in various areas of national activity." In due course, a red-white-and-blue paperback appeared with the commission's report, *Goals for Americans.* Neither the commission nor its goals had the slightest impact on the public or on policy. The juggernaut of change continued to roll through America untouched, as it were, by managerial intelligence.

A far more significant effort to tidy up governmental priorities was initiated by President Johnson, with his attempt to apply PPBS (Planning-Programming-Budgeting-System) throughout the federal establishment. PPBS is a method for tying programs much more closely and rationally to organizational goals. Thus, for example, by applying it, the Department of Health, Education and Welfare can assess the costs and benefits of alternative programs to accomplish specified goals. But who specifies these larger, more important goals? The introduction of PPBS and the systems approach is a major governmental achievement. It is of paramount importance in managing large organization efforts. But it leaves entirely untouched the profoundly political question of how the overall goals of a government or a society are to be chosen in the first place.

President Nixon, still snarled in the goals crisis, tried a third tack. "It is time," he declared, "we addressed ourselves, consciously and systematically, to the question of what kind of a nation we want to be. . . ." He thereupon put his finger on the quintessential question. But once more the method chosen for answering it proved to be inadequate. "I have today ordered the establishment, within the White House, of a National Goals Research Staff," the President announced. "This will be a small, highly technical staff, made up of experts in the collection . . . and processing of data relating to social needs, and in the projection of social trends." . . .

Behind all such efforts runs the notion that national (and, by extension, local) goals for the future of society ought to be formulated at the top. This technocratic premise perfectly mirrors the old bureaucratic forms of organization in which line and staff were separated, in which rigid, undemocratic hierarchies distinguished leader from led, manager from managed, planner from plannee.

Yet the real, as distinct from the glibly verbalized, goals of any society on the path to super-industrialism are already too complex, too transient and too dependent for their achievement upon the willing participation of the governed, to be perceived and defined so easily. We cannot hope to harness the runaway forces of change by assembling a kaffee klatsch of elders to set goals for us or by turning the task over to a "highly technical staff." A revolutionary new approach to goal-setting is needed. . . .

In complex, differentiated societies, vast amounts of information must flow at even faster speeds between the formal organizations and subcultures that make up the whole, and between the layers and sub-structures within these.

Political democracy, by incorporating larger and larger numbers in social decision-making, facilitates feedback. And it is precisely this feedback that is essential to control. To assume control over accelerant change, we shall need still more advanced—and more democratic—feedback mechanisms.

The technocrat, however, still thinking in top-down terms, frequently makes plans without arranging for adequate and instantaneous feedback from the field, so that he seldom knows how well his plans are working. When he does arrange for feedback, what he usually asks for and gets is heavily economic, inadequately social, psychological or cultural. Worse yet, he makes these plans without sufficiently taking into account the fast-changing needs and wishes of those whose participation is needed to make them a success. He assumes the right to set social goals by himself or he accepts them blindly from some higher authority. . . .

Let us convene in each nation, in each city, in each neighborhood, democratic constituent assemblies charged with social stock-taking, charged with defining and assigning priorities to specific social goals for the remainder of the century.

Such "social future assemblies" might represent not merely geographical localities, but social units—industy, labor, the churches, the intellectual community, the arts, women, ethnic and religious groups, students, with organized representation for the unorganized as well. There are no sure-fire techniques for guaranteeing equal representation for all, or for eliciting the wishes of the poor, the inarticulate or the isolated. Yet once we recognize the need to include them, we shall find the ways. Indeed, the problem of participating in the definition of the future is not merely a problem of the poor, the inarticulate and the isolated. Highly paid executives, wealthy professionals, extremely articulate intellectuals and students—all at one time or another feel cut off from the power to influence the directions and pace of change. Wiring them into the system, making them a part of the guidance machinery of the society, is the most critical political task of the coming generation. Imagine the effect if at one level or another a place were provided where all those who will live in the future might voice their wishes about it. Imagine, in short, a massive, global exercise in anticipatory democracy.

Social future assemblies need not—and, given the rate of transience —cannot be anchored, permanent institutions. Instead, they might take the form of ad hoc groupings, perhaps called into being at regular intervals with different representatives participating each time. Today citizens are expected to serve on juries when needed. They give a few days or a few weeks of their time for this service, recognizing that the jury system is one of the guarantees of democracy, that, even though service may be inconvenient, someone must do the job. Social future assemblies could be organized along similar lines, with a constant stream of new participants brought together for short periods to serve as society's "consultants on the future." . . .

All social future assemblies . . . could and should be backed with technical staff to provide data on the social and economic costs of various goals, and to show the cost and benefits of proposed trade-offs, so that participants would be in a position to make reasonably informed choices, as it were, among alternative futures. . . .

Most important of all . . . social future assemblies would help shift the culture toward a more super-industrial time-bias. By focusing public attention for once on long-range goals rather than immediate programs alone, by asking people to choose a preferable future from among a range of alternative futures, these assemblies could dramatize the possibilities for . . . the future—possibilities that all too many have already given up as lost. In so doing, social future assemblies could unleash powerful constructive forces. . . .

Throughout the past, . . . man's awareness followed rather than preceded the event. Because change was slow, he could adapt unconsciously. . . . Today unconscious adaptation is no longer adequate. . . . [M]an must now assume conscious control . . . Avoiding future shock as he rides the waves of change, he must master . . . tomorrow. . . . Instead of rising in revolt against it, he must, from this historic moment on, anticipate and design the future.

Selected References

Burke, John G. (ed.), *The New Technology and Human Values.* Belmont, California: Wadsworth, 1966.
Readings which describe technological changes in various facets of life, how they affect human values, choices which must be made, and suggestions for restoring equilibrium.

Kobrin, Solomon, "The Chicago Area Project—a Twenty-Five Year Assessment," *The Annals of the American Academy of Political and Social Science* 322 (March 1959), pp. 1–29.
The Chicago Area Project was developed from the social disorganization perspective to address the problem of juvenile delinquency in low-income urban areas. Kobrin assesses this program after twenty-five years.

McCorkle, Lloyd W., and Richard Korn, "Resocialization within Walls," *The Annals of the American Academy of Political and Social Science* 293 (May 1954), pp. 88–98.
There is considerable culture conflict, normlessness, and normative breakdown among the inmates, staff, and professionals working in prisons. To rehabilitate prisoners, McCorkle and Korn argue, prisons need to develop clear, consistent, and enforced rules.

McHugh, Peter, "Social Disintegration as a Requisite of Resocialization," *Social Forces* 44 (March 1966), pp. 355–63.
In a highly theoretical argument, McHugh maintains that resocialization may be possible only through a state of deliberate social disorganization.

Sanders, William B., "Criminal Justice and Social Control," in Don H. Zimmerman, D. Lawrence Wieder, and Siu Zimmerman (eds.), *Understanding Social Problems,* New York: Praeger, 1976, pp. 326–53.
Sanders claims that the criminal justice system is currently suffering from serious social disorganization. He discusses the "repairs" that are needed to reinstate effective social organization in this system.

Sennett, Richard, *The Uses of Disorder: Personal Identity and City Life,* New York: Knopf, 1970.
In urban areas that are currently disorganized, Sennett claims, neighbors need to come together to confront one another and to resolve their conflicts. In so doing, he argues, they will get to know one another as individuals, work out accomodations, and develop a new system of social organization.

Toffler, Alvin (ed.), *The Futurists,* New York: Random House, 1972.
Articles by social critics, scientists, philosophers, and planners on the problems of rapid change and on planning for the future.

Von Eckardt, Wolf, "Urban Design," in Daniel P. Moynihan (ed.), *Toward a National Urban Policy,* New York: Basic Books, 1970, pp. 107–8.
Social change has produced social disorganization in America's cities. In this selection, Von Eckardt discusses the need for urban research, urban planning, and urban design to provide for orderly growth and to keep new programs from inadvertently heightening, rather than reducing, social disorganization.

Questions for Discussion

1. Do you agree with Bennis that a new form of organizational leadership is needed? In your opinion, what are the main advantages of the changes Bennis proposes? What, if any, are the

disadvantages? With the type of leadership Bennis proposes, is there a danger of becoming bogged down in "committee-itis"?

2. What do you think are the most controversial aspects of the Davis reading? Do you agree with his proposals? How would a solution from the social pathology perspective differ from the one proposed by Davis?

3. What are the main differences between Toffler's and Bennis's analyses? Do you see any similarities between their proposals? In your opinion, how realistic are their solutions?

4. How do you evaluate the social disorganization perspective and the type of solutions it suggests? Can you identify a contemporary social problem for which this approach seems especially appropriate? If so, outline a solution along the lines suggested by the social disorganization perspective. If not, why not?

4 / VALUE CONFLICT

From both the social pathology and the social disorganization perspectives, society is a unit and social problems are identified in terms of the whole unit. People using these perspectives assume that social problems can be "objectively" identified and scientifically solved, and they usually focus on situations that most people agree to be problems—e.g., mental illness, alcoholism, juvenile delinquency.

Yet there are many times when people cannot agree about how to define a problem, much less what to do about it! Consider the case of striking coal miners, for example. The miners may define the problem as one of low pay, inadequate retirement and health benefits, or unsatisfactory bargaining arrangements. Management may define the problem in an entirely different way. To them it may be a problem of sheer economics (e.g., implementing the strikers' demands may be too costly) or may involve larger symbolic issues (e.g., "creeping socialism" or a breakdown in the work ethic). To the average citizen the problem may be an energy shortage. There may be power cutbacks and rising energy prices. If the strike lasts very long, industries may have to shut down because of fuel shortage. And so another problem emerges—unemployment. Each of these groups, then, defines the problem in a different way, and each advocates a different type of solution.

To the value conflict theorists, such conflicts are natural. According to them, society is not a unit or a system. Rather, it consists of many different groups and factions, each with its own point of view and interests. This is especially true in a pluralistic society like the United States or Canada. Not only is there a very complex economy, which inevitably pits some people's economic interests against others', there is also a diversity of ethnic and cultural groups, religions, lifestyles, ideologies, and allegiances. All these differences create a diversity of *values*. As various groups pursue their own values with regard to one issue or another (e.g., financial profits versus industrial safety), they are often brought into direct *value conflict.*

The value conflict perspective draws on a long tradition of conflict theory in European and American sociology,[1] which often views a stable system of social organization as an organized state of oppression and domination (e.g., slavery or the economic exploitation of unskilled workers by the early industrialists). Thus history and current events tend to be seen in terms of ongoing struggles between groups.

During the twenties and thirties, there were several studies that analyzed social problems from a conflict perspective. Yet throughout this period it was the social disorganization perspective that dominated the study of social problems. With the Great Depression and the approach of World War II, however, conflict between groups became increasingly clear, and around 1940 the value conflict perspective took shape as a cogent way of looking at social problems.

The value conflict apporach to social problems was first presented by Richard C. Fuller and Richard R. Myers in 1941.[2] According to Fuller and Myers, social problems go through a natural career of three stages. In the first stage, *awareness,* a group succeeds in calling public attention to some situation which it defines as a problem. In the second stage, *policy determination*, policies are established to deal with the problem. In the third stage, *reform*,

1. Of special importance for American sociology were Karl Marx and Georg Simmel in Europe, and Albion Small and Robert Park in America. See, for example, Karl Marx and Friedrich Engels, *Selected Works,* 2 Vols. (Moscow: Foreign Languages Publishing House, 1965); Georg Simmel, "The Sociology of Conflict," Albion Small, trans., *American Journal of Sociology* 9 (1903–04), pp. 490–525, 672–89, 798–811; Albion W. Small and George E. Vincent, *An Introduction to the Study of Society* (New York: American Book Company, 1894); Robert E. Park and Ernest W. Burgess, *Introduction to the Science of Sociology* (Chicago: University of Chicago Press, 1921).

2. Richard C. Fuller and Richard R. Myers, "Some Aspects of a Theory of Social Problems," *American Sociological Review* 6 (February 1941), pp. 24–32; Richard C. Fuller and Richard R. Myers, "The Natural History of a Social Problem," *American Sociological Review* 6 (June 1941), pp. 320–28. Important articles leading up to this crystallization include Richard C. Fuller, "Sociological Theory and Social Problems," *Social Forces* 15 (May 1937), pp. 496–502; Richard C. Fuller, "The Problem of Teaching Social Problems," *American Journal of Sociology* 44 (November 1938), pp. 415–28; Richard C. Fuller, "Social Problems, P. I," in R. E. Park (ed.), *An Outline of the Principles of Sociology* (New York: Barnes and Noble, 1939), pp. 3–61.

these policies are administered for a lasting solution. At each of these stages, according to Fuller and Myers, different interest groups are in conflict with one another, and each group seeks to influence events in accord with its own values. Different groups are liable to define the problem differently, advocate different solutions, and have different criteria regarding when a problem can be viewed as solved. Of course, a group's success in controlling each stage is linked to its relative power, whether there is an organized opposition to it, and whether there are institutionalized channels for dealing with such conflicts. It is generally agreed that established channels help to limit the amount of disruption and violence in the process of defining a problem and demanding its resolution, and that such channels may also insure a more equitable resolution. On the other hand, by preventing the eruption of open hostilities, institutionalized channels may also undermine the ability of the protesting group to force concessions from the dominant group.

If each group defines the social problem differently, then what definition should be used in studying social problems? If it is all just a matter of arbitrary values, then how can the student of social problems possibly hope to "objectively" identify or analyze social problems? The answer offered by the value conflict perspective may seem fuzzy, but basically it is this: *a situation is a social problem when people say it is.* Thus it is all a matter of definition. Two criteria must be met for a social problem to be effectively defined. First, people must call attention to the unfavorable situation. Then they must instill a sense of moral indignation about the situation and a hope that the situation can be changed and improved. As long as apathy reigns, the definition process remains incomplete and no action is taken against the problematic situation. When a group succeeds in calling attention to a problem and demanding change, that group has succeeded in defining a new social problem.

In considering the value conflict perspective, three qualities stand out. First, this approach is *group-centered.* Social problems are viewed as being caused neither by immoral individuals (as in the social pathology perspective) nor by lack of coordination or regulation (as in the social disorganization perspective), but rather by a very real and natural conflict between various segments of the population. Social problems are seen as struggles by groups to uphold their rights or to advance their values against opposition. This group-centeredness is reflected in their use of terms such as *allies* and *opponents, factions* or *sides, community, group identity, interests,* and *the movement.*

Moreover, this group-centeredness is seen in the particular problems that value conflict proponents tend to address. This perspective is most often used to deal with social issues that are controversial, that have an identifiable collective "victim," and/or that generate social action and protest. Such problems are well exemplified by issues of group discrimination or exploitation. Recent movements by blacks and other ethnic groups, the women's movement, and the gay rights movement all fall into this category. Other examples include movements generated by a clear conflict of values between different portions of the population—e.g., the antiwar movement of the sixties, and the abortion controversy of the seventies.

Second, the value conflict perspective is *evaluative*. In this regard the value conflict perspective is quite different from the social pathology and social disorganization approaches. Whereas the pathology and disorganization perspectives both suggest "objective," neutral definitions of social problems, the value conflict perspective does not even pretend to be neutral. In fact, conflict theorists point out that what masquerades as neutral, objective definitions of social problems are really themselves value-laden judgments.[3] Thus, they suggest, situations diagnosed as cases of "pathology" or "disorganization" are, more often than not, simply situations that deviate from the canons of middle-class morality. People using a value conflict approach often analyze social problems from an admittedly partisan point of view. Moreover, in contrast to the social disorganization perspective, conflict theorists assume there is nothing wrong with people fighting to uphold their own values against the competing values of other groups, even though this causes a certain amount of disruption or disorganization. In fact, conflict theory often views the prevailing social order as merely a system of oppression designed to preserve the values of the predominant group.

In making their evaluations, people using the value conflict perspective tend to take the side of those with less power and to make judgments against the status quo. They often analyze prob-

---

3. See, for example, Louis Wirth, "Ideological Aspects of Social Disorganization," *American Sociological Review* 4 (August 1940), pp. 472–82; C. Wright Mills, "The Professional Ideology of Social Pathologists," *American Journal of Sociology* 49 (Sept. 1942), pp. 165–80.

lems in terms of *discrimination, domination, exploitation,* or *oppression.* They talk of the oppressed group's *grievances* and its struggles for *community control, equality, freedom, justice, liberation, reform,* and *rights.*

Third, the value conflict perspective is *action-oriented,* i.e., more interested in arriving at effective strategies than at abstract theoretical statements. It is used by people who are especially interested in organizing action to maximize a group's power and effectiveness for a resolution in accord with their values. Their writings and rhetoric are usually rich in terms referring to the realities of confrontation and power—e.g., *action, demands, demonstration, fight, militancy, overthrow, polarization, politics, power, protest, radical, strategy, strike, struggle,* and *tactics.* Or, on a subtler note, they may talk of *bargains, deals, demands,* and *negotiation.*

As noted earlier, the value conflict perspective took shape during the thirties and forties—a time of great conflict and unrest both within and between nations. With the fifties, however, came a period of prosperity and relative tranquility, and the notion of group conflict once again became less salient for sociologists. Yet the value conflict perspective has not died. During the political turmoil and social activism of the sixties, the value conflict perspective once again came into vogue and can still be seen in numerous textbooks and research reports.[4]

The resolution of social problems from the value conflict perspective may range all the way from bargaining and compromise to a naked display of force. In bargaining, the two sides each make certain concessions to arrive at a mutually agreed upon settlement, as is usually the case in collective bargaining. Or the protesting faction might bargain for a recognized voice in the decision-making process (although such a voice is often an ineffective solution if it is not backed up by some kind of power).

Another possible solution (perhaps more desirable than plausible) is consensus. In consensus, the conflict is resolved when the parties find a common ground on which they can agree and lay their conflict aside in pursuit of the agreed-upon values. Political alliances often exemplify this, as do international treaties (e.g., when the Soviet Union allied with Great Britain and the United States during World War II).

4. See, for example, John F. Cuber, William F. Kenkel, and Robert A. Harper, *Problems of American Society: Values in Conflict,* 4th ed. (New York: Holt, Rinehart & Winston, 1964).

If neither negotiation nor consensus can resolve the dispute, the most likely solution is resolution by power or force. This may involve violence or terrorism (e.g., guerrilla actions), or, in other cases, exerting economic power (e.g., withholding rent from slum landlords).

Whatever the particular solution sought for a particular problem, the value conflict perspective suggests several steps a group should take in its own behalf. First, in order for a group to be successful in calling attention to a problem and doing something about it, it is important for it to *organize* in some enduring way. Labor unions are an excellent example of this. By organizing, workers were transformed from an assortment of powerless individual employees to a powerful economic and political force. More recently, welfare rights organizations have tried to make welfare recipients a more powerful force to be taken into account in the legislation and administration of welfare programs.

Organization is facilitated by establishing channels of communication among group members or potential members. Newsletters, meetings, and "underground" networks have all served this purpose for various groups, and at times the mass media have also been utilized to "spread the word" to potential members. A formal structure with officers and representatives may also facilitate the organizing effort, especially if the group wants to influence government or business.

On a more psychological level, organization is facilitated by the development of a group identity. Individuals begin to think of themselves as part of a victimized group, and they develop a sense of communion and concern about the movement. This identification may involve a defiance of conventional values, as is the case when group members develop a new pride and openness about an identity that had formerly been regarded as undesirable or unimportant. The slogan of the Black Power Movement—"Black is beautiful"—was very important in this regard. Similarly, the openness displayed by homosexual activists ("Out of the closets and into the streets!") has helped to undermine the traditional attitude of shame associated with homosexuality.

Another step toward solving social problems according to this perspective is *confrontation*. Demonstrations, marches, picketing, strikes, sit-ins, and teach-ins are examples of confrontation tactics that were used effectively by specific social movements formed around conflict over such issues as the Vietnam war, poverty, and racial injustice. More recently, we have seen the development of still other tactics of confrontation—taking hostages for political demands.

When confronting the opposition, it is important to present an appearance of organization and of serious intention, even if the number and power of the protesting group is not great. One radical leader, with this in mind, suggests that it is wise for the group to adopt an official name, to have formal leaders or spokespersons, and to recruit as many members as possible.[5]

A third step in solving social problems from the value conflict perspective is to *insure a lasting recognition of the group's values.* Initial confrontations must be followed by some more enduring recognition of the group's values by the opposition or the general public. For this reason, people often turn to official change as the final solution to their problem. They may work for legislative action, such as the Civil Rights Bill of 1964 or the Equal Rights Amendment, or they may work to elect sympathetic candidates, assuming that this will result in some lasting changes. They may seek to change administrative policies, and some may urge changes in religious or professional codes.

Whatever the particular solution sought, the crucial point is this: from the value conflict perspective, one cannot trust education or a spirit of cooperation to provide effective solutions to social problems because the underlying conflicts will often remain. Thus some more fundamental and official changes are usually necessary to insure that the old situation will not simply crop up again as soon as the demonstrators have gone home or the terrorists disbanded.

CHARACTERISTICS OF THE VALUE CONFLICT PERSPECTIVE: A SUMMARY

From the value conflict perspective, society is viewed not as an organic or systemic whole but rather as an assortment of groups with different and often conflicting values. Each group pursues its own values, and this brings groups into conflict over a variety of issues. Social problems reflect such conflicts. The specific features of this perspective are as follows:

5. Saul Alinsky, *Rules for Radicals* (New York: Random House, 1971).

Definition.   Social problems are public issues that are incompatible with a particular group's values. When such a group calls public attention to a particular situation and demands a change, then it has succeeded in defining a social problem.

Causes.   Social problems are caused by the conflict between different groups' values. Ultimately, the root cause of most social problems goes back to the economic, social, and cultural diversity of the society.

Conditions.   Direct competition between groups often seems to foster the development of social problems. And once the alarm is sounded, the type of contact and relative power of the groups involved affects the tactics each group is likely to use, how quickly the problem is resolved, and the type of resolution that results.

Consequences.   One consequence of social problems is often a lasting sense of hostility and disrespect between groups. In the most extreme cases this can mean civil war. Another result can be that the group with the most power and force wins—"might equals right." One positive outcome of value conflict may be a greater clarification of the group's values and loyalties.

Solutions.   The solution to a social problem, according to this perspective, lies in group action. Specifically, the group should organize, confront their opponents, and work for lasting changes in policy or legislation. While persuasion and education of the public may be helpful, the ultimate solution is likely to rest on building a base of political and economic power.

BLACKS AND UNEQUAL EDUCATION

Stokley Carmichael and Charles V. Hamilton

Experience has shown that schools in black communities are usually inferior to those in white communities, in part because of poorer financing and in part because of the indifference and insensitivity of white-dominated school boards. To overcome such inequities, most cities have adopted some form of busing for racial desegregation. Carmichael and Hamilton suggest a different type of solution—one formulated along the lines of the value conflict approach. Black education is inferior, they claim, because black parents are politically and economically powerless. Thus Carmichael and Hamilton urge blacks to organize, unite, and demand control over their own communities and institutions. To accomplish this, they claim, blacks must organize independently of white organizations and political parties. Through such a united front, they maintain, blacks could improve the quality not only of their schools but of other aspects of community life as well.

We are aware that it has become commonplace to pinpoint and describe the ills of our urban ghettos. The social, political and economic problems are so acute that even a casual observer cannot fail to see that something is wrong. While description is plentiful, however, there remains a blatant timidity about what to *do* to solve the problems.

Neither rain nor endless "definitive," costly reports nor stop-gap measures will even approach a solution to the explosive situation in the nation's ghettos. This country cannot begin to solve the problems of the ghettos as long as it continues to hang on to outmoded structures and institutions. A political party system that seeks only to "manage conflict" and hope for the best will not be able to serve a growing body of alienated black people. An educational system which, year after year, continues to cripple hundreds of thousands of black children must be replaced by wholly new mechanisms of control and management. We

must begin to think and operate in terms of entirely new and substantially different forms of expression.

It is crystal clear that the initiative for such changes will have to
come from the black community. We cannot expect white America to
begin to move forcefully on these problems unless and until black
America begins to move. This means that black people must organize
themselves without regard for what is traditionally acceptable, precisely
because the traditional approaches have failed. It means that black
people must make demands without regard to their initial "respect-
ability," precisely because "respectable" demands have not been sufficient.

The northern urban ghettos are in many ways different from the
black-belt South, but *in neither area will substantial change come
about until black people organize independently to exert power.*°
. . . [B]lack people already have the voting potential to control the
politics of entire southern counties. Given maximum registration of
blacks, there are more than 110 counties where black people could
outvote the white racists. These people should concentrate on forming
independent political parties and not waste time trying to reform or
convert the racist parties. In the North, it is no less important that
independent groups be formed. It has been clearly shown that when
black people attempt to get within one of the two major parties in the
cities, they become co-opted and their interests are shunted to the
background. They become expendable.

We must begin to think of the black community as a base of
organization to control institutions in that community. Control of the
ghetto schools must be taken out of the hands of "professionals," most
of whom have long since demonstrated their insensitivity to the needs
and problems of the black child. These "experts" bring with them
middle-class biases, unsuitable techniques and materials; these are, at
best, dysfunctional and at worst destructive. A recent study of New
York schools reveals that the New York school system is run by thirty
people—school supervisors, deputy and assistant superintendents and
examiners. The study concluded: "Public education policy has become
the province of the professional bureaucrat, with the tragic result that
the status quo, suffering from many difficulties, is the order of the
day."[1] Virtually no attention is paid to the wishes and demands of the
parents, especially the black parents. This is totally unacceptable.

Black parents should seek as their goal the actual control of the
public schools in their community: hiring and firing of teachers, selection of teaching materials, determination of standards, etc. This can be
done with a committee of teachers. The traditional, irrelevant "See

°Italics added.

Dick, See Jane, Run Dick, Run Jane, White House, Nice Farm" nonsense must be ended. The principals and as many teachers as possible of the ghetto schools should be black. The children will be able to see their kind in positions of leadership and authority. It should never occur to anyone that a brand new school can be built in the heart of the black community and then given a white person to head it. The fact is that in this day and time, it is crucial that race be taken into account in determining policy of this sort. Some people will, again, view this as "reverse segregation" or as "racism." It is not. It is emphasizing race in a positive way: not to subordinate or rule over others but to overcome the effects of centuries in which race has been used to the detriment of the black man.

The story of I.S. 201 in New York City is a case in point. In 1958, the city's Board of Education announced that it would build a special $5-million school in District 4, whose pupils are 90 percent black, 8 percent Puerto Rican, with the remaining 2 percent white. The concept was that students from elementary schools in that district would feed into the new school at the fifth grade and after the eighth grade would move on to high school. This concept, at least according to official policy, was supposed to speed integration.

The parents of children who might be attending the school mobilized in an attempt, once and for all, to have a school adequate for the needs of Harlem. The Board had picked the site for I.S. 201: between 127th and 128th Streets, from Madison Avenue to Park Avenue—in the heart of Central Harlem. The parents argued against this location because they wanted an integrated school, which would be impossible unless it was located on the fringes, not in the heart, of Central Harlem. Their desire clearly points up the colonial relationship of blacks and whites in the city; they knew the only way to get quality education was to have white pupils in the school.

The Board of Education indicated that the school would be integrated, but the parents knew it could not be done and they demonstrated against the site during construction. When they saw that the school would have no windows, they also raised the question of whether this was merely a stylistic or practical innovation, or a means of closing out the reality of the community from the pupils for the hours they would be inside.

During the spring and summer of 1966, some six hundred pupils registered at I.S. 201—all of them black or Puerto Rican. Their parents then threatened that if the school wasn't integrated by fall, they would boycott it. The Board of Education, giving lip service to the parents, passed out and mailed 10,000 leaflets to the white community—in June!

Needless to say, few people go to a school on the basis of a leaflet received while getting off the subway or wherever, and even fewer (white) people want to send their children to school in Harlem. The request for "volunteers" had no effect, and on September 7, the Board of Education finally admitted its "apparent inability to integrate the school." It was the inability of that class . . . "whose primary interest is to secure objects for service, management, and control," the objects in this case being the mothers of I.S. 201. Threatened by a boycott, the school was not opened as scheduled on September 12, 1966.

At this point, the parents—who were picketing—moved in the only way they could: to demand some form of control which would enable them to break out of the old colonial pattern. In view of the fact that whites would not send their children to the school, one parent stated, "We decided we would have to have a voice to ensure that we got quality education segregated-style. We wanted built-in assurances." The parents knew that within a few years, given that pattern, this new school would be like all others which started with fine facilities and deteriorated under an indifferent bureaucracy. The parents' demands thus shifted from integration to control.

On September 16, Superintendent Bernard E. Donovan offered them a voice in screening and recommending candidates for supervisory and teaching positions at the school. An East Harlem community council would be set up with a strong voice in school affairs. The parents also wanted some control over the curriculum, the career guidance system, and financial matters, which the Board deemed legally impossible. Shortly afterward, the white principal—Stanley Lisser—voluntarily requested transfer. A black principal had been one of the parents' key demands. With these two developments, the parents announced that they would send their children to school.

At this point (September 19), however, the United Federation of Teachers bolted. The teachers at I.S. 201 threatened to boycott if Lisser did not stay. Within twenty-four hours, the Board had rescinded its agreement and restored Lisser. (It is contended by many that this was the result of planned collusion between the Board and the U.F.T.) Nine days late, the school opened. The parents became divided; some gladly began sending their children to school while others did the same because they were unaware that the agreement had been rescinded.

The parents' negotiating committee had moved to get outside help, while the city's top administrators, including Mayor Lindsay, entered the picture. A Harlem committee representing parents and community leaders proposed on September 29 that I.S. 201 be put under a special "operations board" composed of four parents and four university educators with another member selected by those eight. This board would pass on the selection of teachers and supervisors, and evaluate the curriculum at I.S. 201 as well as three elementary or "feeder" schools.

But the U.F.T. attacked this proposal. As the struggle dragged on, it became clear that once again efforts by the community to deal with its problems had been laid waste.

Later, in October, the Board of Education offered the parents a take-it-or-leave-it proposal. It proposed a council of parents and teachers that would be purely advisory. The parents flatly rejected this. Father Vincent Resta, a Catholic priest and chairman of the local school board which covered I.S. 201, stated, "In theory the Board's proposal is something that could work. But an advisory role implies trust. And the community has absolutely no reason to trust the Board of Education." The local board later resigned en masse.

But the issue of community control did not end there. It had become clear to the parents that their problems were not restricted to School District 4. When the Board of Education met to discuss its proposed budget in December, 1966, I.S. 201 parents and others came to protest the allocation of resources. Unable to get any response, at the end of one session they simply moved from the gallery into the chairs of those meeting and elected a People's Board of Education. After forty-eight hours, they were arrested and removed but continued to meet in another location, with the Rev. Milton A. Galamison—who had led school boycotts previously in New York City—as President.

At one of its executive sessions on January 8, 1967, the People's Board adopted a motion which stated its goals as:

1. To seek to alter the structure of the school system . . . so it is responsible to our individual community needs, in order to achieve real community control. This may require legislative or state constitutional convention action. This means, of course, decentralization, accountability, meaningful citizen participation, etc.

2. To develop a program which will get grassroots awareness for, understanding of, and support for the goal stated above. It is suggested that we give up top priority to organizing and educating parents and citizens in the poverty areas (approximately 14).

3. That we recognize that power should not rest in any central board, including our own, and that by every means possible we should encourage the development and initiative of local people's groups.

The parents at I.S. 201 failed because they are still powerless. But they succeeded in heating up the situation to the point where the dominant society will have to make certain choices. It is clear that black people are concerned about the type of education their children receive; many more people can be activated by a demonstrated ability to achieve results. One result has already been achieved by the I.S. 201 struggle: the concept of community control has now rooted itself in the consciousness of many black people. Such control has long been accepted in smaller communities, particularly white suburban areas.

No longer is it "white folks' business" only. Ultimately, community-controlled schools could organize an independent school board (like the "People's Board of Education") for the total black community. Such an innovation would permit the parents and the school to develop a much closer relationship and to begin attacking the problems of the ghetto in a communal, realistic way. . . .

Virtually all of the money earned by merchants and exploiters of the black ghetto leaves those communities. Properly organized black groups should seek to establish a community rebate plan. The black people in a given community would organize and refuse to do business with any merchant who did not agree to "reinvest," say, forty to fifty percent of his net profit in the indigenous community. This contribution could take many forms: providing additional jobs for black people, donating scholarship funds for students, supporting certain types of community organizations. An agreement would be reached between the merchants and the black consumers. If a merchant wants customers from a black community, he must be made to understand that he has to contribute to that community. If he chooses not to do so, he will not be patronized, and the end result will be *no* profits from that community. Contractors who seek to do business in the black community would also be made to understand that they face a boycott if they do not donate to the black community.

Such a community rebate plan will require careful organization and tight discipline on the part of the black people. But it is possible, and has in fact already been put into effect by some ethnic communities. White America realizes the market in the black community; black America must begin to realize the potential of that market.

Under the present institutional arrangements, no one should think that the mere election of a few black people to local or national office will solve the problem of political representation. There are now ten black people on the City Council in Chicago, but there are not more than two or three (out of the total of fifty) who will speak out forcefully. The fact is that the present political institutions are not geared to giving the black minority an effective voice. Two needs arise from this.

First, it is important that the black communities in these northern ghettos form independent party groups to elect their own choices to office when and where they can. It should not be assumed that "you cannot beat City Hall." It has been done, as evidenced by the 1967 aldermanic elections in one of the tightest machine cities in the country: Chicago. In the Sixth Ward, an independent black candidate, Sammy Rayner, defeated an incumbent, machine-backed black alderman. Rayner first ran in 1963 and missed a run-off by a mere 177 votes. He then challenged Congressman William L. Dawson in 1964 and lost, but he was building an image in the black community as one who could and would speak out. The black people were getting the message. In 1967, when he ran against the machine incumbent for the City Council, he won handily. Precincts in the East Woodlawn area that he had failed to carry in 1963 (23 out of 26), he now carried (19 out of 26). The difference was continuous, hard, day-to-day, door-to-door campaigning. His campaign manager, Philip Smith, stated: "Another key to Sammy's victory was the fact that he began to methodically get himself around the Sixth Ward. Making the black club functions, attending youth meetings and all the functions that were dear to the hearts of Sixth Ward people became the order of the day."[2]

The cynics will say that Rayner will be just one voice, unable to accomplish anything unless he buckles under to the Daley machine. Let us be very clear: we do not endorse Rayner nor are we blind to the problems he faces. It is the job of the machine to crush such men or to co-opt them before they grow in numbers and power. At the same time, men like Rayner are useful only so long as they speak to the community's broad needs; as we said . . . black visibility is not Black Power. If Rayner does not remain true to his constituents, then they should dislodge him as decisively as they did his predecessor. This establishes the principle that the black politician must first be responsive to his constituents, not to the white machine. The problem then is to resist the forces which would crush or co-opt while building community strength so that more of such men can be elected and compelled to act in the community's interest. . . .

The very least which Sammy Rayner can give the black community is a new political dignity. His victory will begin to establish the *habit* of saying "No" to the downtown bosses. In the same way that the black Southerner had to assert himself and say "No" to those who did not want him to register to vote, now the Northern black voter must begin to defy those who would control his vote. This very act of defiance threatens the status quo, because there is no predicting its ultimate outcome. Those black voters, then *accustomed* to acting independently, could eventually swing their votes one way or the other—but always for *their* benefit. . . .

Let no one protest that this type of politics is naive or childish or fails to understand the "rules of the game." The price of going along with the "regulars" is too high to pay for the so-called benefits received. The rewards of independence can be considerable. It is too soon to say precisely where this new spirit of independence could take us. New forms may lead to a new political force. Hopefully, this force might move to create new national and local political parties—or, more accurately, the first *legitimate* political parties. Some have spoken of a "third party" or "third political force." But from the viewpoint of community needs and popular participation, no existing force or party in this country has ever been relevant. A force which is relevant would therefore be a first—something truly new.

The second implication of the political dilemma facing black people is that ultimately they may have to spearhead a drive to revamp completely the present institutions of representation. If the Rayners are continually outvoted, if the grievances of the black community continue to be overlooked, then it will become necessary to devise wholly new forms of local political representation. There is nothing sacred about the system of electing candidates to serve as aldermen, councilmen, etc., by wards or districts. Geographical representation is not inherently right. Perhaps political interests have to be represented in some entirely different manner—such as community-parent control of schools, unions of tenants, unions of welfare recipients actually taking an official role in running the welfare departments. If political institutions do not meet the needs of the people, if the people finally believe that those institutions do not express their own values, then those institutions must be discarded. It is wasteful and inefficient, not to mention unjust, to continue imposing old forms and ways of doing things on a people who no longer view those forms and ways as functional.

We see independent politics (after the fashion of a Rayner candidacy) as the first step toward implementing something new. Voting year after year for the traditional party and its silent representatives gets the black community nowhere; voters then get their own candidates, but these may become frustrated by the power and organization of the machines. The next logical step is to demand more meaningful structures, forms and ways of dealing with long-standing problems.

We see this as the potential power of the ghettos. In a real sense, it is similar to what is taking place in the South: the move in the direction of independent politics—and from there, the move toward the development of wholly new political institutions. If these proposals also sound impractical, utopian, then we ask: what other real alternatives exist? There are none; the choice lies between a genuinely new approach and maintaining the brutalizing, destructive, violence-breeding life of the ghettos as they exist today. From the viewpoint of black people, that is no choice.

Notes

1. Marilyn Gittell, "Participants and Participation: A Study of School Policy in New York City," New York: The Center for Urban Education. As quoted in the *New York Times,* April 30, 1967, p. E90.

2. Philip Smith, "Politics as I See It," *The Citizen,* Chicago (March 22, 1967).

THE ANTI-RAPE MOVEMENT

Vicki McNickle Rose

One by-product of the feminist movement, according to Rose, has been the development of an anti-rape movement, which claims that rape is not just an individual crime but a broader social problem. According to this view, rape is a male "power trip"—"a means of . . . social control to keep women in their 'place.'" Thus the occurrence of rape and the way rape cases are handled (e.g., by police and the courts) reflect the oppression of women in a male-dominated society. In its short lifetime, Rose suggests, the anti-rape movement has called attention to the problem, sensitized both law enforcement officials and the public to the degrading treatment they inflict upon rape victims, challenged popular assumptions and stereotypes about rape, and succeeded in getting some of the more glaring problems alleviated.

THE DEVELOPMENT OF THE ANTI-RAPE MOVEMENT

The Influence of Feminism. A variety of interest groups have expressed increasing concern over forcible rape, thus contributing to its definition as a social problem. "Anti-rape" and "rape prevention" are terms encompassing several interests, but the most active and vocal groups are those emerging from the women's movement. . . . Those groups adopting a feminist perspective have formulated the ideology of the movement. . . .

Just as the rising rape rate as reflected in official statistics has provided a focal point for feminist rhetoric, so has rape furnished a broadly-based issue for feminism, with attention to the large and geographically dispersed potential-victim population. The first stirrings of the anti-rape movement were apparent during the late 1960's. As women began to meet in consciousness-raising groups and organize to act on other issues, a communications network developed (cf. Freeman,

From Vicki McNickle Rose, "Rape as a Social Problem: A Byproduct of the Feminist Movement," *Social Problems* 25:1 (Oct. 1977), pp. 75–89. Copyright by the Society for the Study of Social Problems. Reprinted by permission of the Society for the Study of Social Problems and the author

1973) which would later become important to the evolution of the anti-rape movement. In the early 1970's, the first rape workshops and conferences were held throughout the country, together with "speak-outs" featuring public testimony by rape victims (Connell and Wilson, 1974). Such conferences provided a means of spreading the feminist ideology, including, for example, the legitimacy of questioning traditional assumptions about rape.

The first rape crisis line for receiving emergency telephone calls from victims, opened by the Rape Crisis Center in Washington, D.C. in July 1972 (Wasserman, 1973), has served as a prototype for subsequent services. Currently, some form of crisis telephone line for rape victims is available in nearly all major cities and college communities, and the National Organization for Women (NOW) has approximately two hundred rape task forces in the United States, including one at the national level (Center for Women Policy Studies, 1975). The continued growth of the movement, however, means that it is impossible to estimate the exact number of anti-rape and rape crisis organizations in existence. The ultimate goal of such groups is the elimination of rape, but rendering assistance to victims and easing the trauma of the experience is considered extremely important.

Accomplishments at the Community Level. The organization of community programs and rape crisis centers designed to aid victims is a major achievement of the anti-rape movement. These centers use similar procedures. Basic features typically include a twenty-four-hour emergency phone line and information concerning what to expect in terms of medical, police and court procedures. Some centers provide volunteer-advocates to accompany victims as their complaints are processed through the criminal justice system.[1] Counseling services are usually provided, and victims are generally encouraged to express anger rather than guilt.[2] Along with this principle, some women have used retaliatory tactics (ranging from harassment to physical attack) against accused rapists (cf. "The Rape Wave," 1973; "Women Against Rape," 1973; "Vigilante Women . . . ," 1975).

Rape prevention groups advocate more sensitive handling by the police and more comprehensive medical treatment for victims. Cooperation among the various agencies managing rape cases is advocated; in fact, their activities are often coordinated by crisis center representatives. The movement seems to have had an impact on law enforcement agencies and medical facilities in many cities ("Revolt Against Rape," 1974; Chappell, 1975). The efforts of anti-rape groups have encouraged more hospitals to treat rape as a public health problem (Wasserman, 1973). However, free medical examinations are seldom available, and many private hospitals have demonstrated reluctance to treat sexual-attack victims.

Despite a reputation for insensitivity in dealing with rape victims (Griffin, 1971), "stories of official [police] indifference are becoming less frequent" (Bart, 1975:101). Many victims report they were asked very personal questions by the police, justified as necessary to ascertain if the case would hold up for the prosecution. Doubts have been expressed, however, that such legal requirements can explain questions such as "Aw, come on, didn't you really enjoy it?" and "How many orgasms did you have?" (cf. Griffin, 1971; Horos, 1974; Connell and Wilson, 1974; Chappell, 1975). The crudeness of the police, enraging feminists, is also exemplified by the statement of one doctor that through improved procedures, the officers he meets no longer enter the emergency room calling, "I got a rape for ya, Charlie!" ("'Code R' for Rape," 1972:75).

According to Grimstad and Rennie (1973:149), the Chicago police training manual, as recently as 1973, instructed officers that "the first thing to do is determine if the woman [who reports the rape] is lying." This suspicion of the victim typically continues throughout the legal process. In spite of the general cynicism embodied in the male-dominated criminal justice system, however, less biased and more humane practices have been instituted in police departments in a number of cities and within the office of the district attorney in a few jurisdictions, largely as a result of the educational and consciousness-raising efforts of anti-rape organizations.

Police departments in some cities have established special sexual-assault and rape-analysis-units, modeled after the New York Police Department's Rape Investigation and Analysis Unit (Lichtenstein, 1974; Waggoner, 1975). Coordinated investigative procedures, the use of female detectives to ease communication with the victim, and other such innovative practices are featured among special police units, but most U.S. law enforcement agencies have not yet instituted such programs, and some resist their development (cf. Cook, 1974).

Although some institutional changes in the processing of rape cases have appeared, advocates of the anti-rape position argue that much more remains to be accomplished. A fifteen-month, nationwide study completed in 1974, prompted the Law Enforcement Assistance Administration (LEAA) to conclude that institutional traditions are often resistant even where reforms are introduced. Longstanding feminist claims were supported by further LEAA conclusions that responses to rape cases and rape victims by police, hospitals and prosecutors tend to be "poor," "inadequate," and "haphazard." The LEAA recommended the development of local programs and procedures to provide more dignified treatment for victims, thereby easing their presentation of evidence against the rapist in court (Brodyaga, et al., 1975; Footlick, et al., 1975; "National Study . . . ," 1975).

Other programs spawned by the anti-rape movement include rape-prevention instruction for women. . . . As with the encouragement of mutual support among women for victims of rape, prevention and self-defense are also important ingredients in anti-rape programs and litera-ture.

Although most anti-rape groups are heavily dominated by feminist interests and female members, some have been founded to counsel the male friends and relatives of rape victims. The male's initial reaction, often one of victimization, has been been interpreted as a result of the cultural lesson that "a woman is his property" ("Gazette," 1975:20). A man's condemnation of rape is frequently dominated by the implication of the decreased "value" of his sexual "possession" (Kanowitz, 1973). Full comprehension of rape is often difficult for men (Weis and Borges, 1973). They may not understand the psychological and physical ex-perience, and they commonly assume, perhaps subconsciously, that it is impossible to rape an unwilling woman (Schwendinger and Schwen-dinger, 1974). Such attitudes and assumptions constitute a focal pont of feminist concerns.

The Feminist Perspective. . . . *In the feminist view, rape is a "power trip"; it is a means of political oppression and social control to keep women in their "place"** (cf. Connell and Wilson, 1974; Davis, 1975; Wasserman, 1973; Brownmiller, 1975; Russell, 1975).

From the feminist perspective, rape is a direct result of our culture's differential sex role socialization and sexual stratification. Traditional notions about sex roles are viewed as the basis of stereotyped attitudes about rape. For example, the association of dominance with the male sex role and submission with the female sex role is veiwed as a signifi-cant factor in the persistence of rape as a serious social problem. Some feel that until patterns of socialization into traditional sex roles are altered, societal processes will continue to prepare women to be "legiti-mate" victims (viewed as deserving, needing, and/or wanting to be raped) and men to be potential offenders (Weis and Borges, 1973; McCaghy, 1975). The American dating system—primarily because of its exchange features—has been identified as a major contributor to the potential for rape (cf. Mulvihill and Tumin, 1969; Weis and Borges, 1973). . . .

A Basis for Further Activism. The anti-rape movement is gradually gaining support from government officials, police and citizens' groups. However, such support is sometimes reluctantly granted and often only after considerable conflict as a result of pressure from rape prevention forces. Nevertheless, the knowledge and expertise gained at the local

*Italics added.

level has served as a basis for activism in the legislative and judicial arenas.

ACTIVITY IN THE LEGISLATIVE ARENA

. . . The argument of many observers, including feminists, is that rape legislation in the United States is primarily based on traditional notions concerning sex roles and sexual standards as well as myths and assumptions about rape, the rapist, and the victim (cf. LeGrand, 1973; Ross, 1973). The fear of the conviction of innocent men has served as a basis for rape legislation since the pronouncement of a 17th-Century British jurist, Sir Matthew Hale, that rape is ". . . an accusation easy to be made, hard to be proved, but harder to be defended by the party accused, though innocent" (The Laws Respecting Women, 1974:312). The "Lord Hale instructions," including a directive to examine the complainant's testimony carefully, are part of the charge given by judges to juries in rape cases in some states, despite the nation-wide trend toward reform of rape laws (Lichtenstein, 1957; Footlick, et al., 1975).

Other legal vestiges in rape cases include corroboration requirements and the notion that a woman with a "reputation" is less likely to resist sexual assault (Wood, 1972). Corroboration requirements are justified by concern for protection of the defendant's rights and suspicion regarding the credibility of the victim's testimony. Some version of corroboration requirement was still on the books of thirteen states as of 1974 ("The Rape Corroboration Requirement . . . ," 1972; "Meskill Signs . . . ," 1974).

Rape laws have been identified by some observers as property laws protecting male interests rather than protecting women from sexual assault:

> . . . rape laws bolster, and in turn are bolstered by, "a masculine pride in the exclusive possession of a sexual object"; they focus a male's aggression, based on fear of losing his sexual partner, against rapists rather than against innocent competitors; rape laws help protect the male from any "decrease in the 'value' of his sexual 'possession,'" which results from forcible violation (LeGrand, 1973:924).

In the feminist view, rape is treated as an affront to the male who dominates the victim (typically her husband or father); rape laws serve to protect his property (Davis, 1975).[3] Further evidence in support of the contention that rape laws are property laws is the legal impossibility for a husband to rape his wife: rape laws must be property laws, it is reasoned, if a man cannot steal what he already "owns" (cf. LeGrand, 1973).[4]

Recommended Changes: Critiques of Traditional Rape Legislation.
Criticisms of traditional rape legislation have provided the basis for
recommended revisions. Model rape laws outlining the changes advocated to redress major injustices have been formulated by various
groups, such as the National Organization for Women (Johnston, 1974)
and are also available in sourcebooks on rape (e.g., Connell and Wilson,
1974).

One common feature of these model laws involves eliminating
the fear of the false complaint incorporated in the law (as with the "Lord
Hale instructions" noted above). In the feminist analysis of rape,
recognition of the victim's status degradation throughout her entire
ordeal in the criminal justice process demonstrates that disincentives
outweigh the temptation of making a false accusation (LeGrand, 1973).
Therefore, it is held, the fear of trumped-up charges should be recognized as an unreasonable one, and the suspicion of female testimony
embodied in the legal system should be expunged. Wood (1972:335–336)
contends that:

> . . . there is no reason to conclude that juries are less able to deal with
> fabrications in rape than they are in any other types of cases . . . [and
> that] . . . the "beyond a reasonable doubt" standard should be ade-
> quate to guard against unjust convictions.

Similarly, model laws assert that insofar as their purposes are largely
served by other legal safeguards, corroboration requirements may be
considered extraneous (cf. "The Rape Corrobation Requirement . . . ,"
1972). Most critics of corroboration requirements advocate the elimination of all special rules concerning rape cases not applicable in other
criminal cases (Ross, 1973). Corroboration of the victim's word is not
required by law in order to convict an offender of any other crime;
therefore, any distinction between an uncorroborated charge of kid-
napping, assault or robbery, and an uncorroborated charge of rape
should be abolished (Wood, 1972; LeGrand, 1973). In this view, the
jury can weigh the credibility of the testimony and determine if there is
enough evidence to support the defendant's conviction. In summary,
"none of the justifications for treating rape cases differently from other
criminal charges stands on solid empirical or theoretical footing" ("The
Rape Corroboration Requirement . . . ," 1972:1390–1391).

Reform laws also urge discarding any notion that the victim's character bears upon whether she consented to sexual intercourse. In contemporary society, numerous women (and men) have nonmarital sexual
relations, and this should have no effect upon the outcome of a rape
case. Another suggestion frequently made is that judges should be
required by law to instruct the jury that a prior acquaintance between
the victim and defendant has no bearing upon the victim's credibility.
However, exceptions are often provided even within new laws de-

signed to limit the courtroom introduction of information concerning the victim's personal sex life or sexual history. . . .

Some suggest that statutory provisions defining degrees of rape (such as the scheme proposed by the National Commission on Reform of Federal Criminal Laws) would result in a greater probability of conviction (for sentences of a shorter duration) in marginal situations where the jury might otherwise acquit (cf. Wood, 1972). Further, shorter (but mandatory) sentences for rape have been recommended (cf. Connell and Wilson, 1974). Some legal experts believe that reducing the sentence for rape will help increase the conviction rate. They assert that a jury is much less likely to avoid convictions if the penalty is only a few years than if there is a possible sentence of death or life imprisonment ("Revolt Against Rape," 1974).

Finally, rape prevention advocates have pressed for the abolition of factors protecting the defendant, the alleged rapist. The traditional fear of convicting innocent men of rape has served as a basis for questioning the "consent" standard—that is, whether a woman's opinion as to whether she consented to sexual intercourse is reliable (LeGrand, 1973; Kanowitz, 1973). Another element traditionally protecting the alleged rapist is the rule that ". . . evidence of another sex crime committed by him at a different time and against another person, having no connection with the crime charged is not admissible. . . ." (LeGrand, 1973: 935). Information concerning the defendant's character becomes an issue only when he chooses to introduce the matter (Hibey, 1972). On the other hand, the sexual experience and practices of the complainant traditionally have been admissible in most jurisdictions. Typically, the defense attorney attempts thereby to discredit her claim that she was forced to submit against her will (Horos, 1974; LeGrand, 1973). The underlying assumption is that a sexually active woman is more likely to consent to intercourse. This is only one area where revisions in rape legislation presently arise largely as a result of the efforts of anti-rape interests.

Legislative Changes: Accomplishments of the Anti-Rape Movement. Corroboration requirements have undergone extensive changes in several states. In 1972, the New York legislature, a pioneer in the reform movement, passed a bill revising what *had* been the strictest corroboration rule in the United States (Lear, 1972). Under the earlier New York statutes, corroboration of each material element of the offense was required—force, penetration, and identity of the accused—by other evidence in addition to the victim's testimony. Corroboration of identity essentially necessitated an eyewitness to the act of sexual intercourse. The new statute was a compromise (some groups were pushing for repeal of all corroboration requirements) so that only the corroboration-of-identity requirement was completely eliminated (cf. Lewis,

1974; "The Rape Corroboration Requirement . . . ," 1972). Further reform legislation, passed in New York in 1973 and 1974 at the urging of feminists, law enforcement officials and civil-liberties groups, and produced largely via lobbying efforts by women's groups, now allows for prosecution without any corroboration, except in cases of statutory rape or consensual sodomy (Andelman, 1974a). A coalition, spearheaded by feminist organizations, sponsored a National Rape Prevention Month in August 1973, held workshops, lobbied, and raised media consciousness in order to gain support for the New York reforms (Lewis, 1974).

Although many states have made or plan to make basic revisions in their rape laws (Lichtenstein, 1975), not all recent changes have taken the direction deemed desirable by the anti-rape movement. Within a four-year time period prior to 1972, "at least two states . . . adopted or substantially broadened statutes preventing a man from being convicted for rape on the uncorroborated testimony of a woman" ("The Rape Corroboration Requirement . . . ," 1972:1374). However, since 1972, other states have followed New York in modifying or eliminating corroboration requirements, as well as making other changes in rape laws to eliminate anti-victim biases.

Other reforms have involved reducing penalties for rape, defining degrees of rape, and establishing rape as a "sexually neutral" crime (i.e., one committable against men as well as women). A number of states have recently passed laws prohibiting inquiries by defense attorneys into a woman's sexual conduct—although with certain limitations.[5] Many of the proposals outlined by anti-rape proponents are being realized, but the rapidity of change, the state-to-state variations, and the lack of any organization to keep tabs on rape legislation revisions (Lichtenstein, 1975) makes accurate and definitive statements about the current nationwide status of rape legislation impossible. But clearly there is a definite trend toward re-examination and revision of legislation concerning the crime of rape, and the anti-rape movement has had a major role in affecting these changes. . . .

Just as experience in local rape crisis groups provided an impetus for the challenge of many traditional rape laws, successful community and legislative experience furnished, in turn, a basis for critiques and demonstrations concerning court-related issues. Thus, the rapid success of the relatively young rape prevention movement has helped extend anti-rape movement critiques and activities into the judicial arena.

ACTIVITY IN THE JUDICIAL SPHERE

. . . Victims whose complaints eventually come to trial find courtroom victimization not uncommon. Bohmer (1974), in fact, found that judges tend to view rape victims as one of three basic types, each associated with a different degree of complainant-credibility. This research evidence disputes the typical assumption of judicial impartiality in rape cases.

Another important element within the context of the trial, the jury's perspective, has been the object of much discussion by advocates of the rape prevention movement. According to many authorities, jury attitudes and composition often inhibit convictions in rape cases. Contrary to popular assumption, the jury's sympathies frequently are extended to the defendant rather than the rape victim (LeGrand, 1973). . . . Further, the tendency of juries to take "contributory behavior" on the part of the victim into account has been established (cf. Kalven and Zeisel, 1966), so that if the jury perceives an "assumption of risk" on the part of the victim, the defendant is typically found guilty of a lesser crime or acquitted ("The Rape Corroboration Requirement. . . ," 1972: 1379). . . .

Representatives of the anti-rape movement entered the debate surrounding two incidents receiving extensive coverage in the media (especially in the feminist press) and attracting nationwide attention to some of the issues surrounding rape. In both instances, the central figures became *causes célèbres* of the anti-rape movement.

The first case involved a thirty-year-old Latina, Inez Garcia, found guilty of the 1974 murder of a three-hundred-pound man who, according to her testimony, held her down while another man raped her. Events surrounding the rape and subsequent shooting death were clouded by several inconsistent accounts, but the Garcia case became a rallying point for feminists. Feminist support was demonstrated by packing the courtroom and demonstrating outside the courthouse during the trial, and calling for a nationwide women's strike following her conviction. Inez Garcia became a "national symbol" for the anti-rape movement (Blitman and Green, 1975), as well as, according to Jaquish (1974), a potential role model for all women because she fought back.

Another woman, Joan Little, also appeared in the national limelight in 1974 as a result of her involvement in a rape case. Little, a black, was tried for the stabbing murder of a white guard at the North Carolina Jail where she was held. Suspicious circumstances surrounding the guard's death supported Little's charge that she was defending herself against sexual attack. For example, the guard's body (when discovered in Little's cell) was nude below the waist, recent sexual activity on his part was revealed by the autopsy, and the murder weapon was the guard's own ice pick. Little's plea of self defense was successful; she was acquitted. Coverage of her plight in the feminist press was extensive, and feminist organizations helped raise funds for her defense. The publicity received by both the Little and Garcia cases attracted more support for the anti-rape movement.

Other less-well publicized events are clearly related to a discussion of activity in the judicial arena. As a result of a civil suit filed against two men convicted of raping her, a Virginia woman was recently awarded $40,000 in compensatory damages and $325,000 in punitive damages, a judgment "believed to be a precedent in American courts" (Pruden, 1976). In contrast, two decisions have been labeled "regressive" by many people involved in the anti-rape movement. Rejecting the arguments of movement proponents, the Supreme Court in 1975 ruled that the media cannot be prohibited by state law from identifying rape victims (Weaver, 1975). Rape prevention advocates maintain that such publicity constitutes invasion of privacy and results in additional unnecessary humiliation for victims. Although victims' names can, of course, be withheld voluntarily by the media, this possibility is unlikely. A second case, which has drawn fire from feminists in particular, is the May, 1975, ruling of a New York judge that a case of rape does not exist where no threats are made and nonviolent means (e.g., deceit) are used to persuade a woman to engage in intercourse ("Rape and Consent," 1975).

Thus, at the judicial level, as well as in community and legislative spheres, opposition to the tenets and objectives of anti-rape forces exists. The outcome of the conflict over issues has not always been in the direction defined as successful by the movement. Nevertheless, the process of defining rape as a critical social problem continues.

SUMMARY AND CONCLUSIONS

Governmental and other institutions have come to recognize the anti-rape movement as a politically effective force:

> Rape has [now] achieved the status of a "serious problem" in the eyes of the Federal Government, law enforcement officials, mental health professionals, social science researchers, and others in positions of power and control. . . . (McDonald, 1976:6).

A significant indicator of the movement's recognition is the 1975 passage by Congress, over President Ford's veto, of a health bill authorizing grants to the states for a variety of public health service programs, including rape prevention and control (Hunter, 1975; Smith, 1975). Women's groups comprised a paramount force in the coalition which lobbied extensively for the override vote (Bowman, 1975). The establishment of a Center for the Prevention and Control of Rape (under the auspices of the National Institute of Mental Health), for funding research on rape causes, prevention and treatment, is an important coup for the movement.

Rape workshops are still held across the country, and more crisis centers are organizing. Institutionalized biases toward rape victims— manifested in attitudes and practices—are increasingly under attack. A number of community interest groups—in addition to feminists—are taking action, addressing medical, legal and social aspects of the problem and efforts are made to debunk rape myths. This overt community support reflects a changing attitude toward the discussion of a once-taboo subject.[6] . . .

Many groups have come to take the position that rape victims deserve more equitable . . . treatment. . . . Changes in laws and procedures have been credited to the increasing pressures from anti-rape forces, especially feminist groups (cf. Wolfe, 1974; Lichtenstein, 1974; Footlick, et. al., 1975). Some of the movement's principles and accomplishments are not without their critics, however, and it remains to be seen whether this resistance will take any organized form. Nevertheless, the anti-rape movement has made considerable progress during its short life-span,[7] largely as a result of the efforts of feminist forces for which the rape issue serves as a nonpartisan, uniting cause. Due chiefly to its accomplishments, more people are becoming aware of the movement's existence and are gradually accepting its definition of rape as a serious social problem.

Notes

1. The women who staff crisis centers usually neither actively encourage nor discourage reporting rape (Wasserman, 1973). However, much of the feminist literature on rape advises victims to report the offense so that the "appalling frequency" of rape will become known, thus facilitating reform of rape laws (cf. Horos, 1974).

2. The expression of anger is epitomized by buttons proclaiming "Castrate Rapists," worn by some proponents of the anti-rape movement.

3. Dueteronomy 22:19 (Holy Bible, 1952) instructs that damages in the amount of fifty silver shekels be paid the father of a violated unbetrothed virgin.

4. The notion that rape is more acceptable when it involves persons who previously have been sexual partners (cf. Ross, 1973; Safilios-Rothschild, 1974) is reflected in police practices (McCaghy, 1975) and public attitudes toward rape (cf. Rossi, et al., 1974), as well as in so-called "reform" legislation. Most of the new legislation limiting cross-examination of the victim concerning her past and present sexual conduct allows exceptions where relevance can be established by the defense—e.g., where there is testimony or evidence of past sexual relations between the complainant and defendant.

5. There are, for example, provisions allowing the admission of evidence or testimony concerning prior sexual activity between complainant and defendant (Footlick, et al., 1975) or complainant's conviction of prostitution within three years of the alleged rape (Narvaez, 1975). Also, such defense inquiries may eventually be allowed in the courtroom if a hearing outside the jury's presence leads to the judge's determination that the evidence is relevant to the case.

6. Note, for example, the recent extensive coverage of rape in media (cf. "Revolt Against Rape," 1975; Footlick, et al., 1975).

7. Increased attention to the incidence and disposition of rape cases, temporal and cultural relativity in attitudes toward rape, and other issues related to the offense are addressed in Rose (1977).

References

American Civil Liberties Union
   1971   The Policy Guide of the American Civil Liberties Union. New York: American Civil Liberties Union.
Andelman, David A.
   1974a   "Assembly votes to drop rape-corroboration rule." New York Times 123 (January 15): 1, 27.
   1974b   "New law on rape signed by Wilson," New York Times 123 (February 20):34.
Bart, Pauline B.
   1975   "Rape doesn't end with a kiss." Viva (June):39–42, 100–101.
Blitman, Nan and Robin Green
   1975   "Inez Garcia on trial." Ms. 3 (May):49–54.
Bohmer, Carol
   1974   "Jucidal attitudes toward rape victims." Judicature 57 (February): 303–307.
Bowman, Elizabeth
   1975   "Congress overrides health services veto." Congressional Quarterly: Weekly Report 33 (August 2):1168–1169.
Brodyaga, Lisa; Margaret Gates; Susan Singer; Marna Tucker; Richardson White
   1975   Rape and Its Victims: A Report for Citizens, Health Facilities, and Criminal Justice Agencies. National Institute of Law Enforcement and Criminal Justice, Law Enforcement Assistance Administration, U.S. Department of Justice.
Brownmiller, Susan
   1975   Against Our Will: Men, Women and Rape. New York: Simon & Schuster.
Center for Women Policy Studies
   1975   Community Anti-Rape Projects. Washington, D.C.: Center for Women Policy Studies. (mimeo)
Chappell, Duncan
   1975   "Forcible rape and the American system of criminal justice." Pp. 85–99 in Duncan Chappell and John Monahan (eds.), Violence and Criminal Justice. Lexington, Massachusetts: D. C. Heath and Company
"'Code R' for rape"
   1972   Newsweek 80 (November 13):75.
Connell, Noreen and Cassandra Wilson
   1974   Rape: The First Sourcebook for Women. New York: New American Library.

Cook, Louise
  1974   "Incidence of rape increasing." Tulsa Daily World (September 29):
         C25.
Davis, Angela
  1975   "Forum: Joanne [sic] Little—the dialectics of rape." Ms. 3(June):74–77.
Footlick, Jerrold K., et al.
  1975   "Rape alert." Newsweek 86 (November 10):70–77, 79.
Freeman, Jo
  1973   "The origins of the women's liberation movement." American Journal
         of Sociology 78 (January):792–811.
"Gazette"
  1975   Ms. 4 (August):20.
Griffin, Susan
  1971   "Rape: the all-American crime." Ramparts 10 (September):26–35.
Grimstad, Kirsten and Susan Rennie (eds.)
  1973   The New Woman's Survival Catalog. New York: Coward, McCann
         and Geoghegan Berkley Publishing Corporation.
Hibey, Richard A.
  1972   "The trial of a rape case: an advocate's analysis of corroboration,
         consent, and character." American Criminal Law Review 11 (Fall):
         309–334.
Holy Bible
  1952   Revised Standard Version. New York: Thomas Nelson & Sons.
Horos, Carol V.
  1974   Rape. New Canaan, Connecticut: Tobey Publishing Co., Inc.
Hunter, Marjorie
  1975   "Congress enacts health measure over Ford's veto." New York Times
         124 (July 30):1, 13.
Jaquish, Barbara
  1974   "¡Viva Inez!" Women's Press (October):1, 15.
Johnston, Laurie
  1974   "NOW elects Syracuse lawyer as head." New York Times 123 (May
         28):29.
Kalven, Harry, Jr. and Hans Zeisel
  1966   The American Jury. Boston: Little, Brown.
Kanowitz, Leo
  1973   Sex Roles in Law and Society: Cases and Materials. Albuquerque:
         University of New Mexico Press.
Lear, Martha W.
  1972   "Q. If you rape a woman and steal her TV, what can they get you for
         in New York? A. Stealing her TV." New York Times Magazine (Jan-
         uary 30):10–11.
LeGrand, Camille E.
  1973   "Rape and rape laws: sexism in society and law." California Law
         Review 61 (May):919–941.
Lewis, Nancy
  1974   "The behind-the-scenes story of the unanimous repeal bill victory."
         Majority Report 3 (March):6–7.

Lichtenstein, Grace
  1974   "Rape squad." New York Times Magazine (March 3):10–11.
  1975   "Rape laws undergoing changes to aid victims." New York Times 124 (June 4):1, 21.
Mauss, Armand L.
  1975   Social Problems as Social Movements. Philadelphia: J. B. Lippincott Company.
McCaghy, Charles H.
  1975   Deviant Behavior. New York: Macmillan Publishing Company, Inc.
McDonald, Nancy
  1976   "Consulting." Feminist Alliance Against Rape 3 (Spring):6–7.
"Meskill signs a rape-corroboration act repealer."
  1974   New York Times 123 (May 7):91.
Mulvihill, Donald J. and Melvin M. Tumin
  1969   Crimes of Violence. Volume 11. A Staff Report Submitted to the National Commission on the Causes and Prevention of Violence. Washington, D.C.: U.S. Government Printing Office.
Narvaez, Alfonso A.
  1975   "Assembly passes sex-crimes bill." New York Times 124 (April 29):31.
"National study says rape only first of indignities to victim"
  1975   Minneapolis Star 97 (October 27):5A.
Pruden, Wesley, Jr.
  1976   "Angry rape victim sues, jury shares her anger." National Observer (February 14).
"Rape consent"
  1975   Time 105 (May 12):55.
"Revolt against rape"
  1974   Time 104 (July 22):85.
"Revolt against rape"
  1975   Time 106 (October 13):48, 53–54.
Rose, Vicki
  1977   "The rise of the rape problem." Pp. 167–95 in Armand L. Mauss and Julie C. Wolfe (eds.) This Land of Promises: The Rise and Fall of Social Problems in America. Philadelphia: Lippincott.
Ross, Susan C.
  1973   The Rights of Women: The Basic ACLU Guide to Women's Rights. New York: Avon Books.
Rossi, Pater H.; Emily Waite; Christine E. Bose; Richard E. Berk
  1974   "The seriousness of crimes: normative structure and individual differences." American Sociological Review 39 (April):224–237.
Russell, Diana
  1975   The Politics of Rape. New York: Stein and Day.
Safilios-Rothschild, Constantina
  1974   Women and Social Policy. Englewood Cliffs, New Jersey: Prentice-Hall, Inc.
Schwendinger, Julia R. and Herman Schwendinger
  1974   "Rape myths: in legal, theoretical, and everyday practice." Crime and Social Justice 1 (Spring-Summer):18–26.

Smith, Robert M.
  1975   "President vetoes health care bill: Senate overrides." New York Times
          124 (July 27):1, 19.
The Laws Respecting Women
  1974   Oceana Publications, Inc. Dobbs Ferry, New York. (Reprinted from
          the J. Johnson Edition-London, 1777.)
"The Rape corroboration requirement: repeal not reform"
  1972   Yale Law Journal 81 (7):1365–1391.
"The rape wave"
  1973   Newsweek 81 (January 29):59.
"Vigilante women who slashed accused rapist still at large"
  1975   Palouse Empire Shopper (July 22).
Waggoner, Walter H.
  1975   "New sexual assault unit is in operation in Newark." New York Times
          124 (July 18):66.
Wasserman, Michelle
  1973   "Rape: breaking the silence." The Progressive 37 (November):19–23.
Weaver, Warren, Jr.
  1975   "High court upsets information curb." New York Times (March 4):
          1,15.
Weis, Kurt and Sandra S. Borges
  1973   "Victimology and rape: the case of the legitimate victim." Issues in
          Criminology 8 (Fall):71–115.
Wolfe, Linda
  1974   "New rape laws ending the anti-victim bias." New York Times 123
          (December 1):IV:10.
"Women against rape"
  1973   Time 101 (April 23):104.
Wood, Pamela Lakes
  1972   "The victim in a forcible rape case: a feminist view." American
          Criminal Law Review 11 (Fall):335–354.

ORGANIZING THE POOR

Jack L. Roach and Janet K. Roach

In this article, Roach and Roach address the problem of poverty from a value conflict perspective. In so doing, they differ somewhat from others with a value conflict perspective in the type of solution they

From Jack L. Roach and Janet K. Roach, "Organizing the Poor: Road to a Dead End."
Social Problems 26:2 (Dec. 1978), pp. 160-63, 166, 167-71. Copyright by the Society for
the Study of Social Problems. Reprinted by permission of the Society for the Study of
Social Problems and the authors.

propose. It is not enough, they claim, for poor people to organize among themselves. They point out that when poor people form their own independent organizations—e.g., the National Welfare Rights Organization—they still lack access to structures of political and economic power. Thus it should not be surprising that such organizations by and large fail to accomplish their objectives. Roach and Roach urge a different solution. The economic problems confronting poor people, they argue, are linked to the problems confronting working people more generally. And the solution they propose is for poor people to join ranks with organized labor—for as organized labor forces improvement in the status of working people generally, the conditions of poor people will be improved as well.

A variety of efforts to organize the poor[1] were made in the 1960s. Whatever the differences in organizational form and strategy, all of them were concerned with fighting poverty and its consequences through collective action by the poor themselves. The basic goal of eliminating or substantially reducing the incidence of poverty was seldom seen as an immediate or short-range possibility; rather the goals pursued and the activities engaged in were seen as intermediate steps towards the ultimate objective. Early antipoverty planners and activists recognized that the poor were a powerless segment of society, and their prescription for this situation was organization. By organizing, other groups had made themselves forces to be reckoned with; the poor, it was contended, could also achieve the clout to have their needs met. A primary objective, then, was to develop the political power of the poor by helping them to organize. "Political power" usually referred to some measure of control over local policy and officials, with influence on national affairs seen as a later step.

The movement to organize the poor and the activities of poor people's organizations have dwindled markedly since the early 1970s. A number of writers have analyzed the movement's success or failure and its strengths and weaknesses. . . .

Frances Fox Piven and Richard Cloward are foremost among those trying to learn from recent and past movements how to construct a more effective future strategy for the poor. Unlike other critics, however, they are not especially interested in the nuances of community organizational theory and practice. Their primary concern is the failure of poor people to win what they should have been able to in the late 1960s, and to demonstrate that conventional organizing itself, rather than insufficient or incorrect organizing, was mainly responsible for this failure. As the most productive future alternative to such organizing, Piven and Cloward propose a "politics of turmoil"—which entails "mobilizing" (not organizing) masses of poor people to engage in sustained disruptive behavior that will force elites to grant significant concessions. [This strategy was exemplified by the National Welfare Rights Organization.] . . .

THE NATIONAL WELFARE RIGHTS ORGANIZATION (NWRO)

NWRO was formed in April 1967.[2] It was a federation of the numerous local welfare rights organizations which had sprung up in the early 1960s as civil rights activists returned north and government funding of community action programs became available. The membership grew from 5,000 in 1967 to a peak of 25–30,000 in 1969. Because most of the members were ADC mothers receiving grants for their children, NWRO estimated it represented 100,000 recipients. . . .

Membership in the national organization was through membership in one of the locals. An unaffiliated individual could not join. NWRO required that members be welfare recipients, former recipients or members of a poor family. The large majority of members were black welfare mothers.

An early NWRO slogan was "Jobs or Income Now—Decent Jobs for Those Who can Work and Adequate Income for Those Who Cannot." The goals were adequate income for all Americans whether or not they were on welfare (a guaranteed annual income) and guarantees that the welfare system accord dignity, justice and democracy to all recipients. The more immediate objectives in pursuit of these goals were amelioration and elimination of restrictive welfare requirements and increasing welfare grants.

Much of NWRO's initial strategy and tactics was a continuation of the sorts of activity the locals had been engaged in: the organization of protest activity around individual grievances and around items recipients generally were entitled to but not receiving. Methods ranged from the preparation of handbooks for clients to advocacy before welfare officials, to sit-ins and demonstrations at welfare departments. The national organization supported these activities both for the gains they might achieve and for the incentive those gains might provide to join the organization, enabling it to pursue its broader goals.

The national organization hoped to facilitate coordination of the activities of local welfare groups, to establish communication among them, and to encourage them in their activities. It further planned to assist in coordinating welfare rights activities (on both the national and local levels) with the activities of related organizations (such as tenants' rights groups). NWRO trained recipients in leadership and organizing. Increasingly its officers acted as spokespersons and negotiators for recipients and participated in conferences with city, state and national officials. The organization brought court tests of welfare law and policy. By 1971, NWRO was lobbying for passage of a guaranteed annual income of $6500 a year for a family of four in opposition to Nixon's penurious Family Assistance Plan.

In 1968, NWRO established the National Self-Help Corporation, a nonpolitical organization to accept grants and contracts. The U.S. Department of Labor gave NASHCO $434,930 to explain to recipients the 1967 amendments to the Social Security Act. Prime among these was the Work Incentive Plan (WIN) which NWRO previously had strenuously opposed. The rationale for this apparent turnabout was that NWRO could see to it that welfare mothers would not be "ripped off."

Further federal grants were not forthcoming. Welfare cutbacks were increasing, initial concessions were being withdrawn, and local membership dropped. By early 1975, NWRO was bankrupt, and the national office closed.

NWRO's Achievements.   NWRO's achievements are difficult to evaluate because several of the organization's goals were expressed in sweeping generalities—for example, to develop a fair and open welfare system that accords respect and dignity to recipients. In all likelihood, pressures brought to bear by NWRO did prod many welfare officials . . . ; but evidence pertinent to attaining this objective is anecdotal, allowing only loose impressions.

Problems also exist in assessing how well NWRO did with respect to such concrete goals as securing benefits for recipients and potential recipients. Steiner (1971:281) concludes that NWRO was relatively successful in "improving access to financial aid and achieving more adequate support levels." Others concur that NWRO played a part in expanding the welfare caseload and increasing benefits; but they qualify this appraisal by suggesting that NWRO's role was mainly supportive of efforts of local welfare groups whose militance gained important concessions long before NWRO's formation (Jackson and Johnson, 1974:44). It is impossible adequately to assess the significance of NWRO's supportive role.

There are no uncertainties concerning the fate of the long-range objectives which were major features of NWRO's first organizing slogan: the call for *decent jobs* or an *adequate guaranteed income*. Following some initial agitation, the call for jobs appears to have been dropped from the agenda and there is no indication of jobs opening up as a consequence of this demand. NWRO directed an increasingly large part of its resources to a campaign for a guaranteed annual income, culminating in a concerted lobbying effort in 1971 for such legislation. The only result that might be viewed as a "gain" connected with this objective was that NWRO's effort may have helped defeat Nixon's punitive version of a guaranteed income. . . .

Piven and Cloward acknowledge with qualification that NWRO did succeed in initiating a militant mass movement among welfare recipients (most notably in New York City and Massachusetts) which resulted in millions of dollars in additional benefits granted to clients. This mass movement turned out to be relatively short-lived; thus, according to Piven and Cloward, NWRO failed to achieve what they regard as its own major objective: "to build an *enduring* mass organization through which the poor could exert influence" (1977:352, emphasis ours). In their opinion, however, the main criterion by which NWRO should be judged is "whether it exploited the unrest among the poor to obtain the maximum concessions possible in return for the restoration of quiescence" (1977:353). In their estimate, NWRO fell far short of meeting this criterion.[3] . . .

PROBLEMS OF SEPARATIST ORGANIZING

While Piven and Cloward's work raises other troublesome questions,[4] we turn now to what we regard as its basic flaw. Like the NWRO organizers before them, Piven and Cloward assume that the *black poor* can achieve significant concessions through independent collective action. (Despite their general references to the working class and the poor, it is apparent that the people on whom Piven and Cloward focus their "mobilizing" are blacks and perhaps Hispanics.) Their organizational and programmatic strategy for "the poor" is yet another example of a more general proclivity of many activists to champion one or another "specially-oppressed groups" and to support and encourage independent struggle on behalf of its needs and interests.

Advocates of separatist organizing, including Piven and Cloward,[5] advance a number of reasons for their position. Some, such as the lack of conventional resources which would make them attractive allies for other groups and the fact that they have unique problems and interests, refer to the nature of the groups themselves. Others refer to barriers erected by the working class and the unions. "Specially-oppressed groups" must go it alone, it is argued, because workers see them as pariahs unworthy of support; because rank-and-file union workers are conservative, self-centered and prejudiced; and because the entrenched union bureaucracy resists the idea of helping them. On such grounds, Piven and Cloward dismiss the possibility of united action with the white working class, particularly organized labor.

We believe that there are many harmful consequences inherent in separatist organizing which no amount of tinkering with organizational form and activities (whether it be called "mobilizing" or otherwise labeled) can remedy. Not the least of these is the exacerbation of further racial divisions in the working class. Especially illustrative here is the history of the call (ardently supported by many white activists) for black control of schools in black communities, which was turned around and used by racist elements in white neighborhoods to oppose the bussing of black students. Television coverage of disruptive protests by black welfare clients did less to win sympathy and support from workers than it did to confirm their view of "lazy niggers wanting everything." White welfare recipients were similarly resentful.[6] Thus, the action intended to secure concrete gains transformed indifference into active hostility.

*The major problem with separatist organizing of "specially-oppressed groups" [such as welfare recipients] is their lack of social power.** This lack is part and parcel of their oppression. Piven and Cloward refer time and again to the poors' lack (i.e., the black poor) of political power, but even so they grossly overestimate that power. *Welfare recipients, and the black poor in general, are an isolated, small fraction of the working class.** Unemployed, or employed in the lowest ranks of service positions, they have no or minimal connection with the "point of production" and thus no access to the social power available to those who are vital to production. Given the only "power" available to them—their ability to disrupt the welfare institution by mass defiance and general disturbance—the best the poor can hope for is some extension of welfare benefits and some . . . reform of the system providing them. The worst they can look forward to—and we maintain, expect—is increasing isolation and hostility from the rest of the working class, and repression by the ruling class.

IMPLICATIONS

What, then, is to be done? Our position, which is implied in our criticism of separatist organizing, is that the *basic task of activists who are concerned about poverty is the promotion of socialist consciousness among the rank and file in the trade unions.* . . .

To many activists our position is tantamount to telling the poor, "starve until the revolution."[7] This interpretation overlooks the extent to which the status of the poor is contingent upon the gains of organized labor. The wages, hours or conditions of work that they win upgrades, to some extent, those of the unorganized work force. Other gains—workmen's compensation, unemployment and disability insurance, pensions—have reduced the devastating impact that unemployment due to cutbacks, illness or age has on one's income. Without these

*Italics added.

gains, the ranks of the poor would be larger and more destitute. Were they to be extended, and new demands won, poverty would be greatly reduced. This desirable outcome can, of course, be achieved and sustained only by a united working class. Thus, many of our comments on a strategy for eliminating poverty will bear on the seemingly unrelated issue of strengthening the trade unions.

Admittedly, strong crosscurrents are always present to deflect the struggle of labor into deceptive short-run gains. Among these are the entrenched union bureaucracy, racism among the workers and a constrictive trade-union consciousness. To the extent to which these forces are resisted, the platform is being prepared for the qualitative jump to socialist consciousness—the willingness to fight for the political/economic changes that could eliminate poverty.

Opposition to regressive forces within organized labor does not come automatically, and the promotion of socialist consciousness entails far more than selling socialist ideas in the abstract. *Accomplishing these tasks will require fuller participation in union activities by the membership, led by socialist militants. The formation of militant caucuses organized around a class-struggle program is the principle role of activists.*[8]*

The rejection of existing trade unions as the locus of struggle for more widespread social change is not confined to liberal social analysts. It is shared by numerous persons on the left, including some self-identified Marxist-Leninists. The latter, while agreeing with us that social power lies at the point of production, argue that the white working class and the trade unions are so riddled with racism as to be incapable of working with and organizing nonwhites, or carrying out a social transformation which would benefit nonwhites. Given this evaluation, the tendency has been very strong among influential left academics and militants in industry and the community to endorse black-separatist organizing in the workplace.[9]

The Struggle Against Racism.   Historically, one of the most divisive and debilitating forces that has afflicted the labor movement is racism. Hostility to nonwhites (especially blacks) is widespread among white workers, often to the point of collaboration in the exploitative discrimination practiced by management. While there are exemplary exceptions, an all too common pattern of leadership in many unions has been to ignore the problem, to deal with it perfunctorily by meting out an occasional disciplinary action, or to sponsor an annual educational forum on race relations. Opportunistic union bureaucrats, eager to demonstrate their "solidarity" with workers and to curry their support,

---

*Italics added.

often tacitly condone incidents of flagrant racism and will exacerbate them, if this appears to be a significant current of sentiment and behavior in the shop.

Such circumstances are discouraging and indicate both the centrality of the issue of racism and the difficulties of the battle needed to eradicate it. One can easily understand why black workers would conclude that their job inequities stemmed from racism in the "white-dominated" unions. But however understandable, this sentiment is not the basis for a successful strategy. Beyond hardening racial divisions among the working class, separatist organizing has often resulted in demands that management and/or government intervene in trade-union affairs. Such intervention both weakens the working class as a whole and confuses the issue of who, or what, is the main enemy of workers.[10] In the short run, some blacks may gain as a result of such actions, but inevitably both blacks and whites lose, because this tactic, born out of desperation, fits into the employer's own divide-and-conquer strategy.

Our position is that while racism constitutes a serious problem in organized labor, the view that it is so virulent as to preclude any potential for black-white unity is unwarranted.[11] Nor is this potential entirely unrealized. Much evidence is at hand showing that the fight against racism is being actively pursued in the trade unions, often by multiracial militant caucuses.[12] Key sectors of organized labor continue to demonstrate, as they have in the past, an encouraging degree of solidarity between black and white workers in their common fight against management.[13] Also, the unions have recently begun a concerted drive to organize the unorganized (many of whom are non-white),[14] a move which many analysts doubted would occur in part because of white racism. Reinforcement and extension of these sorts of activists by militants offers promise of strengthening the trade unions and, in consequence, improving the status of the poor.

Organizing the Unorganized.   The drive to unionize the unorganized has significance beyond its relation to the education of racism. In itself, it is the most immediate action organized labor can take that would be of direct and tangible benefit to the poor. The extension of union membership provides the means of appreciably upgrading the wages and other benefits of millions of workers whose present income places them at or below the poverty line. Further, the strengthening of unions through an increase in numbers and the reduced threat of competition from unorganized workers would facilitate raising and winning such demands as: shorter hours with no loss in pay, hiring more workers, and removal of various restrictions on unemployment insurance benefits. The expansion of the labor market and liberalization of unemployment insurance would benefit immensely those who are now in the vast army of the unemployed. . . .

Other Activities.   We have discussed in some detail two trade-union activities which have a fairly direct bearing on the reduction of poverty and have suggested ways in which militants are, or could be, involved in them. How these activities are carried out has implications for the general strengthening of the working class; and, again, we believe that the ultimate elimination of poverty rests upon that strength. For that reason we have alluded to raising a class-struggle program, opposing separatist organizing and rejecting invitations to management and government to settle grievances or to intervene in union affairs. *Each of these activities is calculated to increase the power of the unions and to raise the level of class consciousness of the rank and file.**

Several similar activities should also be mentioned. These include opposition to wage-freeze legislation and limitations on the right to strike as well as refusal to obey back-to-work court injunctions, and pushing for the general strike. The union bureaucracy has shown a general failure in virtually all of these measures. Indeed, contracts which they have accepted and promoted among the members have often given away some of the unions' most powerful weapons. Thus, there is a pressing need for militants to stimilate these actions.

None of these activities are merely the starry-eyed suggestions of ivory-tower Marxists. In varying degree, all are now being actively pursued.

CONCLUDING REMARKS

Although militants from a variety of socialist groups are in the forefront of the struggle within organized labor to strengthen solidarity and workers' democracy, it would be the height of folly to underestimate the difficulties they face. This is particularly true for those whose activities are geared to raising class consciousness through presentation of a *transitional* socialist program. The infusion of socialist activists into the unions, which began in the late 1960s, has tapered off, and the earlier encouraging prospects are now beclouded.

Large sections of U.S. capital continue to perform poorly. In keeping with the traditional "adjustment mechanism," the squeeze is on labor to shoulder as much of the burden of capitalist anarchy as possible through increased productivity, wage freezes, high unemployment and threats of layoffs. This, then, is a period of retrenchment for labor. Employers are on the offensive. They have been increasingly

*Italics added.

able to dictate contract terms which deny raises and take back numerous previously-won basic and fringe benefits.

The repercussions of this growing assault on the standard of living of unorganized labor have had their inevitable impact on the poor. Inflationary erosion and cutbacks in income as well as health and social services are grim enough for the mainstream of the work force; they spell disaster for the poor. Winning back these losses and resuming movement beyond them would bring an upgrading for all.

The struggle of organized labor against capital, and the limitations imposed by its own trade-union consciousness is enormous; it may come to naught. But in contrast with the alternative of "separatist mobilizing" proposed by Piven and Cloward, that struggle is still the strategy with the greater probability of success. Labor originally organized in periods of profound difficulty, against apparently insurmountable odds; it has weathered other retrenchments. While the outlook today is far from ideal, socialist militants *are* at work in the trade unions, and there *are* signs of growing working-class unity. These encouraging manifestations can be the basis for a resurgence of a collective struggle of the working class which will create the conditions for the final elimination of poverty.

Notes

1. While to us the "poor" refers to people whose income is insufficient to enable them to provide for their basic needs as those needs are defined in our society, many writers' conceptions are much less precise. To some extent our usage reflects the inconsistent referents of the term most flagrantly seen in Piven and Cloward's (1977) work.

2. This account of NWRO leans heavily on descriptions of the organization by Jackson and Johnson (1974) and Steiner (1971).

3. It is important to note that we are dealing more with Piven and Cloward's interpretation of what NWRO's goals *should* have been rather than what NWRO's own explicit goals may have been. The imposition of one's own criteria is, of course, common among critics.

4. Among these are: whether the industrial workers' movement and unemployed workers' movement of the 1930s, the civil rights movement of the 1950s, and the welfare rights movement of the 1960s are sufficiently similar to permit meaningful conclusions; whether a disruption of the relief office by welfare mothers is a suitable analogy to a strike; their dismissal of the probability of massive repression of disruption by the poor; and their interpretation of the actual amount of organization in the movements preceding the welfare rights movement. See Roach and Roach (1978) for a discussion on these and other issues.

5. Their recent work shows no change from their orientation in their 1966 statement. "The black poor do have interests distinct from and more often than not in conflict with those of other groups. Unless they organize along separatist lines it is unlikely that they will have much success in advancing their interest." (Reprinted in Piven and Cloward, 1974:197.)

6. Had white recipients been organized together with blacks, this problem would have been eliminated, but it would have done little to enhance welfare clients in workers' eyes.

7. Designating militant trade union activity as the main arena for the fight against poverty does not exclude vigorous opposition to policies which reduce either the standard of living or dignity of poor people and critical support of reform measures. We are not advocating abandonment of the poor.

8. We differentiate multiracial militant caucuses from the "dual" or "oppositional" caucuses (virtually mini-unions) usually formed by blacks. These inevitably end in pitting sections of the work force against each other, further exacerbating divisiveness, exposing all to increased exploitation.

9. For many leftists, their conclusions on the extent, depth and tenacity of white racism and hence the tendency to write off organized labor as a potential ally are strongly influenced by various "Third World" perspectives, which hold that the "most oppressed" (e.g., black workers) are the best hope for the vanguard of a revitalized socialist revolution (see, for example, Allen, 1974).

10. The unhappy consequences of acting upon this identification of the main enemy are amply illustrated in the rise and fall of the League of Revolutionary Black Workers, a coalition of black groups in the auto industry in the late 1960s and early 1970s. Ostensibly the League was formed to increase black solidarity (and Marxist-Leninist consciousness) in the fight against racism—whether fostered by the union or management. But the League's literature and activities disclose an overriding preoccupation with fighting real and alleged racism of the UAW as an organization and of the white membership. Geschwender (1977) lists some of the concrete accomplishments of the League (e.g., an increase in black foremen and black union stewards). However, he suggests that these outcomes are relatively unimportant compared to the legacy of struggle that was provided black workers who "came together and developed a sense of solidarity and unity of interests [and] perceived the existence of a common enemy. . . . They won some victories through collective effort and solidarity. These experiences leave memories that will be activated the next time there is an effort to organize black workers in the plants (Geschwender, 1977:185–86)." What is left out of this appraisal of the League's accomplishments is the legacy of the illusory and destructive conviction that blacks must win *their* struggle alone, and then can go on to fulfill their destiny as *the* vanguard in a general proletarian revolution. The legacy we refer to is the greatly heightened hostility of white workers, which erects increased obstacles to black-white unity against the bosses.

11. While Wilson's recent appraisal (1978) of the "declining significance of race" may be overly sanguine, he does present evidence and interpretation indicating a significant reduction in racial conflict in the work place, and a shift to the

sociopolitical order. See also Foner (1974:430–32) who points to much less discrimination against blacks in unionized versus the nonunionized labor market.

12. Accounts of these struggles—some very encouraging, others not—can be found over the past few years in various issues of socialist publications such as *Workers Vanguard, The Guardian* and *Radical America.*

13. For example, the solidarity between black and white miners in the recent UMW strike and the presence of black leaders among rank-and-file miner organizations.

14. For a general description of this current massive organizing drive see the New York Times, "Week in Review" (1978:3).

References

Allen, Robert L.
    1974   Reluctant Reformers. Washington: Howard University Press.
Foner, Philip S.
    1974   Organized Labor and the Black Worker. New York: Praeger.
Geschwender, James A.
    1977   Class, Race and Worker Insurgency. Cambridge: Cambridge University Press.
Jackson, Larry R. and William A. Johnson
    1974   Protest by the Poor. Lexington: Heath.
Piven, Frances Fox and Richard A. Cloward
    1974   The Politics of Turmoil. New York: Pantheon.
    1977   Poor People's Movements. New York: Pantheon.
Roach, Janet K. and Jack L. Roach
    1978   "Turmoil in command of politics: Organizing the poor." Mimeo.
Steiner, Gilbert Y.
    1971   The State of Welfare. Washington: The Brookings Institute.
Wilson, William J.
    1978   The Declining Significance of Race. Chicago: Chicago University Press.

Selected References

Alinsky, Saul A., *Rules for Radicals: A Practical Primer for Realistic Radicals,* New York: Random House, 1971.
A handbook for organizing a community in order to protect its interests and values. Alinsky clearly states the need for a spirit of partisanship and a willingness to fight for one's own values.

Buckout, Robert, and eighty-one concerned Berkeley students (eds.), *Toward Social Change: A Handbook for Those Who Will,* New York: Harper & Row, 1971.

This text-reader diagnoses many contemporary social problems from the value conflict perspective and prescribes remedies for them along the lines suggested by this perspective.

Daniels, Arlene Kaplan, "From Lecture Hall to Picket Line," in Arlene Kaplan Daniels, Rachel Kahn-Hut, and associates (eds.), *Academics on the Line: The Faculty Strike at San Francisco State,* San Francisco: Jossey-Bass, 1970, Ch. 3.
This fascinating personal chronicle presents the unfolding history of the San Francisco State University strike of 1969 and a faculty member's involvement in it.

Love, Sam (ed.), *Earth Tool Kit: A Field Manual for Citizen Activists,* New York: Pocket Books, 1971.
This is a handbook for organizing, confronting, and solving ecological problems. Strategies range from the traditionally acceptable to the traditionally unacceptable. The tactics outlined are easily generalized to other social problems.

Organizer's Manual Collective, *The Organizer's Manual,* New York: Bantam Books, 1971.
Boston University students organized and wrote this book during the national student strike in May 1970. Clearly in the value conflict tradition, it deals with the principles of organizing and the constituencies to be organized.

Piven, Frances F., and Richard A. Cloward, *Poor People's Movements: Why They Succeed, How They Fail,* New York: Pantheon, 1977.
Piven and Cloward discuss various attempts to organize poor people along lines suggested by the value conflict perspective. Included is a discussion of the National Welfare Rights Organization (NWRO).

Schrag, Philip, "Consumer Rights," in Henry Etzkowitz (ed.), *Is America Possible?: Social Problems from Conservative, Liberal, and Socialist Perspectives,* St. Paul: West Publishing Co., 1974.
The abuse of consumers is based on inequality of bargaining power and an inability to press claims. Schrag discusses methods for equalizing the power of producers and consumers and for effectively pressing claims. Class action suits are among his proposed solutions.

Questions for Discussion

1. Rose analyzes rape from a value conflict perspective. How would a social pathologist analyze the rape problem? How would a social pathology perspective differ from the steps advocated by the antirape movement? Which approach to this problem do you prefer? Why?

2. Carmichael and Hamilton advocate a separatist solution to the problem of racial inequality. Why do Roach and Roach disagree with such a strategy? Which view makes more sense to you? Why?

3.   With regard to the problem of unequal educational opportunities for blacks, compare the solution proposed by Carmichael and Hamilton with the one which has been mandated in most American cities, namely, bussing for school integration. What are the key differences between the two solutions? In the long run, which do you think has more chances of succeeding?

4.   How do you evaluate the value conflict perspective and the type of solutions it suggests? Many social problems are currently being identified and tackled by groups using this perspective (consciously or unconsciously). How many examples can you think of?

5 / DEVIANT BEHAVIOR

From World War I to the 1950s, the social disorganization perspective remained the dominant approach to the study of social problems.[1] During the fifties, however, a fourth perspective supplanted both the social disorganization and the value conflict approaches. As noted in the preceding chapter, the fifties was a period of relative prosperity and tranquillity. Concern with group conflict diminished. There was less overt social or political conflict than there had been in the thirties, and less than there would be in the sixties. The national mood was a smug one. On the one hand, there was a sense of satisfaction with "the good life" that prosperity and technology had brought. Middle-class values and lifestyle were touted as a dream come true. Anyone choosing another lifestyle or different values (e.g., the beatniks) was regarded at best as misguided and more typically as subversive or criminal. The McCarthy era (in which Senator Joseph McCarthy accused many people of being un-American or communist) stands as a regrettable monument to this attitude of suspicion against anyone who by choice or birth was "different."

Critics have described the fifties as a period of mass conformity, and the pursuit of conformity is reflected in the sociology of the period as well. The perspective that came into vogue during this time is called the deviant behavior perspective, which viewed social behavior in terms of *conformity* versus *deviant behavior*. Conformity and deviant behavior were defined in terms of prevailing middle-class *norms*—i.e., expectations as to what is appropriate behavior.

In many ways the deviant behavior perspective builds on social disorganization theory. It looks at many of the same types of social

1. Perhaps the most influential textbook on social problems during this period was Mabel Elliot and Francis Merrill, *Social Disorganization* (New York: Harper, 1931).

problems (e.g., delinquent gangs, alcoholism, drug use, street crime). Yet the deviant behavior perspective goes beyond the disorganization approach. Given a backdrop of social disorganization, the deviant behavior perspective goes on to ask how various deviant roles arise and how some people come to adopt those roles while other people adopt more conventional roles. Note that the focus is on *deviant roles,* not on isolated deviant acts.

In addressing these questions, the deviant behavior perspective links deviant roles to the larger social environment and social structure. Two major theories were drawn together in the deviant behavior perspective to explain social problems in these terms. First, there was Robert K. Merton's *anomie theory.*[2] The notion of anomie, introduced by the Frenchman Emile Durkheim, refers to the stress and problems caused by rising but unmet expectations.[3] In our society, Merton suggests, almost everyone is socialized to the "great American dream" of opportunity and success. People in some segments of society, however, find themselves unable to materialize that dream through legitimate channels. A lower- or working-class background may not provide them with the skills and resources necessary for success. Or perhaps they are handicapped by racial or ethnic discrimination. According to this line of thought, there is a condition of discrepancy in the social structure—specifically, disparity between cultural goals and the actual opportunities many working- and lower-class people have for realizing those goals. This disjunction between aspirations and opportunities creates frustration and stress, which in turn may lead to deviant behavior.

In Merton's theory deviant behavior is seen as an adaptation to this disjunction. Merton delineated several different forms this adaptation may take. One deviant adaptation, called *innovation,* involves the use of unconventional or criminal channels for attaining the goals that one cannot attain by conventional means. If a person is shut out of the business or professional world, for example, s/he might turn to theft or drug peddling to get the desired money and lifestyle. Note that it is not the goal (making money and enjoying "the good life") but rather the means for attaining that goal that are deviant. A second type of adaptation is called *ritualism,* which

2. Robert K. Merton, "Social Structure and Anomie," *American Sociological Review* 3 (October 1938), pp. 672–82.
3. Emile Durkheim, *Suicide: A Study in Sociology*, John A. Spaulding and George Simpson, trans. (New York: The Free Press, 1951).

occurs when people scale down their dreams to match their means. People using this adaptation, Merton suggests, are in a rut. They play it safe, avoid competition, shun new ideas, and cling desperately to conventional rules. The zealously conforming bureaucrat, Merton says, is an example. A third type of adaptation is called *retreatism.* Here, a person rejects the conventional goals ("I never really wanted money or a nice home anyway!") and instead tries to find an escape. Drug use, alcoholism, and becoming a hermit were all considered by Merton to be examples of retreatism. A fourth response is *rebellion*, where people reject both conventional goals and conventional means. Instead, they create their own goals and adopt unconventional means for accomplishing their new goals. Withdrawing their allegience from the established order, they seek to bring about a new order. Rebellion does not necessarily produce social problems (many religious movements, for example, could be classified as rebellion), but it does if it involves flouting the law and seeking to change society through illegal means. Political terrorism is an example of this.

The second major theory that was incorporated into the deviant behavior perspective is Edwin H. Sutherland's theory of *differential association.*[4] Sutherland pointed out that deviant roles, like conformist roles, are *learned* behaviors. And like conformist roles, they are learned in interaction with other people. If people have contact mainly with criminal or delinquent behavior patterns, then they are likely to learn ways of thinking that are favorable to crime and to take on a criminal or delinquent role themselves. On the other hand, if they associate chiefly with more conventional patterns of behavior, they are likely to learn ways of thinking that are unfavorable to crime and to adopt a more conventional role.

Therefore, according to this theory, the roles we enact are mainly a function of the learning and reinforcement we get in relationships with other people, and whether we adopt deviant or conventional roles depends on the balance of deviant and conventional influences on us. Primary groups, such as family and friends, are thought to be especially important in this regard, and the deviant behavior perspective puts particular emphasis on the influence of the peer group.

Both Merton's and Sutherland's theories were proposed in the late 1930s. It was not until the fifties, however, that they were drawn

---

4. Edwin H. Sutherland, *Principles of Criminology* (Philadelphia: J. B. Lippincott, 1939).

together and incorporated into a common perspective on social problems. This was accomplished by sociologists who related both theories to the issue of deviant subcultures. One sociologist traced subcultures of delinquency to the blocked opportunities that Merton talked about.[5] Extending Merton's theory, others pointed out that one must consider not only the legitimate opportunity structure but also the illegitimate opportunity structure (i.e., whether or not one has access to criminal opportunities.)[6] Some communities contain criminal subcultures providing a good illegitimate opportunity structure, while others provide neither legitimate nor illegitimate opportunities. A boy in Appalachia, for example, may have few legitimate opportunities but also few opportunities to "make it" through crime. Similarly, some types of deviant behavior can be carried out without any involvement in a deviant subculture (rape is one example), while other crimes, such as drug use or professional crime, usually require a supportive subculture.

From the deviant behavior perspective, blocked legitimate opportunities, access to illegitimate opportunities, and informal social relations all join together to produce social problems. Like its predecessors, the deviant behavior perspective has its own vocabulary. Merton's anomie theory is reflected in terms like *access, anomie, ends, goals, life chances, means, opportunities, social structure,* and *status.* From Sutherland's differential association theory comes an assortment of terms dealing with a person's social circle—*bad company, companions, example, group, peers, role model,* and *significant others*—and the learning of deviant roles—*commitment, conversion, socialization, resocialization,* and *self-image.* During the fifties, as attention began to focus on the importance of subcultures in creating and sustaining deviant roles, the following types of terms also became characteristic: *criminal subculture, delinquent subculture, deviant subculture, illegitimate opportunity structure, retreatist subculture,* and *risks.*

The deviant behavior perspective follows the social disorganization approach in its concern with advancing sociology as a discipline. Sociologists using the deviant behavior approach were as concerned with developing basic sociological theory and doing empirical research as they were with solving particular problems.

5. Albert K. Cohen, *Delinquent Boys: The Culture of the Gang* (New York: The Free Press, 1955).
6. Richard A. Cloward and Lloyd E. Ohlin, *Delinquency and Opportunity: A Theory of Delinquent Gangs* (New York: The Free Press, 1960).

These sociologists found an approach that was fertile for generating sociological theory and a set of concepts that were more easily applied than the very abstract concepts of the social disorganization perspective. The deviant behavior perspective seemed more useful in explaining how people come to participate in so-called social problems, in formulating programs to solve social problems, and in taking action to prevent social problems. Thus the deviant behavior approach spawned a great deal of theory about social problems, empirical research on a variety of forms of deviant behavior, and programs for practical remedial action.

Of the five perspectives, the deviant behavior approach has probably been the most widely used in actual attempts to solve social problems. This perspective has figured prominently in efforts to "rehabilitate" various types of deviant individuals, and it sometimes underlies efforts to open up opportunities for disadvantaged groups. It should be noted, however, that this perspective cannot be applied to solving *all* social problems. It is applicable only to persons who risk becoming (or have become) "career" deviants—i.e., who take on deviant roles in association with other deviants or in response to blocked opportunities. This perspective would be much more useful in attempts to rehabilitate members of delinquent gangs, for example, than it would be for solving other types of social problems such as discrimination, pollution, or slum housing. Also, since the deviant behavior perspective deals with deviant behavior as a social phenomenon, its solutions are best carried out in a group context and are less applicable to situations of individual counseling or therapy.

The central assumption in the deviant behavior perspective is that all roles, whether conforming or deviant, are learned through participation in primary groups. If people have learned a deviant role through participation in deviant groups, then they can learn or relearn conformist roles through participation in more conformist groups. To rehabilitate deviants, one should construct conformist groups in which they can simultaneously unlearn deviant patterns and learn conforming ones. To accomplish such learning, one should reduce the deviant's contact with illegitimate conduct and increase contact with conventional patterns, provide opportunities for learning conformist roles, and supply a group context that offers a new, legitimate role and self-image in exchange for conforming conduct.

Such attempted solutions have taken a variety of forms. One

form is found in self-help groups set up by former deviants. Alcoholics Anonymous, Synanon (as it was set up in the 1950s for drug addicts), Parents Anonymous (for child abusers), Mistress' Anonymous, and Gamblers' Anonymous are examples of such groups. These groups offer a specific set of goals and norms. They also provide a context of primary group support and help in accomplishing these goals by the prescribed norms. In this manner they seek to resocialize deviants into more conforming ways and, when needed, to gain their reentry into conventional society. Such programs tend to develop informally under the charismatic leadership of a former deviant. These groups are generally interested in practical results, not sociological theory, and concordance with the deviant behavior perspective is usually just coincidental. Yet in drawing on their own personal experiences and knowledge, such leaders at least implicitly take into account the type of factors that concern the deviant behavior perspective.

There are also programs in which sociologists seek to formally apply the deviant behavior perspective to rehabilitate deviants. Such programs abound in the field of juvenile delinquency—e.g., Essexfields, Highfields, Provo, and Silverlake. While professionals provide assistance in the rehabilitation process, the primary group remains the core of the program, and organizational conditions foster primary groups that encourage conventional behaviors and self-image. These programs are sometimes used for research as well as rehabilitation. Delinquents in a formal sociological program, for example, may be compared with those receiving more traditional treatment in order to weigh the relative effectiveness of the program.

In both self-help programs and formal rehabilitation programs operating along lines suggested by the deviant behavior perspective, one point should be noted. The primary emphasis is on changing *roles*, not personality, and this is best achieved through group interaction, not individual counseling.

The deviant behavior perspective suggests yet another kind of remedy to social problems. Insofar as social problems reflect a blocked opportunity structure, they can be reduced by opening up opportunities for success to disadvantaged groups and individuals. Such opportunities include both economic opportunities (e.g., job training) and cultural or educational opportunities. Many government programs have been initiated to provide learning experiences and job training, thus helping such people succeed in middle-class institutions. The Job Corps, Mobilization for Youth, Headstart, and Upward Bound are but a few examples.

CHARACTERISTICS OF THE DEVIANT BEHAVIOR PERSPECTIVE: A SUMMARY

In the deviant behavior perspective, society is viewed as including deviant roles and cultures as well as conforming, or conventional, roles and culture. Social problems are conceptualized primarily in terms of these deviant roles and analyzed in relation to the larger society. The central characteristics of this perspective are as follows:

Definition.   Social problems consist of deviant behavior on the part of individuals or groups—i.e., behavior that violates the prevailing norms of the society. Social problems, then, reflect violations of normative expectations.

Causes.   Deviant behavior is caused by inappropriate socialization. Within primary groups such as family or peer groups, people learn deviant or conventional ways. When socialization to deviant patterns outweighs socialization to conventional ones, deviant behavior results.

Conditions.   In a society such as ours, a discrepancy between goals and opportunities lays the groundwork for much deviant behavior. When people are taught to have high aspirations for success but have limited opportunities for achieving success, they may turn to deviant behavior as an alternative source of rewards. Illegitimate opportunity structures (e.g., criminal or delinquent subcultures) are also important background conditions because they determine which role models and opportunities are available and thus the particular type of deviant role one might adopt.

Consequences.   Deviant behavior can be costly. The victims may suffer bodily injury or material loss, and deviant subcultures may develop that perpetuate and strengthen the deviant roles.

Solutions.   The principle solution is to resocialize, or "rehabilitate," deviants to conform to middle-class norms. The deviant's primary group can be manipulated so that conforming behaviors are rewarded while deviant behaviors are punished. Contact with deviant roles should be decreased while contact with conventional roles is increased. Legitimate opportunities for deviants should be increased (e.g., through job training). Finally, illegitimate opportunities should be decreased, either by removing the deviant from that setting or by eradicating the deviant subculture or group.

A HALF-WAY HOUSE
FOR THE MENTALLY ILL

George W. Fairweather, David H. Sanders,
David L. Cressler, and Hugo Maynard

According to Merton's anomie theory, mental illness represents a form of retreatism, whereby the mentally ill are unwilling or unable to pursue traditional goals and participate in conventional roles. In this article, Fairweather, Sanders, Cressler, and Maynard describe an innovative program designed to reintegrate mentally ill patients into the larger society. In this program mental patients live in a half-way house and work, if they are able, in the larger community. The program is structured in a way that emphasizes the goals and values of the larger society—e.g., work, ownership, and upward mobility. Patients are also taught how to conform to conventional roles outside the half-way house. Rehabilitation is accomplished, according to this program, when patients can once again participate in the larger society.

This study was carried out as a direct result of preceding studies which showed a high recidivism rate among hospital patients who had been institutionalized for considerable periods of time (Fairweather, 1964). It was designed to test several hypotheses mainly concerned with the effects that a living and working situation established in the community might have upon reducing this high recidivism rate and enhancing the chronic mental patients' social status. A working-living social subsystem [the lodge] was established which linked the hospital to a dormitory located in the community. Here the individuals lived and operated a business. . . .

After planning the experiment, which included the creation of the assessment devices and the research design, all individuals on a selected

From George W. Fairweather, David H. Sanders, David L. Cressler, and Hugo Maynard, *Community Life for the Mentally Ill: An Alternative to Institutional Care*, 1969, pp. 5–6, 168–82, 321. Reprinted by permission of George W. Fairweather.

open ward were questioned about volunteering to live in the lodge society. Those who volunteered were randomly assigned to either the lodge group or its control group. Those who refused to volunteer constituted the experimental group used later to discover the effects of the act of volunteering itself.

On a prearranged date, the action phase of the study began. Initial testing was completed for all individuals in the sample, and group meetings by the potential lodge members to plan the imminent move into the community were begun. The members decided who their leaders would be, what procedures for purchasing food were needed, and the type of work each member would do. At the end of 30 days, the lodge group moved into its community residence. . . . As with most plans, changes needed to be instituted immediately. Difficulties soon arose concerning the taking of tranquilizing medication, and a system whereby a lodge member gave medication to those persons who would not take it was instituted. The planned janitorial and gardening work was not done well by the members. Work habits learned in the hospital seemed to have been more oriented toward avoiding than carrying out work. Accordingly, work-training programs were initiated. Problems arose in obtaining food and preparing it. Finally, one member who demonstrated an interest in cooking emerged from the group and eventually became the lodge member continuously responsible for preparing and serving meals.

But management of the food problem was only the first step toward achieving full autonomy in the community. It was soon discovered that the members worked best in teams. Each work team had a leader who became responsible for its work. A business manager emerged with the responsibility for keeping the business records of the organization. To aid the members in establishing competence in the various areas of living and work, the services of a number of consultants also were obtained. Thus the medical problems of the lodge were handled by a house physician, an accountant consulted the business manager about the manner in which the books should be kept, and a janitorial consultant aided the lodge group in improving its work methods.

Initially, extensive supervision of the lodge society was required. This was provided by a coordinator, a psychologist with many years of professional experience in the mental health field. According to the research plan, he was replaced by a graduate student with much less experience, while at the same time a governing body, composed of lodge members, was given increased autonomy in the management of both the social and work life of the lodge members. After several months of leadership under the graduate student coincident with increasing autonomy of the governing body, the student was replaced by lay leaders, responsible only for the work aspect of the lodge. The member governing body at this point became totally responsible for the development and operation of the lodge. This committee of lodge members established policy for governing the members and for allocating lodge resources. For example, they set salary levels, approved vacations, determined how the organization's money would be spent, and disciplined troublesome members. Under joint lay and member leadership, an extensive business was created, and lodge living conditions became more attractive to the members. Eventually, the lodge building was closed and the remaining members became a completely autonomous group residing on their own in a new location. Despite the physical change, they continued the work and living arrangements of the lodge organization without the aid of lay or professional persons. Occasionally lodge members did request help from these persons, who then functioned as their consultants.

What did this new society achieve? Did it fulfill the expectations of those who established it? Several questions like these asked at the outset of the study were answered once the full sequence of events leading to autonomy of the lodge society was completed. . . .

By establishing such a dual-purpose residence in the community, return to or remaining in the hospital were both drastically reduced and employment greatly improved. But a reduction in recidivism and increased employment were not the only benefits. Such constructive living was accompanied by strong feelings of pride that the members had about the organization, themselves, and their accomplishments. And these accomplishments were attained with little professional support and at a minimum cost to the public when contrasted with the cost of mental hospital care. More important, perhaps, the new working-living subsystem was integrated into society without encountering difficulties with other members of society. Most members of society accepted the ex-patients and respected them as responsible citizens. *But perhaps the most important result of this study was that the newly created participating social statuses for the ex-patients generated an identification with the usual goals of the society by a group of its members who previously had been generally isolated from it and who in the past had little regard for it.** This study created a living system which largely negated the social marginality which was such a characteristic feature of the background of most of the lodge members. In addition to recognizing these concrete benefits, it is also important to place these results in a broader perspective, especially since this experiment has shown that new social statuses *can* be created for the mentally ill and that such persons *can* live durably in the community. The question naturally arises: What principles of organization can be

*Italics added.

abstracted from the experience of operating this new social subsystem that may help future workers with this or other marginal social groups? Certain features undoubtedly created this successful outcome. These features may be viewed as operating principles for social subsystems that can be established to provide a more responsible and rewarding social position for chronic mental patients.

The *first principle* that is of primary importance in creating such a new status concerns the degree of ego-involvement that the participants must develop in order to make the subsystem work. The experimental evidence clearly suggests that ego-involvement is directly related to *the "stake" that the participants have in the social subsystem*. The tasks performed by the members must be meaningful to them. Throughout the course of the experiment presented here, the lodge members typically thought their work was important, and they became increasingly proud of their organization. They wanted the organization to succeed. The members often remarked that the janitorial and gardening service was *their* business. The feeling of identification with the success of the organization was enhanced by their ownership of the business. *Such ownership is important when placed in the perspective of contemporary American culture.** In America, great value is placed upon the ownership of property. Individuals who have *not* achieved a rewarding social status in this culture—such as the chronic mental patients described here—tend to attach great importance to the ownership of property. Thus, an organization which they manage and control leads to perceptions of personal success in terms of social values that are an accepted part of the culture. When such perceptions occur, the feelings of personal accomplishment are often positive and intense. . . .

A *second principle* derived from the research results is that *any subsystem must give as much autonomy to its members as is possible, consistent with their behavioral performance*. While autonomy of action contributes to each member's "stake" in the organization, it is such an important aspect of the conduct of social subsystems that it is treated here as a separate and independent principle. When the participants in any developing social organization are not initially capable of assuming full autonomy, organizational procedures must be structured by someone else who does not "belong." The leadership roles of such "outsiders," however, should be relinquished as quickly as possible. The degree of autonomy that members . . . can assume must be based upon empirical testing of their capacities for responsibility, rather than arbitrary guesswork. This is especially important with members of the mental health professions who often perceive the chronic mental

*Italics added.

patient as being far less capable than he actually is. . . . Only when real-life trials indicate that the members of such a subsystem are incapable of performing responsibly should the professional staff assume responsibility for them. When they do, repeated trials aimed at more complete autonomy for the members should be immediately instituted and continuously maintained.

Thus, in accordance with this principle, control over lodge affairs was gradually given to the members. By the end of the study the group had become completely autonomous. . . . Redelegation of citizenship responsibilities gradually and by continuous trial is one way to find the maximum possible level of responsibility for each such person participating in a social subsystem. Such trials can ascertain the level of autonomy that is possible for each individual, without inviting the personal failure which has always been observed to have such a disastrous psychological and social impact upon former inmates of such total institutions.

There are several practical ways in which staff authority can gradually be transferred to subordinate members. Jurisdiction over disciplinary problems among peers can be turned over to a committee of the membership. Such matters as who should hold particular statuses within the organization, such as crew chief and worker statuses in the lodge, can be determined by the membership. They can also be charged with the responsibility for handling the financial affairs of the organization and altering organizational procedures when necessary to meet the changing needs of its members. The administration of rewards and punishments should be put in the hands of the members as quickly as possible. Autonomy can also be achieved by placing operations that are essential to the daily functioning of the subsystem, such as bookkeeping, the dispensing of medication, and the purchase of food in the case of the lodge, under the direct control of the membership.

Not all these responsibilities can or need to be delegated at once. They can and probably should be delegated gradually, so that the assumption of a second set of responsibilities is contingent upon adequate performance in carrying out the first, the third upon adequate performance of the second, and so on. Such a step-wise system of progressive and graded responsibility was a feature of the hospital ward from which the lodge members came (Fairweather, 1964). However, it should not be overlooked that the delegation of *all* responsibilities should be the ultimate goal of the staff. This should be completed as quickly as possible because autonomy increases the "stake" that each member has in the social organization of which he is a member. The foresighted professional staff will not hesitate to turn over to the members of any such social organization those activities which its members are capable of assuming when determined by actual trial. Such a method of determination gives confidence in the members' capabilities to the staff as well as to the members. At the same time, the responsible staff must itself be willing to assume responsibility in those areas where the members demonstrate an incapacity to do so, and without using failures at such independent attempts as an excuse to perpetuate the members' subordinate status.

The subsystem should have a vertical organization so that both a division of labor is possible and a meaningful role can be found for all members. This *third principle* was exemplified in the vertical social organization of the lodge, which permitted upward mobility *within* the lodge society. Those members who were motivated and capable of assuming higher social statuses did so and, at the same time, a meaningful social position was established for those members who were not capable or did not aspire to higher social positions within the organization. *Thus, it was possible for each member to find a social position commensurate with his abilities and interests.** Any particular social status, however, was not permanent, and changes continuously occurred in the social position of lodge members—workers became crew chiefs and crew chiefs became workers.

Different types of work for the participants should be provided within the subsystem. The greater the diversity of tasks involved, the more likely it is that work which has meaning for every member can be found. In the lodge, the diversity of tasks was pronounced. Jobs for the kitchen crew included cooks, helpers, and the administrator of the kitchen; janitorial crews had crew chiefs, workers, and marginal workers; gardening crews had the same three work statuses; other jobs such as bookkeeper and truck driver provided so much diversity of employment that every member of the lodge society found a job that was acceptable to him.

A social subsystem with vertical mobility also provides a social organization whose different statuses can be ranked in order of their degree of responsibility. *The highest statuses can be given the highest rewards, so that motivation toward more responsible social positions can be maintained.** Each member can thus aspire to the highest status of which he is capable and can be rewarded accordingly. It is also important to note here that when higher rewards are linked with higher statuses, it is much easier for the participants within the subsystem to deal with the jealousies and rivalries that inevitably occur. Because the rewards are attached to the status, the individual occupying a given status receives the rewards commensurate with it, irrespective of who he might be.

Any created social subsystem must be compatible with the environment in which it is implanted. Its internal social organization and its physical location must be compatible with the broader society, ac-

---

*Italics added.

cording to this *fourth principle.* The entire social organization of any potentially successful new social subsystem must be as close a facsimile of the broader society as it is possible to make it, consistent with the capabilities of its participants. This is necessary because some individuals who participate in such organizations will leave and reenter the larger society. For this reason, life in the subsystem must stress those behaviors that will permit any resident of the subsystem to make this transition without undue stress. The more identical the subsystem is to the society, the easier such transitions become.

For example, *vertical organization and division of labor just mentioned are modeled upon the larger society.* ° A meaningful system of rewards and real-life tasks were also attributes of the lodge society that were compatible with the larger society. The type of work done by members of such a subsociety should be work for which society has a need. In such cases, those behaviors learned while the person is a participant in the subsystem can be directly transferred to other community situations. *It is, therefore, important that the social organization of the created subsystem represent statuses and role behaviors that exist and are accepted in the society at large.* °

Social subsystems established to give new social statuses and roles to the mentally ill will typically not be completely identical with those in the society. Certain behaviors that are acceptable within such model societies may not be compatible with the behavioral norms of the larger society. As an example, the establishment of the lodge executive committee which dealt with violations of norms internal to the subsystem was the means by which the behavior of its members was regulated so that the larger society would not reject it. Few homes or organizations in the larger community have such specifically organized regulatory social processes. From this example, however, it may be inferred that social processes solely internal to a social subsystem do not have to be compatible with the greater social environment, but social processes that cross the boundaries into the community must be compatible with the larger society. As another example, despite differences between the lodge and the surrounding community in the methods for distribution of income, a bookkeeping procedure was established in the lodge which was the same as bookkeeping procedures everywhere. This was necessary because auditors from the community supervised the lodge's business books. It is at such points of contact with the community that practices which are compatible with the larger society must be maintained.

Subsystem compatibility with the geographical location in which it is implanted is also necessary. It is highly questionable whether the

°Italics added.

lodge could have survived if it had been implanted at the outset in an upper middle-class neighborhood. Although it was unusual, some members did venture into the surrounding community evidencing odd behaviors which were either ignored by the neighbors or were considered not much different than that which might be expected from any resident there. Trucks and other heavy equipment were commonplace in the neighborhood. Thus the appearance of trucks filled with workers was not perceived as different from what might occur at any place of business in the locale. The group was also racially integrated, and racially mixed groups were common in the area where the lodge was located.

It seems logical that while every social subsystem for chronic mental patients that is implanted in the larger community will necessarily differ from the community itself in certain respects, there is only a certain degree of deviation that can occur at any one time without so disrupting the typical social processes of its locale that antagonism against the subsystem will occur. In instances where these tolerances are exceeded, the implanted subsystem may be rejected or destroyed.

Since chronic mental patients often exhibit behavior that is not acceptable in society at large, the *fifth principle* requires that *subsystems designed for mental patients must establish internal norms that are tolerant of the deviant behavior that is normative for that particular population.* Many mentally ill persons do not behave in ways that are acceptable to the society at large, but such behavior is normative for them. It is difficult, if not impossible, for individuals who have been continuously hospitalized to discard aberrant behaviors immediately upon entry into a community if, indeed, such behavior can be totally extinguished at all. The members of the subsystem must be tolerant of these behaviors. In the lodge, for example, members often hallucinated while talking with other members within the confines of the lodge itself. To take an extreme example of such toleration, one member who openly hallucinated within the lodge and enroute to work was informed by his crew chief upon arival at the work site that no talking was permitted on the job. Usually he was silent during work hours but upon entry into the truck for the trip back to the lodge, he began hallucinating again—an acceptable behavior for his peers.

Leaders of such subsystems should be able to differentiate clearly the behavior norms of the greater society from those of the subsystem. *Eventually the behavior within the subsystem tends to become somewhat similar to that required for community living.** There was a trend in this direction from the opening of the lodge to the eventual assimilation of its members into the community. But it does appear from this

*Italics added.

experience that some persons may never be able to assume completely the responsibilities of full citizenship. Each person within the subsystem should be expected to contribute whatever he is capable of giving but, at the same time, other members of the subsystem must be aware and understanding of the fact that some persons have certain rather permanent incapacities which prevent them from active and full participation in the usual citizen's role.

A *specific communication system needs to be devised for each subsystem,* according to a *sixth principle.* The importance of continuous information feedback to members of such social subsystems about their performance cannot be overstressed. An almost continuous input of information to lodge members was necessary in order for them to achieve acceptable job performance and to maintain such performance. The curve of performance for all members was variable. According to the lodge experience, therefore, it is at the point of a generalized downturn in performance that information about such a decrement in performance is urgently needed. The input of information should be maximized at the point where deterioration in performance begins, because such information often prevents further deterioration of performance and aids in reestablishing more adequate levels of performance that have often been achieved in the past.

In the lodge subsystem, the dining area of the lodge served as the place for continuous exchanges of informal information about one's self and others. This continuous informal communication served to clarify interpersonal conflicts that might otherwise have become serious threats to the continuation of the organization. Information about problems among members was presented to the executive committee by lodge members and by the professional staff. Once the executive committee assumed its proper role, it almost always arrived at adequate solutions when the board of peers had accurate factual information about such real-life problems. As time passed, these solutions became more and more appropriate in terms of society's mores. In the initial stages of the lodge's operation, the staff supervisor retained a veto power over the executive committee's decisions and, in the infrequent case where their decision was unacceptable, his veto created an atmosphere for further deliberation which eventually resulted in an acceptable solution. Thus, through continuous information feedback (including the fact a veto had been used), the executive committee eventually reached a level of judgment so reasonable that supervisory vetoes became unnecessary. . . .

Other forms of communication can also be used to provide such needed information. For example, the consultants to the lodge were a constant and valuable source. The janitorial consultant gave the lodge members continuously updated information about the use of new janitorial techniques that could be of use to the organization. The crew chiefs inspected the work of each crew and rated their performance. Their ratings were in turn evaluated by a staff member, particularly during the developmental stages of the organization. For the first six months of the lodge's operation, weekly meetings were held in which any personal problems that the members had were discussed and reviewed. This meeting served initially as a source of information to the participants in the lodge which eventually was no longer needed. . . . Another form of information feedback was the annual customer questionnaire, which requested information from them about the adequacy of the work performed by the janitorial and gardening service. Of course, the immediate feedback by customers while the work crews were on the job was perhaps the most valuable source of information. And information feedback from crew chiefs to new members during work training sessions was helpful in creating good work habits.

Some persons will want to enter and some will want to leave such a subsystem. *Mobile entry and exit from the subsystem should be possible without penalty to the individual* is the *seventh principle* of subsystem operation. If the community subsystem is voluntary, there will be continuous entry into and exit from it. Free access to the larger community should be provided for residents in such social subsystems. For this reason, training for living in the larger community should be one of the primary aims of the subsystem. A social atmosphere conducive to venturing forth into the community without attaching penalties to such movements should be provided. This is important because the member leaders of such autonomous social subsystems will often feel an obligation to their group. This sense of obligation may cause them to hesitate in leaving the group, even though they are capable of such a move into the larger society. The social norms of the subsystem should encourage such departures when they are clearly warranted and it can do this by attaching no sanctions to exit from it.

But it is equally important that no penalty be attached to remaining in the subsystem if a person is incapable of completely independent living. The research results of this study showed that certain members were able to perform quite adequately in the lodge setting but rapidly became disorganized or otherwise incapacitated when they attempted to live independently in the community. It seems plausible, therefore, that for some individuals a dormitory type of life constitutes maximally independent living for them. It is therefore critical that the norms governing movement into the broader community also do not punish those who have achieved their highest level of adjustment within the created social subsystem, in acknowledgement of the fact that their probability of movement into the broader community is slight.

The *eighth principle* for such subsystems requires that *persons should perform as groups wherever possible.* From earlier studies and the one presented here, it appears that membership in a reference group is very important in maintaining the chronically disturbed person in the community, as well as in the mental hospital (Fairweather, 1964). Furthermore, the norms of such groups reflect realistic performance standards for the members. This is essential with chronic mental patients, who often are unable to behave within socially acceptable limits without the support of a group. Many examples can be cited from life at the lodge. The work crews comprised of three or more men were able adequately to perform on the janitorial or yard job. Each member of the crew had a particular task which he typically completed. The usual composition of such a crew was a leader (crew chief), worker, and a marginal worker. It was the marginal worker whose work was constantly brought up to acceptable standards by the working example of the supervisor and worker. Without the framework of the group and the supervision and help of the crew chief, the marginal worker often failed.

But it was not in work alone that the group served to structure the social situation, for the group improved decision-making processes as well. The executive committee, which made the major decisions concerning the lives of the members, was an excellent decision-making group. The consensus arrived at through their discussions of the problems facing the members was often more realistic than one individual's opinion. And, in addition, such discussions focused on decisions about real-life problems also brought about group cohesiveness. Group decision-making and mutual work led to shared pride in the organization, which emphasized the worth of every individual and resulted in high group morale.

Only a limited number of people should participate in any subsystem constitutes the *ninth principle.* It is important that close interpersonal contact be established for the members of such a subsystem because it promotes identification with the subsystem and its goals. Interpersonal experience with others also yields a personal knowledge of them which can serve as the basis for decision-making by peers. Large organizations tend to become impersonal. For example, the greatest number of individuals at the lodge at any one time was 33. When the number of 33 was reached, the lodge members own executive committee asked that it not be exceeded, because the organization was becoming "large like the hospital." Even though a different physical plant might have permitted more participants while still maintaining its home-like social atmosphere, it seems clear that too many people would have tended to make the organization too impersonal for the members both to perceive their peers as a reference group and to identify with the organization and its goals.

New social subsystems need to be implanted in the community so that they are not dependent for their existence upon the good will of the community in which they are implanted. The *tenth principle* stresses that while it is important that the social subsystem be compatible with the environment in which it is placed, it is also important that it should be financed and supported by agencies or groups who are *not* directly dependent upon the immediate neighborhood for their financial support. Chronic mental patients who return to the community need time to become self-sufficient and they also need protection against community pressures that might destroy the embryonic social organization to which they belong. The lodge did not become self-sufficient until its fourth year of operation. The members were sustained through the formative stages, when great insecurity prevailed, by the strong support of two interested and devoted staff coordinators. The financial support, work organization, and relations in the community were established through a federal agency, a local university, and a rehabilitative non-profit corporation. It was the combined efforts of these three organizations that offered support for the fledgling organization when it could have been most easily destroyed.

The social organization of the social subsystem must be so arranged that individuals may substitute for other individuals when required. It was a recurrent experience in the community-lodge work situation that a particular person might not be available for work on a particular day. That experience is the source of this *eleventh principle*. It was most important that another person be able to take his place when this occurred, in order that lodge operations not suffer. In order to appreciate the significance of this, one needs to imagine the entire group as a work force where several individuals are trained for the same role and each one is capable of assuming it on short notice. For example, it was not uncommon that an alcoholically inclined person would not be available for work on a particular day because of excessive indulgence, although he might have been perfectly capable of working the following day and for several days thereafter. Psychotic persons with psychosomatic complaints often were unable to work on a particular day or during a particular time period. On the other hand, such persons frequently recovered quickly and asked to be returned to their work. It is, therefore, essential that every function in the social subsystem be so organized that any person can be replaced by another on very short notice. In other terms, this might be called the *principle of substitution*. . . .

A social subsystem for the chronically disturbed person should emphasize equally both rehabilitative and work norms. This represents the *twelfth principle* of subsystem operation. The history of the lodge revealed that in the initial stages of development the emphasis of the members was upon a deep concern for the adjustment of their fellows. Thus, in the early days of the lodge, it was a common practice for the members to try to persuade any member who wanted to return to the hospital that he should make a more diligent attempt to remain in the community. Helpfulness among the members was common and a bond of being adventurers together in a new situation was the *Zeitgeist*. As the lodge became more and more similar to the community, work norms became the dominant behavioral guide lines. There was less and less concern for one's fellows. Eventually, it was necessary for the lodge supervisors to reestablish the work-rehabilitation balance in values. If social subsystems are to be established that adequately meet the needs of the total chronic ex-patient population—a goal that seems both realistic and desirable—a continuing balance between rehabilitative and work norms seems essential.

The *thirteenth principle* is: *Any social subsystem for chronically disturbed persons must establish an appropriate mechanism for handling medication.* Shortly after the lodge was activated, one member failed to take his medication and was returned to the hospital. From that point on, the members themselves assumed the responsibility for seeing that the offending members took their prescribed medication. When any member was not taking his medication, it soon became obvious to the residents of the lodge, because his behavior became more disorganized. The members then quickly informed the offender that his medication would be given to him. After this plan was developed, little further difficulty was experienced with members failing to take their medication.

The thirteen principles set forth here are a synthesis of the information gained from study of the lodge society. These principles may have general applicability to the entire national population of hospitalized mental patients. Two examples provide the evidence suggesting this possibility. During the latter stages of the lodge society's existence, one of the investigators was requested by a large hospital in a predominantly rural southern state to work with their staff toward establishing a community work-living situation. Through the use of funds from different sources than the lodge's research staff had used, a program in the community was established for persons who averaged 13.8 years of previous psychiatric hospitalization. Both men and *women* patients are included in the nine groups which have been formed up to the present time. Through close consultation with the person who helped establish the prototype lodge society itself, the hospital personnel were able to adapt most of the lodge procedures to the new setting. Men and women lived in dormitories in the community. Men worked at golf courses and other such places in teams doing gardening, landscaping, and groundskeeping work. The women worked in groups at several nursing homes, as well as in motels and restaurants in the local area. They have all provided much needed services for the local society. So much so, that requests from other potential employers, such as large hotels, federal natural resource agencies, and farm operators, could not be filled in favor of requests by the original employers for additional groups of workers. Some of the outcomes of this program, which at this writing has been in existence more than 24 months, has been: 72 such chronic patients have left the hospital; of the 8 who have returned to the hosptial since the beginning of the program, 6 have remained there but 2 have again reentered the community; 6 have gone on to other community-living situations from their community dormitories. . . .

The results of this study indicate that the traditional concept of mental illness needs to be replaced. A more meaningful, action-directed concept that could lead to more general social acceptance of those who are emotionally different would simply define each person's adjustment as the degree to which he was a responsible, participating member of his society. In such a case, *the emotionally disturbed person could be viewed as having certain social deficits** that a particular social situation could be created to alleviate. This conception would not fail to recognize the utility of medication or other new biochemical agents for permitting greater accessibility to that specially devised social situation.

With these assumptions about emotional disturbance, *the goal of rehabilitation would become the maximization of such a person's participation in the larger society** to the extent possible at a particular time, without punishing those not currently capable of it. Such a change in conceptual direction is urgently needed in order for such programs to be successful, for the results of this study show that chronic schizophrenic ex-patients only slightly modify their actual behavior. This slight modification, however, is sufficient for living in the society if the person's perception of himself is positive and the social situation in which he finds himself is adequately planned to take account of his personal deficiencies. Whatever new treatment programs *are* developed for the emotionally disturbed, especially those more severely afflicted, it seems clear that they should provide each person with maximum participation in the decision-making processes of the program. Such processes as assuming responsibility for fellow members, developing work techniques, and having control of money allow such persons to participate more realistically in their ongoing life situation. Participation in such processes is the very essence of citizenship which has so often eluded the returning mental patient. It is to be hoped that the operating principles outlined in this chapter will en-

*Italics added.

courage many responsible persons in our society to work toward providing such responsibilities to these persons who can now be looked upon as capable of holding them alongside any other citizen they may encounter in the community.

Reference

Fairweather, G. W. (ed.),
    1964   Social Psychology in Treating Mental Illness: An Experimental Approach. New York: John Wiley & Sons.

ALCOHOLICS ANONYMOUS

Milton A. Maxwell

Alcoholics Anonymous is a classic example of a rehabilitation program fashioned along the lines suggested by Sutherland's theory of differential association. In this reading, Maxwell describes Alcoholics Anonymous as a new subculture with its own rules and values, which the alcoholic learns through face-to-face contact with other A.A. members. Thus, A.A. utilizes not professional therapy but peer influence to socialize new members to a sober lifestyle. Typical of many kinds of self-help groups set up by lay people to address various kinds of deviant behavior, the parallels between the A.A. program and differential association theory are inadvertent rather than deliberate. Nonetheless, A.A. continues to illustrate the efficacy of Sutherland's model.

It is probable that more contemporary alcoholics have found sobriety through the fellowship of Alcoholics Anonymous than through all other agencies combined. Yet the "A.A. recovery program" remains an unknown quantity to many, and at least something of an enigma to most. It is agreed that, for many alcoholics, the A.A. program "works," but what makes it work? What are the therapeutic dynamics? At this point, even social scientists and clinicians close to the alcoholism problem are often baffled. They find it difficult to reconcile what they know or think they know about A.A. with their theoretical assumptions about the nature of alcoholism on the one hand, and the imperatives of the therapeutic processes on the other. The interpretation that follows— limited and incomplete as it must be—is based on the assumption that . . . the A.A. program "makes sense" in the light of contemporary social science concepts and assumptions. . . .

THE TWELVE-STEP PROGRAM

Many of the elements of the Twelve-Step Program are seen . . . in the original formulation of the steps by which Bill, A.A.'s cofounder, achieved sobriety. These are: you admit you are licked; you get honest with yourself; you talk it out with somebody else; you make restitution to the people you have harmed; you try to give of yourself without stint, with no demands for reward; and you pray to whatever God you think there is, even as an experiment, to help you to do these things.[1]

In this series of steps will be seen the admission of "powerlessness over alcohol." . . . Also implicit is the hope of a way out—faith in potential resources and complete reliance upon these resources. The other steps constitute quite an additional order: honest self-analysis and catharsis; the mending of social fences; the practice of out-going, giving, productive behavior for its own sake and not for ego-defense or reassurance; and, finally, the cultivation of the "potential resources" as understood by the individual. Much could be written about the therapeutic value of these steps, for there is wide consensus about the importance of an honest facing of oneself and the unburdening of guilts, fears, and repressed material in the presence of an accepting person, and about the importance of cultivating the desired attitudes and practicing the desired patterns of behavior. However, the Twelve Steps do not exhaust the A.A. program. *The interpersonal and group aspects of the A.A. fellowship also play a very important therapeutic role.** . . .

THE A.A. GROUP AND ITS SUBCULTURE

Kurt Lewin and Paul Grabbe[2] have provided us with a bridge in their suggestion that a change in personality may be conceptualized as a change in culture. Specifically, they suggested that to change is to accept a change in "facts" which are accepted as true, a change in values, and a change in the perception of self and others in a social field. To this we could add that the personality changes may also be seen as the acceptance of new norms—folkways and mores, new role-

*Italics added.

status system, a new charter, and new sanctions. These are all aspects of culture—of a group-shared way of life.

*We may accordingly conceptualize the alcoholic's recovery in A.A. as the joining of a new group and, in that group, gradually learning that group's culture.** The A.A subculture, moreover, constitutes a way of life which is more realistic, which enables the members to get closer to people, which provides one with more emotional security, and which facilitates more productive living. *Thus, the A.A. group becomes an important new reference group**—a new point of orientation.

The A.A. group must also be seen as a primary group which provides exceptionally favorable learning conditions for the internalizing of this new way of life. Primary groups were so called by Cooley because they are more influential than other groups in shaping our attitudes. Among primary groups, however, some are more influential than others. The more intimate the group and the more totally involved its members become in each other and the group life, the greater is the influence of the group upon its members.

The writer's experience as a participant observer in an A.A. group for a summer impressed upon him the unusual quality of relationship to be found there—the intimacy, mutual acceptance, and identification. Unless these qualities of relationship are recognized and unless the "relearning potency" of such a group experience is appreciated, the observer will miss something very important about A.A.

To summarize the points just made: *the A.A. group is to be understood as an unusually intimate primary group which sponsors, in a potent learning situation, a new way of life—a new subculture.** Within this frame of reference, it is possible to analyze the content of this new learning and how it deals with the linkage of stress to alcohol drinking.

First, the A.A. subculture provides the member with much more objective knowledge about alcohol and particularly about alcoholism. This includes a redefinition of alcoholism as an illness rather than as moral degeneracy.

Second, the A.A. subculture requires and facilitates an honest facing of the connection between drinking and stressful situations; the alcoholic begins to define his disorder as involving an obsession of the mind. The impotency of willpower to handle the obsession and the necessity of other help are emphasized. Myths and rationalizations concerning drinking are debunked. The "screwy alcoholic thinking" is dissected and exposed, frequently in a humorous fashion.

Anxieties against drinking are buttressed. Alcohol is associated with all the harm it has done to the alcoholic and with the tragic increase rather than the solution of problems. The member is given perspective on the first drink—that he will always be just one drink from a drunk,

*Italics added.

and that he can never again drink socially. He is taught that he can "arrest" his problem but that he will always remain an alcoholic. This fact is reinforced each time he presides and introduces himself with "I'm Joe Doakes and I'm an alcoholic." Then, to handle the anxiety aroused by the dread of a lifetime without alcohol, he is provided with the "24-hour plan"—sobriety just one day at a time. Because of his association and identification with sobriety models, the A.A. system is made easier to accept and learn. Then when he steps out to help a new prospect (Twelfth-Step calls), he furthers his learning by becoming a teacher and a representative of the A.A. way of thinking and acting. Thus, the A.A. ideology not only attacks vigorously the use of alcohol for the relief of stress, it provides alternative methods of tension relief.

Important is the A.A. structuring of the freedom and the formal and informal opportunities to gain relief from tensions by the "talking-out" process. Important also are the club activities: the fellowship of the coffee bar, the bull sessions, the games, the parties, or the hours of private conversations over a cup of coffee somewhere. In countless ways, A.A. provides the rewards of satisfying social activities to replace the rewards previously sought in a drinking group, or simply sought in the bottle itself.

Outgoing activity in the form of "Twelfth-Step" work—working with other alcoholics—is another important mode of tension relief expected in A.A. In addition, the A.A. culture encourages the cultivation of hobbies, interests, and other means of tension relief. Included are meditation and prayer.

Not only does A.A. provide and encourage the learning (or re-learning) of alternative relief methods, but the A.A. way of life also reduces the amount of stress for which relief is needed. When the compounding of stress through years of alcoholic drinking is considered, the reversal of the isolation, anxiety, and rationalization trends adds up to a substantial reduction of stress. In addition, acceptance of the A.A. way of life reduces the predrinking level of stress. This is done by providing the group member with values and norms and ways of perceiving his social world which are simply less anxiety-producing, which enable him to relate more satisfyingly to other people and, in general, to find more of the satisfactions of a productive orientation.

Other stress-reducing aspects of the A.A. way of life can be mentioned. There are the slogans repeated in the literature and usually posted in meeting places. "Live and let live" reminds the member of the importance of tolerance for others. "Keep an open mind" asks for tolerance of new ideas. "Easy does it" suggests relaxation in various tension-producing contexts. "But for the Grace of God" expresses thankfulness and reminds him of his dependence upon more than his own efforts. The value placed upon "honesty" and "humility" are a constant encouragement to a greater objectivity with regard to himself.

To be rated also are the low-pressure methods encouraged in A.A. This permissiveness has the function of reducing initial resistance. It constantly encourages respect for the rights of the other fellow—even his right to get drunk if he wants to.

Many other aspects of the A.A. way of life could be cited, but the above are sufficient to illustrate the present frame of reference through which the changes in the A.A. member's personality are seen as the learning of culture—a new way of life—in the favorable learning milieu of an exceptionally intimate primary group. . . .

Not least remarkable is the fact that its program was worked out not by professional therapists but by a group of alcoholics themselves. A.A.'s success alone demonstrates that these laymen did indeed weave together a very effective pattern. Their lay language and spiritual concepts, however, have made it difficult for some social scientists and clinicians to appreciate fully the dynamics involved.[3]

Notes

1. *Alcoholics Anonymous Comes of Age: A Brief History of A.A.*, New York: Alcoholics Anonymous Publishing, 1957.

2. Lewin, Kurt, and Grabbe, Paul, "Conduct, Knowledge, and Acceptance of New Values," in Gertrud W. Lewin (ed.), *Resolving Social Conflicts*, New York: Harper & Row, 1948, pp. 56–68.

3. Ritchie, Oscar W., "A Sociohistorical Survey of Alcoholics Anonymous," *Quart. J. Stud. Alc.*, 9:119–156, 1955.

DRUG REHABILITATION

Rita Volkman and Donald R. Cressey

While Alcoholics Anonymous illustrates one type of self-help group fashioned along lines suggested by differential association theory, Synanon illustrates another, and more comprehensive, program. Synanon was set up in 1958 to provide a setting in which drug addicts, living

From Rita Volkman and Donald R. Cressey, "Differential Association and the Rehabilitation of Drug Addicts," *American Journal of Sociology* 69 (Sept. 1963), pp. 129–42. Copyright © 1963 by the University of Chicago Press. Reprinted by permission.

together in a total community, could help one another "kick the habit" and learn a new way of life. Former addicts served as role models for newcomers, and the entire community was organized in such a way that conventional goals and behaviors were encouraged and rewarded while criminal or deviant behaviors were not tolerated. The strongest influences toward rehabilitation came from the rehabilitated addicts themselves, who insisted that newcomers not just "dry out" physically but also change the attitudes and ways of behaving that could lead them once again into drug use.

Volkman and Cressey show how this program, albeit inadvertently, illustrates the sociological principles derived from Sutherland's differential association theory. It should be noted, however, that Synanon has changed significantly in recent years, and that this description applies to Synanon as it operated in earlier years.

In 1955 Cressey listed five principles for applying Edwin Sutherland's theory of differential association to the rehabilitation of criminals.[1] While this article is now frequently cited in the sociological literature dealing with group therapy, "therapeutic communities," and "total institutions," we know of no program of rehabilitation that has been explicitly based on the principles. The major point of Cressey's article, which referred to criminals, not addicts, is similar to the following recommendation by the Chief of the United States Narcotics Division: "The community should restore the former addict to his proper place in society and help him avoid associations that would influence him to return to the use of drugs."[2]

Cressey gives five rules (to be reviewed below) for implementing this directive to "restore," "help," and "influence" the addict. These rules, derived from the sociological and social-psychological literature on social movements, crime prevention, group therapy, communications, personality change, and social change, were designed to show that sociology has distinctive, non-psychiatric theory that can be used effectively by practitioners seeking to prevent crime and change criminals. Sutherland also had this as a principal objective when he formulated his theory of differential association.[3]

Assuming, as we do, that Cressey's principles are consistent with Sutherland's theory and that his theory, in turn, is consistent with more general sociological theory, a test of the principles would be a test of the more general formulations. Ideally, such a test would involve careful study of the results of a program rationally designed to utilize the principles to change criminals. To our knowledge, such a test has not been made.[4] As a "next best" test, we may study rehabilitation programs that use the principles, however unwittingly. Such a program has been in operation since 1958. Insofar as it is remarkably similar to any program that could have been designed to implement the principles, the results over the years can be viewed as at least a crude test of the principles. Since the principles are interrelated, the parts of any program implementing them must necessarily overlap.

"Synanon," an organization of former drug addicts, was founded in May 1958, by a member of Alcoholics Anonymous with the assistance of an alcoholic and a drug addict. . . .

THE PROGRAM

Admission.   Not every addict who knocks on the door of Synanon is given admission. Nevertheless, the only admission criterion we have been able to find is *expressed willingness* to submit one's self to a group that hates drug addiction. Use of this criterion has unwittingly implemented one of Cressey's principles:

If criminals are to be changed, they must be assimilated into groups which emphasize values conducive to law-abiding behavior and, concurrently, alienated from groups emphasizing values conducive to criminality. Since our experience has been that the majority of criminals experience great difficulty in securing intimate contacts in ordinary groups, special groups whose major common goal is the reformation of criminals must be created.

This process of assimilation and alienation begins the moment an addict arrives at Synanon, and it continues throughout his stay. The following are two leaders' comments on admission interviews; they are consistent with our own observations of about twenty such interviews.

> 1. When a new guy comes in we want to find out whether a person has one inkling of seriousness. Everybody who comes here is what we call a psychopathic liar. We don't take them all, either. We work off the top spontaneously, in terms of feeling. We use a sort of intuitive faculty. You know he's lying, but you figure, "Well, maybe if you get a halfway positive feeling that he'll stay. . . ." We ask him things like "What do you want from us?" "Don't you think you're an idiot or insane?" "Doesn't it sound insane for you to be running around the alleys stealing money from others so's you can go and stick something up your arm?" "Does this sound sane to you?" "Have you got family and friends outside?" We might tell him to go do his business now and come back when he's ready to do business with us. We tell him, "We don't need you." "You need *us.*" And if we figure he's only halfway with us, we'll chop off his hair.
>
> It's all in the *attitude.* It's got to be positive. We don't want their money. But we may just tell him to bring back some dough next week. If he pleads and begs—the money's not important. If he shows he really cares. If his attitude is good. It's all in the attitude.

2. Mostly, if people don't have a family outside, with no business to take care of, they're ready to stay. They ain't going to have much time to think about themselves otherwise. . . . Now, when he's got problems, when he's got things outside, if he's got mickey mouse objections, like when you ask him "How do you feel about staying here for a year?" and he's got to bargain with you, like he needs to stay with his wife or his sick mother—then we tell him to get lost. If he can't listen to a few harsh words thrown at him, he's not ready. Sometimes we yell at him, "You're a goddamned liar!" If he's serious he'll take it. He'll do anything if he's serious.

But each guy's different. If he sounds sincere, we're not so hard. If he's sick of running the rat race out there, or afraid of going to the penitentiary, he's ready to do anything. Then we let him right in. . . .

This admission process seems to have two principal functions. First, it forces the newcomer to admit, at least on a verbal level, that he is willing to try to conform to the norms of the group, whose members will not tolerate any liking for drugs or drug addicts. From the minute he enters the door, his expressed desire to join the group is tested by giving him difficult orders—to have his hair cut off, to give up all his money, to sever all family ties, to come back in ten days or even thirty days. He is given expert help and explicit but simple criteria for separating the "good guys" from the "bad guys"—the latter shoot dope. Second, the admission process weeds out men and women who simply want to lie down for a few days to rest, to obtain free room and board, or stay out of the hands of the police. In the terms used by Lindesmith, and also in the terms used at Synanon, the person must want to give up drug *addiction,* not just the drug *habit.*[5] This means that he must at least *say* that he wants to quit using drugs once and for all, in order to realize his potentials as an adult; he must not indicate that he merely wants a convenient place in which to go through withdrawal distress so that he can be rid of his habit for a short time because he has lost his connection, or for some other reason. He must be willing to give up all ambitions, desires, and social interactions that might prevent the group from assimilating him completely.

If he says he just wants to kick, he's no good. Out with him. Now we know nine out of ten lie, but we don't care. We'd rather have him make an attempt and *lie* and then get him in here for thirty days or so—then he might stick. It takes months to decide to stay.

Most fish [newcomers] don't take us seriously. We know what they want, out in front. A dope fiend wants dope, nothing else. All the rest is garbage. We've even taken that ugly thing called money. This shows that they're serious. Now this guy today was sincere. We told him we didn't want money. We could see he would at least give the place a try. We have to find out if he's sincere. Is he willing to have us cut off his curly locks? I imagine cutting his hair off makes him take us seriously. . . .

Although it is impossible to say whether Synanon's selective admission process inadvertently admits those addicts who are most amenable to change, no addict has been refused admission on the ground that his case is "hopeless" or "difficult" or that he is "unreachable." On the contrary, before coming to Synanon, twenty-nine of the fifty-two addicts had been on drugs for at least ten years. Two of these were addicted for over forty years, and had been in and out of institutions during that period. The average length of time on drugs for the fifty-two was eleven years, and 56 per cent reported less than one month as the longest period of time voluntarily free of drugs after addiction and prior to Synanon.

Indoctrination.   In the admission process, and throughout his residence, the addict discovers over and over again that the group to which he is submitting is antidrug, anticrime, and antialcohol. At least a dozen times a day he hears someone tell him that he can remain at Synanon only as long as he "stays clean," that is, stays away from crime, alcohol, and drugs. This emphasis is an unwitting implementatin of Cressey's second principle:

The more relevant the common purpose of the group to the reformation of criminals, the greater will be its influence on the criminal members' attitudes and values. Just as a labor union exerts strong influence over its members' attitudes toward management but less influence on their attitudes toward say, Negroes, so a group organized for recreation or welfare purposes will have less success in influencing criminalistic attitudes and values than will one whose explicit purpose is to change criminals.

Indoctrination makes clear the notion that Synanon exists in order to keep addicts off drugs, not for purposes of recreation, vocational education, etc. Within a week after admission, each newcomer participates in an indoctrination session by a spontaneous group made up of four or five older members. Ordinarily, at least one member of the Board of Directors is present, and he acts as leader. The following are excerpts from one such session with a woman addict. The rules indicate the extreme extent to which it is necessary for the individual to subvert his personal desires and ambitions to the antidrug, anticrime group.

> Remember, we told you not to go outside by yourself. Whenever anybody leaves this building they have to check in and out at the desk. For a while, stay in the living room. Don't take showers alone or even go to the bath room alone, see. While you're kicking, somebody will be with you all the time. And stay away from newcomers. You got nothing to talk to them about, except street talk, and before you know it you'll be splitting

[leaving] to take a fix together. Stay out of the streets, mentally and physically, or get lost now.

No phone calls or letters for a while—if you get one, you'll read it in front of us. We'll be monitoring all your phone calls for a while. You see, you got no ties, no business out there any more. You don't need them. You never could handle them before, so don't start thinking you can do it now. All you knew how to do was shoot dope and go to prison.

You could never take care of your daughter before. You didn't know how to be a mother. It's garbage. All a dope fiend knows how to do is shoot dope. Forget it.

There are two obvious illustrations of the antidrug and anticrime nature of the group's subculture. First, there is a strong taboo against what is called "street talk." Discussion of how it feels to take a fix, who one's connection was, where one took his shot, the crimes one has committed, or who one associated with is severely censured. One's best friend and confidant at Synanon might well be the person that administers a tongue lashing for street talk, and the person who calls your undesirable behavior to the attention of the entire group during a general meeting.

Second, a member must never, in any circumstances, identify with the "code of the streets," which says that a criminal is supposed to keep quiet about the criminal activities of his peers. Even calling an ordinary citizen "square" is likely to stimulate a spontaneous lecture, in heated and colorful terms, on the notion that the people who are *really* square are those that go around as bums sticking needles in their arms. A person who, as a criminal, learned to hate stool pigeons and finks with a passion must now turn even his closest friend over to the authorities, the older members of Synanon, if the friend shows any signs of nonconformity. If he should find that a member is considering "sneaking off to a fix somewhere," has kept pills, drugs, or an "outfit" with him when he joined the organization, or even has violated rules such as that prohibiting walking alone on the beach, he must by Synanon's code relinquish his emotional ties with the violator and expose the matter to another member or even to the total membership at a general meeting. If he does not do so, more pressure is put upon him than upon the violator, for he is expected to have "known better." Thus, for perhaps the first time in his life he will be censured for *not* "squealing" rather than for "squealing."[6] He must identify with the law and not with the criminal intent or act.

The sanctions enforcing this norm are severe, for its violation threatens the very existence of the group. "Guilt by association" is the rule. In several instances, during a general meeting the entire group spontaneously voted to "throw out" both a member who had used drugs and a member who had known of this use but had not informed the group. Banishment from the group is considered the worst possible punishment, for it is stressed over and over again that life in the streets "in your condition" can only mean imprisonment or death.

That the group's purpose is keeping addicts off drugs is given emphasis in formal and informal sessions—called "haircuts" or "pull ups"—as well as in spontaneous denunciations, and in denunciations at general meetings. The "synanon," discussed below, also serves this purpose. A "haircut" is a deliberately contrived device for minimizing the importance of the individual and maximizing the importance of the group, and for defining the group's basic purpose—keeping addicts off drugs and crime. The following is the response of a leader to the questions, "What's a haircut? What's its purpose?"

> When you are pointing out what a guy is doing. We do this through mechanisms of exaggeration. We blow up an incident so he can really get a look at it. The Coordinators [a coordinator resembles an officer of the day] and the Board members and sometimes an old timer may sit in on it. We do this when we see a person's attitude becoming negative in some area.
>
> For a *real* haircut, I'll give you myself. I was in a tender trap. My girl split. She called me on the job three days in a row. I made a date with her. We kept the date and I stayed out all night with her. Now, she was loaded [using drugs]. I neglected—or I refused—to call the house. By doing this I ranked everybody. You know doing something like that was no good. They were all concerned. They sent three or four autos looking for me because I didn't come back from work. You see, I was in Stage II.
>
> X found me and he made me feel real lousy, because I knew he worked and was concerned. Here he was out looking for me and he had to get up in the morning.
>
> Well, I called the house the next morning and came back. I got called in for a haircut.
>
> I sat down with three Board members in the office. They stopped everything to give the haircut. That impressed me. Both Y and Z, they pointed out my absurd and ridiculous behavior by saying things like this—though I did not get loaded, I associated with a broad I was emotionally involved with who was using junk. I jeopardized my *own* existence by doing this. So they told me, "Well, you fool, you might as well have shot dope by associating with a using addict." I was given an ultimatum. If I called her again or got in touch with her I would be thrown out.
>
> ("Why?")
>
> Because continued correspondence with a using dope fiend is a crime against *me*—it hurts *me*. It was also pointed out how rank I was to people who are concerned with me. I didn't seem to care about people who were trying to help me. I'm inconsiderate to folks who've wiped my nose, fed me, clothed me. I'm like a child, I guess. I bite the hand that feeds me.
>
> To top that off, I had to call a general meeting and I told everybody in the building what a jerk I was and I was sorry for acting like a little punk. I just sort of tore myself down. Told everyone what a phony I had been. And then the ridiculing questions began. Everybody started in. Like,

"Where do you get off doing that to us?" That kind of stuff. When I was getting the treatment they asked me what I'd do—whether I would continue the relationship, whether I'd cut it off, or if I really wanted to stay at Synanon and do something about myself and my problem. But I made the decision before I even went in that I'd stay and cut the broad loose. I had enough time under my belt to know enough to make that decision before I even came back to the house. . . .

Group Cohesion.   The daily program at Synanon is consistent with Cressey's third principle, and appears to be an unwitting attempt to implement that principle:

The more cohesive the group, the greater the member's readiness to influence others and the more relevant the problem of conformity to group norms. The criminals who are to be reformed and the persons expected to effect the change must, then, have a strong sense of belonging to one group: between them there must be a genuine "we" feeling. The reformers, consequently, should not be identifiable as correctional workers, probation or parole officers, or social workers.

Cohesion is maximized by a "family" analogy and by the fact that all but some "third-stage" members live and work together. The daily program has been deliberately designed to throw members into continuous mutual activity. In addition to the free, unrestricted interaction in small groups called "synanons," the members meet as a group at least twice each day. After breakfast, someone is called upon to read the "Synanon Philosophy," which is a kind of declaration of principles, the day's work schedule is discussed, bits of gossip are publicly shared, the group or individual members are spontaneously praised or scolded by older members. Following a morning of work activities, members meet in the dining room after lunch to discuss some concept or quotation that has been written on a blackboard. Stress is on participation and expression; quotations are selected by Board members to provoke controversy and examination of the meaning, or lack of meaning, of words. Discussion sometimes continues informally during the afternoon work period and in "synanons," which are held after dinner (see below). In addition, lectures and classes, conducted by any member or outside speaker who will take on the responsibility, are held several times a week for all members who feel a need for them. Topics have included "semantics," "group dynamics," "meaning of truth," and "Oedipus complex."

There are weekend recreational activities, and holidays, wedding anniversaries, and birthdays are celebrated. Each member is urged: "Be yourself," "Speak the truth," "Be honest," and this kind of action in an atmosphere that is informal and open quickly gives participants a strong sense of "belonging." Since many of the members have been homeless drifters, it is not surprising to hear frequent repetition of some comment to the effect that "This is the first home I ever had."

Also of direct relevance to the third principle is the *voluntary* character of Synanon. Any member can walk out at any time; at night the doors are locked against persons who might want to enter, but not against persons who might want to leave. Many do leave.

Holding addicts in the house once they have been allowed to enter is a strong appeal to ideas such as "We have all been in the shape you are now in," or "Mike was on heroin for twenty years and *he's* off." It is significant, in this connection, that addicts who "kick" (go through withdrawal distress) at Synanon universally report that the sickness is not as severe as it is in involuntary organizations, such as jails and mental hospitals. One important variable here, we believe, is the practice of not giving "kicking dope fiends" special quarters. A newcomer kicks on a davenport in the center of the large living room, not in a special isolation room or quarantine room. Life goes on around him. Although a member will be assigned to watch him, he soon learns that his sickness is not important to men and women who have themselves kicked the habit. In the living room, one or two couples might be dancing, five or six people may be arguing, a man may be practicing the guitar, and a girl may be ironing. The kicking addict learns his lesson: these others have made it. This subtle device is supplemented by explicit comments from various members as they walk by or as they drop in to chat with him. We have heard the following comments, and many similar ones, made to new addicts lying sick from withdrawal. It should be noted that none of the comments could reasonably have been made by a rehabilitation official or a professional therapist.

> It's OK boy. We've all been through it before.
> For once you're with people like us. You've got everything to gain here and nothing to lose.
> You think you're tough. Listen, we've got guys in here who could run circles around you, so quit your bull____ .
> You're one of us now, so keep your eyes open, your mouth shut and try to listen for a while. Maybe you'll learn a few things.
> Hang tough, baby. We won't let you die.

Status Ascription.   Cressey's fourth principle is:

Both reformers and those to be reformed must achieve status within the group by exhibition of "pro-reform" or anti-criminal values and behavior patterns. As a novitiate . . . he is a therapeutic parasite and not actually a member until he accepts the group's own system for assigning status.

This is the crucial point in Cressey's formula, and it is on this point that Synanon seems most effective. The house has an explicit program for distributing status symbols to members in return for staying off the drug and, later, for actually displaying antidrug attitudes. The resident, no longer restricted to the status of "inmate" or "patient" as in a prison or hospital, can achieve any staff position in the status hierarchy.

The Synanon experience is organized into a career of roles that represent stages of graded competence, at whose end are roles that might later be used in the broader community. Figure 1 shows the status system in terms of occupational roles, each box signifying a stratum. Such cliques as exist at Synanon tend to be among persons of the same stratum. Significantly, obtaining jobs of increased responsibility and status is almost completely dependent upon one's attitudes toward crime and the use of drugs. To obtain a job such as Senior Coordinator, for example, the member must have demonstrated that

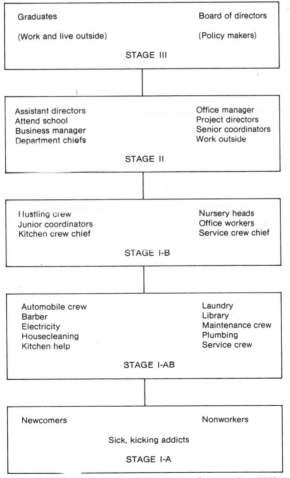

Fig. 1. **Division of labor and stratification system, Synanon, June, 1962.**

he can remain free of drugs, crime, and alcohol for at least three to six months. Equally important, he must show that he can function without drugs in situations where he might have used drugs before he came to Synanon. Since he is believed to have avoided positions of responsibility by taking drugs, he must gradually take on positions of responsibility without the use of drugs. Thus, he cannot go up the status ladder unless his "attitudes" are right, no matter what degree of skill he might have as a workman. Evaluation is rather casual, but it is evaluation neverthe-less—he will not be given a decent job in the organization unless he relinquishes the role of the "con artist" and answers questions honestly, expresses emotions freely, co-operates in group activities, and demon-strates leadership. . . .

An analogy with a family and the development of a child also is used. Officially, every member is expected to go through three "stages of growth," indicated by Roman numerals in Figure 1. Stage I has two phases, "infancy" and "adolescence." In the "infancy" phase (I-A) the member behaves like an infant and is treated as one; as he kicks the habit "cold turkey" (without the aid of drugs) in the living room, he is dependent on the others, and he is supervised and watched at all times. When he is physically and mentally able, he performs menial tasks such as dishwashing and sweeping in a kind of "preadolescent" stage (IAB) and then takes on more responsible positions (I-B). In this "adolescence" phase he take on responsibility for maintenance work, participates actively in group meetings, demonstrates a concern for "emotional growth," mingles with newcomers and visitors, and accepts responsibilities for dealing with them. In work activities, for example, he might drive the group's delivery truck alone, watch over a sick addict, supervise the dishwashing and cleanup crews, or meet strangers at the door.

Stage II is called the "young adult stage." Here, the member is in a position to choose between making Synanon a "career," attending school, or going to work at least part time. If he works for Synanon, his position is complex and involves enforcing policy over a wide range of members. In Stage III, "adult," he moves up to a policy-making position in the Board of Directors or moves out of Synanon but returns with his friends and family for occasional visits. He can apparently resist the urge to resort to drugs in times of crisis without the direct help of Synanon members. One man described this stage by saying, "They go out, get jobs, lose jobs, get married, get divorced, get married again, just like everyone else." However, the group does maintain a degree of control. Graduates are never supposed to cut off their ties with their Synanon "family," and they are expected to return frequently to display themselves as "a dope fiend made good."

 . . . [S]eniority in the form of length of residence (equivalent to the number of "clean" days) is an important determinant of status. As time of residence increases, responsibilities to the group, in the forms of work and leadership, tend to increase. . . . The longer one lives at Synanon, the "cleaner" he is, the more diffuse the roles he performs, and the higher his status.

It is also important to note that high status does not depend entirely upon one's conduct within the house. Before he graduates to Stage III a member must in some way be accorded an increase in status by the legitimate outside community. This is further insurance that status will be conferred for activities that are antidrug in character. In early 1960, the members began to take an active part in legitimate community activities, mostly in the form of lectures and discussion groups. Since Synanon's inception, more than 350 service groups, church groups, political groups, school and college classes, etc., have been addressed by speakers from Synanon. Such speeches and discussions gain community support for the organization, but they further function to give members a feeling of being important enough to be honored by an invitation to speak before community groups. Similarly, members are proud of those individuals who have "made good" in the outside community by becoming board members of the P.T.A., Sunday-school teachers, college students, and members of civic and service organizations. Over thirty-five Synanon members are now working full or part time in the community, holding a wide range of unskilled (janitor, parking attendant), skilled (truck driver, carpenter, electrician), white-collar (secretary, photographer), and executive (purchasing agent) posts. . . .

The "synanon."   Synanon got its name from an addict who was trying to say "seminar." The term "Synanon" is used to refer to the entire organization, but when it is spelled with a lower-case *s* it refers only to the meetings occurring in the evenings among small groups of six to ten members. Each evening, all members are assigned to such groups, and membership in the groups is rotated so that one does not regularly interact with the same six or ten persons. The announced aim of these meetings is to "trigger feelings" and to allow what some members refer to as "a catharsis." The sessions are not "group therapy" in the usual sense, for no trained therapist is present. Moreover, the emphasis is on enforcing anticriminal and antidrug norms, as well as upon emotional adjustment.[7] These sessions, like the entire program, constitute a system for implementing Cressey's fifth principle, although they were not designed to do so.

The most effective mechanism for exerting group pressure on members will be found in groups so organized that criminals are induced to join with noncriminals for the purpose of changing other criminals. A group in which criminal A joins with some noncriminals to change criminal B is probably most effective in changing criminal A, not B; in order to change criminal B, criminal A must necessarily share the values of the anticriminal members.

In the house, the behavior of all members is visible to all others. What a member is seen to do at the breakfast table, for example, might well be scrutinized and discussed at his synanon that evening. The synanon sessions differ from everyday honesty by virtue of the fact that in these discussions one is expected to *insist on* the truth as well as to tell the truth. Any weapon, such as ridicule, cross-examination, or hostile attack, is both permissible and expected. The sessions seem to provide an atmosphere of truth-seeking that is reflected in the rest of the social life within the household so that a simple question like "How are you?" is likely to be answered by a five-minute discourse in which the respondent searches for the truth. The following discussion is from a tape recording of a synanon session held in June, 1961. It should be noted that an "innocent" question about appearance, asked by an older member who has become a non-criminal and a non-addict, led to an opportunity to emphasize the importance of loyalty to the antidrug, anti-crime group.

What are you doing about losing weight?
Why? Is that your business?
I asked you a question.
I don't intend to answer it. It's not your business.
Why do you want to lose weight?
I don't intend to answer it.
Why?
Because it's an irrelevant and meaningless question. You know I had a baby only three weeks ago, and you've been attacking me about my weight. It's none of your business.
Why did you call your doctor?
Why? Because I'm on a diet.
What did he prescribe for you?
I don't know. I didn't ask him.
What did you ask for?
I didn't. I don't know what he gave me.
Come on now. What kind of pills are they?
I don't know. I'm not a chemist. Look, the doctor knows I'm an addict. He knows I live at Synanon. He knows a whole lot about me.
Yeah, well, I heard you also talking to him on the phone, and you sounded just like any other addict trying to cop a doctor out of pills.
You're a goddamned liar!
Yeah, well X was sitting right there. Look, does the doctor know and does the Board know?
I spoke to Y [Board member]. It's all been verified.
What did Y say?
I was talking to . . .
What did Y say?
Well, will you wait just a minute?

What did Y say?

Well, let her talk.

I don't want to hear no stories.

I'm not telling stories.

What did Y say?

That it was harmless. The doctor said he'd give me nothing that would affect me. There's nothing in it. He knows it all. I told Y.

Oh, you're all like a pack of wolves. You don't need to yell and scream at her.

Look, I heard her on the phone and the way she talked she was trying to manipulate the doctor.

Do you resent the fact that she's still acting like a dope fiend and she still sounds like she's conning the doctor out of something? She's a dope fiend. Maybe she can't talk to a doctor any differently.

Look, I called the doctor today. He said I should call him if I need him. He gave me vitamins and lots of other things.

Now wait a minute. You called to find out if you could get some more pills.

Besides, it's the attitude they heard over the phone. That's the main thing.

Yeah, well they probably projected it onto me.

Then how come you don't like anyone listening to your phone calls? Are you feeling guilty?

Who said?

Me. That's who. You even got sore when you found out X and me heard you on the phone, didn't you? You didn't like that at all, did you?

Is that so?

(*Silence.*)

I don't think her old man wants her back.

Well, who would? An old fat slob like that.

Sure, that's probably why she's thinking of leaving all the time and ordering pills.

Sure.

(*Silence.*)

My appearance is none of your business.

Everything here is our business.

Look, when a woman has a baby you can't understand she can't go back to normal weight in a day.

Now *you* look. We're really not interested in your weight problem now. Not really. We just want to know why you've got to have pills to solve the problem. We're going to talk about that if we want to. That's what we're here for.

Look, something's bugging you. We all know that. I even noticed it in your attitude toward me.

Yeah, I don't care about those pills. I want to know how you're feeling. What's behind all this? Something's wrong. What is it?

(*Silence.*)

Have you asked your old man if you could come home yet?

(*Softly.*) Yes.

What did he say?

(*Softly.*) He asked me how I felt. Wanted to know why I felt I was ready to come home. . . .

(*Silence.*)

(*Softly.*) I did it out of anger. I wasn't happy. (*Pause.*) A day before I tried [telephoning him] and he wasn't there. (*Pause.*) Just this funny feeling about my husband being there and me here. My other kid's there and this one's here. (*Pause.*) A mixed-up family.

Why do you want to stay then? Do you want to be here?

No. I don't want to be here. That's exactly why I'm staying. I need to stay till I'm ready.

Look, you've got to cut them loose for a while. You may not be ready for the rest of your life. You may not ever be able to be with those people.

(*Tears.*)

I know. . . .

After the synanon sessions, the house is always noisy and lively. We have seen members sulk, cry, shout, and threaten to leave the group as a result of conversation in the synanon. The following comments, every one of which represents the expression of a pro-reform attitude by the speaker, were heard after one session. It is our hypothesis that such expressions are the important ones, for they indicate that the speaker has become a reformer and, thus, is reinforcing his own pro-reform attitudes every time he tries to comfort or reform another.

Were they hard on you?

I really let him have it tonight.

I couldn't get to her. She's so damned blocked she couldn't even hear what I was trying to tell her.

Hang tough, man; it gets easier.

One of these days he'll drop those defenses of his and start getting honest.

Don't leave. We all love you and want you to get well.

At Synanon, disassociating with former friends, avoiding street talk, and becoming disloyal to criminals are emphasized at the same time that loyalty to non-criminals, telling the truth to authority figures, and legitimate work are stressed. We have no direct evidence that haircuts, synanons, and both formal and spontaneous denunciations of street talk and the code of the streets have important rehabilitative effects on the actor, as well as (or, perhaps even "rather than") on the victim. It seems rather apparent, however, that an individual's own behavior must be dramatically influenced when he acts in the role of a moral policeman and "takes apart" another member. It is significant that older members of Synanon like to point out that the "real Synanon" began on "the night of the big cop out" (confession). In its earliest days, Synanon had neither the group cohesiveness nor the degree of control it now has. Some participants remained as addicts while proclaiming their loyalty to the principle of antiaddiction, and other participants knew of this condition. One evening in a general meeting a man spontaneously stood up and confessed ("copped out") that he had sneaked out for a shot. One by one, with no prompting, the others present rose to confess either their own violations or their knowledge of the violations of their friends. . . .

CONCLUSIONS

Synanon's leaders do not claim to "cure" drug addicts. . . . [A person] can be helped to stay away from drugs, however, and this seems to be the contribution Synanon is making. In this regard, its "success" rate is higher than that of those institutions officially designated by society as places for the confinement and "reform" of drug addicts. . . .

We cannot be certain that it is the group relationships at Synanon, rather than something else, that is keeping addicts away from crime and drugs. However, both the times at which dropouts occur and the increasing antidrug attitudes displayed with increasing length of residence tend to substantiate Sutherland's theory of differential association and Cressey's notion that modifying social relationships is an effective supplement to the clinical handling of convicted criminals. Drug addiction is, in fact, a severe test of Sutherland's sociological theory and Cressey's sociological principles, for addicts have the double problem of criminality and the drug habit. The statistics on dropouts suggest that the group relations method of rehabilitation does not begin to have its effects until newcomers are truly integrated into the antidrug, anticrime group that is Synanon.

Notes

1. Donald R. Cressey, "Changing Criminals: The Application of the Theory of Differential Association," *American Journal of Sociology,* LXI (September, 1955), pp. 116–20 (see also Cressey, "Contradictory Theories in Correctional Group Therapy Programs," *Federal Probation,* XVIII [June, 1954], pp. 20–26).

2. Harry J. Anslinger, "Drug Addiction," *Encyclopaedia Britannica,* VII (1960), pp. 677–79.

3. Edwin H. Sutherland and Donald R. Cressey, *Principles of Criminology* (6th ed.; Philadelphia: J. B. Lippincott Co., 1960), pp. 74–80.

4. See, however, Joseph A. Cook and Gilbert Geis, "Forum Anonymous: The Techniques of Alcoholics Anonymous Applied to Prison Therapy," *Journal of Social Therapy,* III (First Quarter, 1957), pp. 9–13.

5. Alfred R. Lindesmith, *Opiate Addiction* (Bloomington: Principia Press, 1947), pp. 44–66.

6. See Lewis Yablonsky, "The Anti-Criminal Society: Synanon," *Federal Proba- tion,* XXVI (September, 1962), pp. 50–57; and Lewis Yablonsky, *The Violent Gang* (New York: Macmillan Co., 1962), pp. 252–63.

7. See Cressey, "Contradictory Theories in Correctional Group Therapy Pro- grams," *op. cit.*

Selected References

Empey, Lamar R., and Steven G. Lubeck, *The Silverlake Experiment: Testing Delinquency Theory and Community Intervention,* Chicago: Aldine- Atherton, 1971.
Empey and Lubeck describe an attempt to solve delinquency problems by rigorously applying the principles of the deviant behavior perspective.

Klein, Malcolm W., *Street Gangs and Street Workers,* Englewood Cliffs, New Jersey: Prentice-Hall, 1971.
Two projects to prevent gang delinquency are described. Each of these projects sought to provide gang members with legitimate opportunities and to change their values and roles.

McCorkle, Lloyd W., Albert Elias, and F. Lovell Bixby, *The Highfields Story: An Experimental Treatment Project for Youthful Offenders,* New York: Holt, 1958.
A program to help juvenile delinquents by means of guided group interac- tion, applying Sutherland's principles of differential association, is des- cribed.

Ohlin, Lloyd E., Robert B. Coates, Alden D. Miller, "Radical Correctional Reform: A Case Study of the Massachusetts Youth Correctional System," *Harvard Educational Review* 44 (1, 1974), pp. 74–111.
The authors describe a correctional reform movement in which Massa- chusetts replaced its juvenile correctional institutions with community- based treatment programs. They report on some of the preliminary ac- complishments of these programs and note that this move was based solidly on the deviant behavior perspective.

Sagarin, Edward, *Odd Man In: Societies of Deviants in America,* Chicago: Quadrangle Books, 1969.
Sagarin's collection shows attempts to help alcoholics, midgets and dwarfs, homosexuals, gamblers, drug addicts, convicted criminals, mental patients, and transvestites through associations that reflect, intentionally or in- advertently, the principles of anomie and differential association theory.

Short, James F., Jr., "The Natural History of an Applied Theory: Differential Opportunity and 'Mobilization for Youth,'" in N. J. Demerath III, Otto Larsen, and Karl F. Schuessler (eds.), *Social Policy and Sociology,* New York: Academic Press, 1975, pp. 193–210.
This author documents some of the problems the Mobilization for Youth program faced in applying opportunity theory to the juvenile delinquency problem.

Questions for Discussion

1.   Fairweather et al. describe a program that is organized along the lines suggested by anomie theory. Do you see elements of differential association in it as well? Synanon and Alcoholics Anonymous, on the other hand, are described in terms of differential association theory. Do you see elements of anomie theory in these programs?

2.   What similarities are there between the three programs described in the readings in this chapter? What are the major differences, aside from the fact that they deal with different types of deviant behavior? How would you evaluate these three programs?

3.   How do you think someone using the social pathology approach would evaluate the three programs described in this chapter? Someone using the value conflict approach? How might the solutions suggested by the social pathology perspective or the value conflict perspective differ from those described in this chapter?

4.   How do you evaluate the deviant behavior perspective and the type of solutions it suggests? From this perspective, how would you evaluate the practice of imprisoning criminals? From this perspective, how would you evaluate the idea of using work-release centers for criminals?

6 / LABELING

"Beauty lies in the eye of the beholder." We have all heard this saying, and its truth is obvious. What is beautiful to one person may seem ordinary to another, and what is ugly to some people may be pretty to others. What is true of beauty is also, in many instances, true of social problems. What seems a problem for one group (e.g., marijuana use, working mothers) may be quite acceptable or even desirable to another. Similarly, a condition that is tolerated by most people (e.g., food additives) may be seen as a great unrecognized problem by others (e.g., "health food" advocates). Thus whether or not something is a social problem depends on whom one asks and on which definition of the situation one employs.

As we noted in earlier chapters, most sociologists believe social problems consist of both an objective condition and a subjective definition. Some perspectives place more emphasis on the objective elements. In the deviant behavior perspective, for instance, certain behaviors are seen as objectively undesirable (e.g., crime and delinquency), and that perspective looks for the objective social economic conditions that give rise to such behaviors or that can be used to prevent or correct them.

According to the labeling perspective, social problems are all a matter of subjective definition. A situation becomes a social problem, for instance, not because of some inherent evil or undesirability, but rather because someone has succeeded in getting it so defined. Likewise, people become "deviants" not because of particular behaviors that they have committed, but because they have been labeled as deviant by others.

According to the labeling perspective, a social problem is not a property or quality inherent in the behavior or situation but a status that is *conferred* by other people. Thus a social problem is defined not by the alleged situation itself but by people's *reactions* to it. If they treat it as a problem, then from a sociological point of view it *is* a problem. And if they treat a person or group as deviant, then they *are* deviant sociologically (i.e., their social relations are affected).

The labeling perspective was christened by Howard S. Becker in the 1960s[1] (although some of its core concepts had been developed earlier). It reflected a growing dissatisfaction with the deviant behavior perspective, which regarded certain behaviors as criminal or delinquent, and classified people who commit these crimes as criminals and delinquents. From the deviant behavior approach, agents of social control (such as the police and the courts) detect and punish such deviant behaviors in a straightforward way.

Yet we are all aware that the laws are only selectively enforced. Likewise, people who do violate the law are only selectively punished. Police in many cities, for example, routinely close their eyes to the violations of organized crime, or of the influential and wealthy. Even if they are caught committing the same crime, higher-status citizens usually receive less severe treatment than do less powerful or lower-status citizens. Moreover, the laws themselves tend to shield some types of crime (e.g., white-collar crime) while responding strongly to other types (e.g., street crime).

Because of such inconsistencies and ironies, some sociologists began to regard any "objectivist" definition of social problems as inadequate, and they began to focus not on those who commit certain behaviors but on *how other people define and react to them.* Do they define a behavior as problematic and severely punish it? Or do they overlook it with little response at all? Do they castigate people and single them out? Or do they continue to act toward them as they did before? Do they interpret a behavior as a type of illness, or sin, or downright mean? And when they stigmatize or sanction a person, how does this affect the person's later life?

In seeking to answer questions such as these, those holding the labeling perspective look at the social interaction by which particu-

---

1. Becker crystallized this view in 1963 when he wrote:
   Deviance is not a quality of the act the person commits, but rather a consequence of the application by others of rules and sanctions to an "offender." The deviant is one to whom that label has successfully been applied; deviant behavior is behavior that people so label.

Quoted from Howard S. Becker, *Outsiders: Studies in the Sociology of Deviance* (New York: The Free Press of Glencoe, 1963), p. 9.

lar people or situations come to be defined as problematic, the interaction between the labelers and the labeled (e.g., between police officers and the accused), and the interaction among so-called deviants (e.g., among members of a cult). In other words, attention is directed both to the social processes by which a person or situation becomes defined as a social problem and to the consequences of such definitions.

This approach draws upon a school of sociology called *symbolic interactionism.* Building on the works of George Herbert Mead[2] and others, symbolic interactionism emphasizes the importance of people's conceptual schemes, beliefs, language, and other symbolic meanings in determining their actions. Thus symbolic interactionist proponents emphasize not so much the objective features of a situation but rather how the participants *view* and interact in a particular situation. Because of its ties to symbolic interactionism, there is a growing trend to dub this approach "the interactionist perspective."[3]

Sociologists in the labeling school see the definition of a social problem or the labeling of a deviant as a complex and variable process taking place over a period of time and affected by many factors besides the "objective" characteristics of the so-called problem. First, there is the label itself. Before people can define and take collective action against a social problem, there must be a socially recognized label to apply, and as a rule any particular label is a cultural and historical development. Some labels have ceased to be popular (e.g., heresy, witchcraft, cuckold, Mongoloid idiot), while others have more recently come into vogue (e.g., mental illness, juvenile delinquency, spouse abuse, workaholic). And the very same state of affairs can be defined as acceptable at one time but problematic at another (e.g., what was considered to be merely "discipline" a century ago is defined as child abuse today). When people define a situation to be a social problem, they do so in terms of the labels that are available in their own cultural milieu.

How does a particular situation come to be defined as a social problem? From the labeling perspective, social problems can be defined by anyone who succeeds in influencing public opinion and official action. Often this is done through the legal system. Various

2. George Herbert Mead, *Mind, Self, and Society from the Standpoint of a Social Behaviorist* (Chicago: University of Chicago Press, 1934).
3. This name was first used by Earl Rubington and Martin S. Weinberg, *Deviance: The Interactionist Perspective* (New York: Macmillan, 1968).

laws define a whole range of activities as illegal, and such laws can be invoked to label and sanction people who allegedly engage in those activities. In many cases, legal definitions change. Previously legal activities become illegal (e.g., air or water pollution), while previously illegal activities are decriminalized (e.g., abortion, parimutual betting).

The mass media also play an important role in defining or redefining social problems. Popular books, for example, can sway public opinion toward a particular definition; news media are also important for informing the public about new or different definitions. In the 1950s, for instance, news coverage of the McCarthy hearings had a powerful impact on the public's definition of communism as a social problem. News coverage of the Vietnam war protests undoubtedly did much to sway the public to regard that war, if not militarism more generally, as a social problem. And the mass media were also instrumental in getting the public to recognize child abuse as a social problem.[4]

Sociologists have noted that new legal definitions often result from the "symbolic crusades" of middle-class reformers, or "moral entrepreneurs" as one sociologist has called them. The WCTU (Women's Christian Temperance Union), for example, crusaded in turn for the abolition of slavery and for temperance, which contributed to redefinitions of both via Constitutional amendments.[5] Similarly, middle-class women at the end of the nineteenth century campaigned for a legal redefinition of young criminals. As a result of these efforts, young offenders were redefined as "juvenile delinquents," and a special institution—the juvenile court—was set up to deal with them.[6] Turning to more recent examples, Ralph Nadar launched a successful moral crusade to define inadequate consumer protection as a social problem, and singer Anita Bryant launched a moral crusade against homosexuality, denouncing it as both "sinful" and "sick."

On an individual level, the definition process takes place whenever a person is labeled and treated as a "deviant" of one kind or another. This may occur informally, as when people gossip about a "promiscuous woman" or a "crazy" person.

4. Stephen J. Pfohl, "The 'Discovery' of Child Abuse," *Social Problems* 24 (Feb. 1977), pp. 310–23.
5. Joseph R. Gusfield, *Symbolic Crusade* (Urbana: University of Illinois Press, 1963).
6. Anthony M. Platt, *The Child Savers: The Invention of Delinquency* (Chicago: University of Chicago Press, 1969).

On an official level, labeling occurs when agents of social control type people as one kind of deviant or another and then process them accordingly. When police type a person as "suspicious-looking," when the courts convict, when a youth is judged "delinquent" or a person diagnosed "mentally ill"—all these are examples of the labeling that goes on every day in official agencies. In such settings, people are in the business of diagnosing problems and applying labels. They confront so many cases that their handling of cases becomes routine, and they quickly peg a case as this type or that type. Typing may be guided by professional training or by practical experience and advice, but in either case it is a matter of definition and interpretation.

It should be noted that labeling (whether official or informal) need not reflect a person's true behavior. Deviant behavior may be overlooked for years and the corresponding label never applied (e.g., the "discrete silence" surrounding the private lives of high public officials). In other cases, labeling may reflect mere allegation with no basis in fact. Once people begin to think of a person as being a particular type of deviant and act differently because of it, however, the person has been effectively labeled deviant whether the labeling is true or not!

Often, it should be noted, the labeler has something to gain by labeling others. For instance, labeling may result from the actions of people whose job it is to apply labels (e.g., journalists, police officers, psychiatrists) and for whom assigning labels may be a mark of occupational success or competence. In other cases, people may try to clear their own image by calling attention to the defects of others (as occurred during the Watergate scandal when the Republican administration called attention to earlier abuses by Democratic administrations). Occasionally, a person may even stand to gain by labeling himself (e.g., reporting oneself to be homosexual to gain a discharge from the military).

People using the labeling perspective are especially interested in the consequences of labeling. Sometimes the labeling can later be outgrown or "neutralized"; sometimes it cannot. Publicity, official records, the nature of the label, and the person's particular situation are some of the variables effecting how permanent the labeling may be. In the most extreme cases, of course, labeling can lead to harsh punishment or even death (e.g., when convicted murderers are executed). Even when the effects are less extreme, labeling can have great consequences for a person's social relations and self-concept. Soon people start interpreting the so-called deviant's every action in light of what they have heard or concluded, and they start acting differently toward the person in question. Deviants usually experience stigma, which blatantly or subtly sets them apart from more conventional people. The stigma may also, however, drive them to the side of their fellow deviants, with whom they begin to feel more accepted. People may begin to expect the worst of the so-called deviant, and such reactions only reinforce the deviant role. A boy who is labeled delinquent by teachers or police, for example, may begin to think of himself in those terms and may soon begin to act out a full-fledged delinquent or criminal role. Similarly, a girl who is labeled promiscuous may find that "nice" boys no longer ask her out and that boys who do take her out are always after sex. She may find herself under inordinate pressure to act "promiscuously," and she may eventually begin to comply out of sheer social pressure! Deviance that is prompted or reinforced by such labeling is called *secondary deviation*.[7] Thus, instead of deterring further deviance, in some cases labeling seems to facilitate the development of a deviant career.

The labeling perspective has also led sociologists to question other effects of labeling—particularly when it is enacted into law. Vice laws, for example, reflect a certain notion of morality more than anything objectively harmful. They tend to be enforced only sporadically and selectively, and in the end they seem to encourage police corruption and reinforce the rise and maintenance of deviant subcultures.

As with the other perspectives, labeling is characterized by its own vocabulary. The interactionist focus is reflected in terms such as *social interaction* and *symbolic interaction*, and the focus on people's reactions is reflected in such words as *labeling, social reaction*, and *societal reactions.* The concern with subjective definitions is reflected in such terms as *constructed reality, definition of the situation, interpretations, normalizing, reconstitution, retrospective interpretation, situated meanings, social construction of reality, typification*, and *typing.* As noted above, the process of legally defining or redefining problems as a central interest is reflected in terms like *criminalization, decriminalization, moral entrepreneurs*, and *symbolic crusade. Control agent, defining agent, normal case* (or *normal crime*), *official agency, official records, of-*

7. Edwin M. Lemert, *Social Pathology: A Systematic Approach to the Theory of Sociopathic Behavior* (New York: McGraw-Hill, 1951), p. 76.

fical statistics, and *organizational processing* all refer to the role of official agents of social control (such as the police) in defining and labeling deviants. Terms reflecting the consequences of labeling for the person labeled deviant include *deviant career, deviant identity, life chances, moral career, secondary deviation, self-fulfilling prophecy, self-image, status degradation,* and *stigma.*

In the labeling perspective, sociologists tend to sympathize with the "deviants" and to see them as victims of labeling. By concentrating on the consequences of labeling, this approach points up the discrimination and suffering that comes from stigma and official sanctions. The solutions suggested by this perspective generally center around efforts to minimize the amount or effects of labeling.

One type of solution suggested by the labeling perspective is to convince both the lay public and official agents of social control to be more hesitant to apply deviant labels. It would discourage the labeling of people with different lifestyles or values as "crazy," "immoral," or "sick" (e.g., homosexuals, Moonies, antiwar demonstrators, or polygamists). The labeling approach suggests that people be especially hesitant to label an individual when such labeling will lead to stigma or special treatment—e.g., when a child is labeled retarded and put into special classes for slow learners. Refraining from gossip would be another step that most labeling theorists would endorse, since gossip often serves to label people on an informal level. With greater moderation in labeling, this approach suggests, secondary deviation could be lessened and the human costs resulting from stigma could be averted.

Another type of solution suggests the repeal of certain laws—particularly laws against so-called "victimless" crimes such as gambling, prostitution, homosexuality, abortion, and drug use. In some instances we have seen a trend toward decriminalization of victimless crimes. For example, the Netherlands has decriminalized prostitution, and some forms of prostitution are legal in Nevada. Gambling has become legal, in certain forms, in several states, and moves are now underway in various areas of the United States to decriminalize marihuana use and homosexuality. By repealing laws against victimless crimes, it has been argued, people who participate in these activities would not be thrown into a criminal underworld, would not risk the stigma of arrest, and would be less likely to develop a criminal self-concept.

Changes in professional or official definitions of deviance are also urged. In 1973, for instance, the American Psychiatric Association removed homosexuality from its official list of "mental ill-nesses," which was heralded as a great victory for homosexuals wanting to be freed from stigma. Similarly, the movement among many psychologists to regard their clients as having "problems in living" rather than "emotional disturbances" also reflects a trend toward less stigmatizing professional definitions.

The labeling perspective offers suggestions for correctional programs and agencies as well. The first would be one of *noninter-vention*. A recent book titled *Radical Nonintervention* suggests that the best thing to do about delinquents is nothing.[8] By refusing to intervene, the book argues, we can lessen the chances of secondary deviation and make it easier for those youths to later adopt a more conventional status and lifestyle. Second, the labeling approach suggests that any diagnoses or records made by an official agency would best be kept private and short-lived—again, to make it easier for the "deviant" to adopt a more conventional status. It has been argued, for example, that the rehabilitation of ex-convicts would be helped if they could "erase" their past criminal records through good behavior.

CHARACTERISTICS OF THE LABELING PERSPECTIVE: A SUMMARY

The labeling perspective views social problems as a matter of subjective definition, rather than of objective conditions. Thus it focuses on the development, application, and consequences of social definitions (or labels) by various groups and agents, and on the social interaction between various people and groups. The principle elements of the labeling perspective are as follows:

Definition. People or situations are social problems when others react to them as such. They are defined not by any inherent harm or evil but rather by the condemnation or stigma others attach to them.

Causes. In contrast to earlier approaches, the labeling perspec-tive is concerned not with the cause of an alleged situation but in how people label and respond to it and the consequences of their responses.

8. Edwin M. Schur, *Radical Nonintervention: Rethinking the Delinquency Problem* (Englewood Cliffs, N.J.: Prentice-Hall, 1973).

Conditions.   A number of background conditions influence the course of the labeling process. First, there must be a socially recognized label to apply. Second, the labeling process is affected by the relative power of the labeler and the labeled. (Official agents of social control are usually powerful in making labels stick, especially when they label children or other people with little political or economic clout; they may find their efforts undermined if they try to label people who are powerful or influential.) Other conditions influencing the labeling process include the amount of publicity given to the labeling and the amount of stigma attached to it.

Consequences.   The labeling of a person or situation as socially problematic usually leads to a reordering of social relations. For example, an alleged deviant is singled out, differentiated from the "normal" population, and put into a social category with other "deviants." People may try to take corrective action against a person so labeled, but the labeling approach suggests that such action often only serves to promote further "deviance." An ex-convict, for instance, may be unable to find a job because of the stigma of having been in prison; thus he may return to crime as a way of making a living. Another consequence of labeling includes the development of deviant subcultures, as deviants come together for mutual aid and support. In some cases, police corruption or abuse may also result. This is thought to be especially true with regard to the so-called victimless crimes (e.g., gambling, prostitution). These are defined as illegal, but because of widespread demand and tolerance for these activities, the police tend to "look the other way" and may even develop cooperative relationships (e.g., by accepting bribes) with the criminals involved.

Solutions.   The labeling perspective suggests two types of solutions. The first solution is to *change definitions*—e.g., by decriminalizing activities such as marihuana use, or by educating the public to be more tolerant and understanding of diverse lifestyles. The second solution is to *limit labeling*—e.g., by not categorizing youths as "delinquent," or by taking the occupational incentive out of labeling. Presumably, such steps would decrease the suffering and problems that result from such labeling and would lessen the development of career deviance.

LIBERALIZING MARIHUANA LAWS

John F. Galliher and Linda Basilick

*Proponents of the labeling perspective often urge that laws against
marihuana use and other victimless crimes be abolished or greatly
liberalized. By defining these relatively harmless acts as felonies, they
argue, such laws define large segments of the population as criminal
and, in so doing, breed secondary deviance and disrespect for the law.
In keeping with this line of thinking, several states have reduced the
penalties for possession of marihuana. In this reading, Galliher and
Basilick describe the processes by which such legislative changes were
brought about in the state of Utah. In that state, they point out, the
normally conservative Mormon community rallied behind the liberal-
izing of marihuana laws as the best way to protect their young people.
In other words, they saw harsh criminal records and penalties as more
harmful than marihuana itself to Mormon youngsters and the Mormon
community.*

Most states have revised their marihuana control laws within the past
decade, reducing the penalty for first-offense possession from a felony
to a misdemeanor. One of the first states to make such a change in its
laws was Nebraska (Galliher *et al.*, 1974) . . . Utah was also a leader
becoming . . . the third state to pass such legislation.

If a leadership role in such legislation was unexpected for Nebraska,
it surely was for Utah. Utah is a contemporary Mormon equivalent of
historical theocracies. Erikson (1966) claims that in another theocracy,
the Massachusetts Bay colony, crisis periods arose from time to time
when citizens lacked a clear notion of the group's collective self-
identity. By punishing specific behavior, colonists asserted that as a

part of their collective self-definition, they would not tolerate certain actions. In the case of Utah, much of the collective self-identity comes from a Mormon prohibition against not only tobacco and alcohol, but tea and coffee as well. The last two prohibitions obviously separate Mormons (Latter-day Saints) from most other Christians. Joseph Smith (*Doctrine and Covenants*, 1974:154–155), the LDS Church's founder, advocated these prohibitions as a means to protect the human body, and according to O'Dea (1957), the Church expends considerable effort to demonstrate the harmful effects of these substances. Surely in Utah, tolerance of marihuana would not be expected.

The Church opposition to drugs has been emphasized by Church President Spencer W. Kimball (1969) as well as numerous other Church leaders. As might be expected, the Mormon clergy's attitudes toward drug laws are much more restrictive than clergy from other religious groups. In a survey of Catholic, Protestant and Mormon clergy, Jolley (1972) found that a higher percentage of Mormons felt possession of such drugs as marihuana, amphetamines, LSD and heroin should be punished as a felony. Non-Mormon clergy were more likely to choose either legalization or misdemeanor penalties.

The term *deseret* is widely used by Mormons as are the bee and beehive symbols, and all three are used to denote industry, hard work and perseverance. Mormons emphasize the importance of the family, as they do education, and believe that patriotism is a religious duty (O'Dea, 1957). However, Suchman (1968) found a radically different world view among drug users which he has called the "Hang-loose Ethic." The hang-loose ethic is irreverent toward Christianity and patriotism, legal and educational institutions, marriage, premarital chastity, and the right and competence of parents to make decisions for children—in short, it repudiates the Establishment. Such attitudes surrounding drug use directly contradict Mormon values, making Utah an unlikely place to find leadership in reductions in drug law penalties.

The conservative nature of the Mormon faithful is reflected in the Utah state government. . . . The Utah legislature is indeed very conservative and is typically 90–95 percent Mormon (Jones, 1969) compared with only 70 percent of the population of the state which are Church members. Three-term Utah governor Calvin L. Rampton (1976) contends this Mormon overrepresentation in the state legislature is because Mormons vote for friends who are Church members. Rampton observes that not only are more Mormons elected, but LDS Church officials are especially likely to be elected. So the Utah legislature is not merely controlled by Mormons but by Church officials who would seem even more likely than other members to follow Church teaching. . . .

STATUTES

Until 1967, drugs and drug laws were apparently not an important issue for the Utah state legislature. . . .

In 1969, penalties were dramatically increased for most drug offenses. One bill (SB 143) dealt with narcotics including opium and coca products and also with marihuana. First-offense possession of these drugs was defined as a misdemeanor punishable by six months to one year in the local jail or probation. A second conviction of marihuana possession was punishable by six months to five years in prison. A second conviction for possession of the other drugs covered in SB 143 required five to twenty years. The other bill (SB 164) covered depressant, stimulant and hallucinogenic drugs and provided no possibility of parole and 60 days to ten years for first-offense possession.

In 1971 (SB 101) penalties were reduced for all drug offenses. For first-offense possession of any controlled substance, including marihuana, the maximum penalty was reduced from one year to six months in jail. For the second offense, the maximum was reduced from up to twenty years to one year in the county jail. Subsequent convictions were reduced from a maximum of twenty years to a maximum of five years in prison. All these bills passed both houses of the Utah legislature either unanimously or at least by wide margins reflecting the homogeneity of this group. Since 1971, legislative changes have been limited to a few minor technical modifications of the state's drug control statutes.

BACKGROUND INFORMATION ON STATUTES

1967 Legislation. . . . In March of 1967 the people and legislature of Utah . . . felt that no drug problem existed in their state and therefore high penalties were not required. The attorney who drafted SB 86 put it this way: "At the time [1967] the Salt Lake City police said that they knew of one addict and a little glue-sniffing. The Utah law was a response to California's and New York's drug problems, not Utah's." Another local attorney said: "The law [SB 86] was simply a first step. The effects of amphetamines and barbiturates were obscure at the time here." And finally, the former governor observed: "That law was designed just to draw people's attention to it—an introductory law." . . .

1969 Legislation. In 1969, SB 164 and SB 143 were introduced which dramatically increased penalties for most drug offenses except first-offense possession of opium, cocaine and marihuana. . . . The pattern of drug arrests shows large increases from 1967 to 1969. It is understandable that concern about drugs was growing at this time in the state legislature, local newspapers, and LDS Church Publications. In 1968–1969, more articles appeared on drugs [in Utah newspapers] . . . and both newspapers noted the high social class and youth of many users and the dramatic increase in overall drug use. . . . Both the *Salt Lake City Tribune* and later the *Deseret News* voiced editorial opposition to the original blanket minimum penalties for first-offense drug possession, the *Tribune* doing so by quoting a prominent local psychiatrist, a juvenile court judge and a Salt Lake City attorney (Halliday, 1969). The head of the local state university's Department of Psychiatry was quoted:

> This could be destructive, crippling many lives. Treating users as felons and confining them in prison would cause a great deal more harm than the good to be obtained from any deterrent effect of the measures.

The Head of the Committee on Dangerous Drugs and Narcotics of the Utah Bar Association (Halliday, 1969) said; "*We would run the risk of classifying vast numbers of our children as felons, with the extremely serious consequences that brand carries.*"* He noted that a felony conviction would mean loss of civil rights, the right to vote, rights of admission to many colleges, to government employment and employment in many private concerns. The attorney continued, "The requirement for mandatory minimum prison terms displays a lack of confidence in the courts and in the appropriate use of discretionary power by the judges." A local juvenile court judge (Halliday, 1969) said, "The courts involved should be given discretion to handle each case according to its degree of seriousness and rehabilitation potential. . . ." While the *Deseret News* did not attempt to pressure the legislature to change the original legislation as did the *Tribune,* it did give editorial support to the legislation once it was amended and passed:

> When critics objected to the mandatory jail sentence that had been provided by the drug control bills before the Utah legislature, they performed a useful service.

> California tried mandatory sentences only to find that court convictions and penalties fell off, even though drug abuses were increasing. Evidently, judges and juries hesitated to send youthful first offenders to prison where they could be brutalized by experienced criminals and induced to make crime a way of life.

> As a result, the Utah bills were modified to give the courts more discretion in sentencing so that drug users could be rehabilitated rather than hardened (1969, March 10:12A). . . .

---

*Italics added.

The reasoning behind the 1969 misdemeanor provision for marihuana, opium and cocaine . . . elicited diverse opinion from LDS members and non-Mormons in the interviews. Non-Mormons had the following observations about the origins of the 1969 drug legislation. The assistant county attorney explained the lack of public reaction to the misdemeanor provisions: "The legislature masked this change with massive increases in other penalties." The *Tribune* newsman who wrote an article critical of the original high penalties for possession of drugs observed that:

> As a liberal I'm glad that I feel my story stopped the bill in its tracks. The author of the bill came to me and asked "what will you settle for?" I was concerned with the high mandatory penalty for marihuana possession.

An attorney who lobbied in the Utah Senate for reduction in penalties for drug possession explained the lack of opposition:

> . . . Marihuana was the symbol of our concern. It was our major concern because that was the drug for which amateurs were being arrested. If the Senate hadn't originally passed such an outrageous marihuana penalty the misdemeanor law might not have passed so soon. *We merely asked the senators if they really wanted to sentence people who are really not criminals—kids and so on. "These are your kids after all," we told them.* . . .

Another attorney involved in the lobbying effort said:

> We sat down with the legislators and said that this would only put kids in the state prison at a youthful age and hurt them. We also pointed out that the courts would be reluctant to convict in marihuana possession cases since the marihuana problem was hitting middle-class families and Mormon youth. For example, I was a federal magistrate judge at the time when a prominent Utah banker's son was arrested for possession of large quantities of marihuana.

Other explanations came from Mormon respondents in several occupational roles—state representative, vice squad captain, Senate committee member and the bills' co-sponsor. All emphasized that the LDS Church attempted not to force its values on others but also echoed the enforcement problems. . . . And, the 1969 bills' LDS Senate co-sponsor claimed that with felony marihuana penalties: "We would be punishing kids, and anyway, judges wouldn't enforce it." In all, three themes are reflected in these interviews: (1) LDS claims of tolerance of other groups' behavior; (2) concern for the young, especially LDS young people; and (3) the unwillingness of the courts to enforce punitive drug possession laws.

*Italics added.

1971 Legislation.   On April 4, 1969, approximately two weeks after the drug law passed and the state legislature adjourned, the Utah governor appointed a Citizen Advisory Committee on Drugs. The main purpose of the Committee was to study Utah's drug problem and make recommendations for the control of drugs. According to the former governor who appointed the committee:

> There was at the time [1969] a growing concern with drugs in Utah among the citizens and their elected representatives and the 1969 drug legislation reflected this concern. The committee's task was to determine to what extent these concerns were justified.

The committee distributed a statewide anonymous questionnaire to high school and college students and also held hearings on the drug abuse problem in Utah and issued its report in September, 1969. Some of the study's conclusions were:

> If marihuana is included in a survey, then it can be said that no junior or senior high school in Salt Lake City has not had drugs. The age is lowering when arrests can be made in the sixth grade (Governor's Citizens Advisory Committee, 1969:9).

> There has been a 300 percent increase in the past two years in drug abuse admissions at the State Hospital (Governor's Committee, 1969:16).

> Economic status is no deterrent to obtaining drugs and youngsters of all economic levels are involved (Governor's Committee, 1969:18).

> High school students in Utah report that 33.7 percent of them can obtain drugs quite readily, while 31.6 percent *think* [emphasis added] they can do the same thing (Governor's Committee, 1969:21).

Based on testimony from the Salt Lake City Chief of Police, the Committee concluded that the mandatory minimum sentences in the 1969 drug laws resulted in judges throwing out cases in some instances (Governor's Committee, 1969:27). The Committee recommended that discretion be returned to the courts by dropping mandatory minimum sentences so consideration could be given to "the nature and seriousness of the offense, the prior record of the offender and other relevant circumstances" (Governor's Committee, 1969:30–31). The Committee also specifically recommended lowering the penalty for possession of marihuana (Governor's Committee, 1969:32).

After the 1969 legislature adjourned, the Utah Bar appointed a committee composed of judges, prosecutors and defense attorneys to make recommendations for the revision of Utah's criminal code. Immediately after the Advisory Committee Report on Drug Abuse was published in September 1969, the governor asked the Bar committee as its first order of business to make recommendations for the revision of Utah's drug control statutes. The Bar committee proposed the 1971 legislation (SB 101) and the Committee representative defended the legislation before the Utah legislature as follows (Senate, March 1, 1971):

> It was the feeling that there are a lot of people and young people [sic] who are experimenting and it didn't make a lot of sense to throw 18 and 19 year olds kids who are merely experimenting in prison for terms where they may come out hardened criminals.

The 1971 bill (SB 101) dropping the mandatory minimum penalties for *all*° drug offenses was justified by its Senate sponsor as necessary because judges refused to cooperate with the old law. He observed: "This bill gives the judges the permission to exercise some discretion in the case of young people and people who are first offenders" (SB 101, Senate, March 1, 1971). During the floor debate, it was also mentioned that the Salt Lake County Prosecuting Attorney supported the bill. . . .

Unlike the interviews regarding the reasons for earlier drug legislation, now there appears nearly complete consensus regarding the reasons for the 1971 drug law. While the theme of LDS tolerance continues, the common interpretation of the 1971 drug legislation was that the 1969 law had to be scrapped because it was not enforceable due to its overly high penalties which could not and should not be levied against youthful offenders. The attorney who represented the Utah bar on behalf of the proposed 1971 legislation observed:

> With lesser penalties available defendents will plead guilty and get probation. So with lower penalties you get more convictions by [guilty] pleas and more supervision. The 1969 legislature was *taking our high school kids and putting them with men who were rapists and big drug dealers.*° These criminals were treated the same as our sons and daughters.

The assistant county attorney put it this way:

> The [1971] law was passed very quietly with judges, prosecutors and defense attorneys behind it. Practitioners dealing with the law know better than to believe that high penalties increase crime control—juries simply find the defendant not guilty.

A vice squad captain complained that: "Even if we had a case that was a lead-pipe cinch, we couldn't get a jury conviction." In fact, the former governor observed:

°Italics added.

The [1969] drug study showed widespread drug use in Utah—more than people thought—in all school ages. But marihuana is not worse than alcohol so a jury would not convict what they saw as misguided kids.

A former city narcotics officer claimed: "After the 1969 law passed, enforcing the law became easier because with the high penalties we didn't bother with users and only went after dealers." In other words, the law worked well only because the police made fewer arrests by ignoring possession cases. As indicated earlier, marihuana arrests do show the greatest increase in 1972 while non-marihuana arrests show a considerable bulge in 1971, the year the 1969 laws were repealed. So the high minimum penalties of the 1969 laws may have discouraged drug arrests as the police officer suggested. As might be expected given the high number of drug arrests, LDS concern continues to be reflected in a large number of Church publications on drugs during the early 1970's.

CONCLUSION

. . . The *Deseret News* editorial indicates that a primary reason for Church support for elimination of high mandatory marihuana penalties [in the 1969 law] was that this would increase the probability of conviction. However the same *Deseret News* editorial supported judicial discretion in sentencing due to a concern for protecting "youthful first offenders" from "experienced criminals" so the former can be "rehabilitated rather than hardened." These themes of punishment and protection of offenders dominated legislative considerations as well. . . .

As was true of the 1969 laws, the bill in 1971 was passed by the Utah legislature both to punish and protect drug users. Having already declared its opposition to high minimum penalties in drug laws in 1969, the Church's publications now stated no position. The themes of punishment and protection appear again in Nebraska (Galliher *et al.*, 1974) where a powerful conservative state legislator sponsored a radical decrease in the marihuana possession penalty for the stated purpose of increasing the percentage of convictions in such cases, but also incidentally to *protect* a prosecutor's son who had been arrested. It might be tempting for some observers to claim that legislators and others in Utah and Nebraska conceal their true motivations in an effort to pacify observers of diverse persuasions. Rather than looking for hidden motivations, it is probably safest to take respondent explanations at face value. These respondents indeed appear to want both punishment and protection of drug users. They want punishment, but only that punishment they see as appropriate for these youthful and often affluent law violators—not long prison sentences.

References

Annual Report: Salt Lake City Police Department
    1962   Salt Lake City, Utah
Deseret News
          March 1, 1966-March 31, 1967
          March 1, 1968-March 31, 1969
          March 1, 1970-March 31, 1971
Doctrine and Covenants
    1974   Salt Lake City, Utah: The Church of Jesus Christ of Latter-day Saints.
Erikson, Kai T.
    1966   Wayward Puritans: A Study in the Sociology of Deviance, New York: Wiley.
Galliher, John F., James L. McCartney and Barbara Baum
    1974   "Nebraska's marijuana law: A case of unexpected legislative innovation." Law and Society Review 8:441–455.
Governor's Citizens Advisory Committee
    1969   Report on Drug Abuse. Utah. September.
Halliday, Robert S.
    1969   "Experts criticize severity of drug bill's penalties." Salt Lake City Tribune. March 2.
Jolley, Jerry Clyde
    1972   "Clergy attitudes about drug abuse and drug abuse education: A case study." The Rocky Mountain Social Science Journal 9:75–82.
Jonas, Frank H.
    1961   "Utah: Crossroads of the west." Pp. 273–302 in F. H. Jonas (ed.), Western Politics. Salt Lake City: University of Utah Press.
    1969   "Utah: The different state." Pp. 327–379 in F. II. Jonas (ed.), Politics in the American West. Salt Lake City: University of Utah Press.
Kimball, Spencer W.
    1969   The Miracle of Forgiveness. Salt Lake City: Bookcraft.
Latter-day Saints Church Index to Publications
          January 1, 1960–December 31, 1975.
McKay, David O.
    1969   "Address to the 139th semi-annual Church conference." Improvement Era 72:29–31.
Moore, William Howard
    1974   The Kefauver Committee and the Politics of Crime 1950–1952. Columbia: University of Missouri Press.
O'Dea, Thomas F.
    1957   The Mormons. Chicago: University of Chicago Press.
Rampton, Calvin L.
    1976   "Suggested remarks to Interstake Business and Professional Association." Los Angeles, California, December 13.
Salt Lake City Tribune
          March 1, 1966–March 31, 1967
          March 1, 1968–March 31, 1969
          March 1, 1970–March 31, 1971

Suchman, Edward A.
  1968 "The 'hang-loose' ethic and the spirit of drug use." Journal of Health
        and Social Behavior 9:146–155.
Utah Senate
  1967 Hearings, SB 86, February 21.
  1969 Hearings, SB 143, February 24.
  1971 Hearings, SB 101, March 1.

HOMOSEXUALITY AND STIGMA

Martin S. Weinberg and Colin J. Williams

According to Weinberg and Williams, the real social problem is not homosexuality but society's rejection and condemnation of homosexuals. Because so many people view homosexuality as "sick" or "sinful," homosexuals are stigmatized, with unfortunate consequences for both the homosexual minority and the heterosexual majority. Weinberg and Williams advocate a number of concrete changes aimed at lessening prejudice and discrimination against homosexuals. They urge a number of institutional changes (e.g., in law enforcement, employment, and religion) as well as a change in attitudes (e.g., through sex education and the mass media). Finally, they encourage homosexual individuals to quit "passing" and become more open about the fact that they are homosexual. Running throughout their numerous proposals is one common thread: that the public must rethink its conceptualization of homosexuality and get rid of stigmatizing stereotypes. Only in this way, they suggest, will the real social problem be solved.

It is evident that among homosexuals, psychological and social functioning is affected by the perception and internalization of societal rejection. Prejudice and discrimination do exist. It seems obvious, therefore, that a major strategy in alleviating some of the homosexual's problems is to alter reactions to homosexuals. We now discuss what can be done toward this end. . . .

INSTITUTIONS

Research on racial minorities has shown that one of the more effective ways to make societal reactions less negative is to change the institutions that sustain discrimination. When this is done, a change in individuals' attitudes often follows.[1] Therefore, those aspects of social organization that support the moral meanings of homosexuality as sinful, immoral, dangerous, perverted, revolting, or sick should be a primary target for change. The following arenas are seen by most commentators—homosexual and heterosexual alike—as most in need of change.

Law and Law Enforcement. . . . [The] law and its enforcement descriminate against adult consenting homosexuals, despite the absence of evidence that such behavior is harmful to the persons involved or to society in general. Not only does this reinforce negative evaluations of homosexuality among the general public, but it causes great hardship for many individual homosexuals.

In the United States, for example, if one has ever been arrested for a homosexual offense, whether convicted or not, he may find his employment opportunities limited. Many employers, both public and private, ask whether a job applicant has ever been arrested. If the answer is "yes," the employer can obtain the specific offense from court records. In those cases where arrests do not lead to conviction, arrest records should be expunged. Otherwise, the employment chances of many persons are unjustly limited, and this is especially true for homosexuals.[2]

In addition, antihomosexual laws and law enforcement practices extract a price from the heterosexual majority. Proponents of homosexual law reform point out, for example, that civil liberties in general are threatened by such intrusions into the realm of private morality.[3] This realm, the Wolfenden Committee states bluntly, is "not the law's business."[4] Sodomy laws are considered by many to be unconstitutional in that they exceed the legitimate police powers of the state and attempt to sustain religious dictates.[5]

Perhaps more important than the sodomy laws are laws against soliciting, lewd conduct, and so forth, under which American homosexuals are most often actually prosecuted. To obtain evidence, the police resort to entrapment and such devices as decoys, peepholes, and one-way mirrors in public restrooms. Such practices degrade the ideals of the law and law enforcement, to say the least, and often make for police corruption. In addition, they are a waste of the time and resources of law enforcement agencies. We also see no reason why behaviors such as homosexual solicitation should be a matter for the criminal law.

In conclusion, we recommend the repeal of antihomosexual laws and that the employment of other laws to harass homosexuals be stopped. Fears regarding the possible negative consequences of doing this are not supported by logic or data. Moreover, the burden of proof regarding the harmful effects of homosexuality should lie on the shoulders of those who insist on such laws and legal practices.[6]

The Federal Government.   Government policies and practices in the United States attempt to exclude homosexuals from federal employment. The basis for such a position was a Senate report in 1950 (during the Communist scare) which claimed that homosexuals are unsuitable for government employment.[7] The report assumes that homosexuals are emotionally unstable, attempt to seduce heterosexuals, have a "corrosive" influence on other employees, attempt to hire other homosexuals for government jobs, and are susceptible to blackmail. The recommendations of that report became part of Civil Service policy, resulting in the removal or exclusion of suspected homosexuals from employment by the federal government.[8]

Exclusion of homosexuals from federal employment on such dubious grounds is clearly discriminatory. Furthermore, although there may be truth in some of the allegations—for example, susceptibility to blackmail—it is often overlooked that the same logic applies to others, such as married heterosexuals having extramarital affairs, and the government policy of firing persons found to be homosexual itself contributes to the potential for blackmail.[9]

Nonfederal Government and Private Business.   Although other employers may not have formal regulations to exclude homosexuals, informal procedures often discriminate against them. In many states, homosexuals are not allowed to be teachers, and arrests for homosexual acts (regardless of conviction) often disqualify a person from legally practicing certain professions, such as medicine, dentistry, and law. (Also, professional licenses are usually denied or withdrawn without a hearing.)

With private employers, the situation is no better. Even in a relatively liberal place like New York City:

> It is currently the practice of many companies . . . to refuse jobs to homosexuals, supposedly to "protect company morale" when, in reality, the applicant is rejected for being homosexual per se in spite of his qualifications and mode of behavior.
> Employers use several devices to discover whether an applicant is homosexual: special arrangements with employment agencies in which the agencies use a code to indicate whether, to their knowledge, the job seeker is homosexual; a request on the application form for the release of draft records, which disclose any references to homosexual behavior; a

request for information regarding the draft classification of applicants who have not served in the military, and the marital status of all persons seeking employment; and employers sometimes contact private agencies whose sole purpose is to gather information on applicants in order to determine anything which might not be in what the firm considers its best interests.[10]

In this atmosphere, most homosexuals, and especially those in the more prestigious occupations, feel forced to hide or deny their homosexuality. Except perhaps for disclosure of one's homosexuality to his family, the threat to employment is probably (for the American homosexual) the most serious consequence of being publicly labeled homosexual. . . .

Religion. . . . [R]eligious dogma has played a large part in initiating and sustaining negative definitions of homosexuality in the Western world. And although today religion has less influence on people's daily lives, many of our customs and moralities are implicitly based upon religious codes. We believe that religion must be a primary target for change because the persons who are most negative toward homosexuals are often religious and because religious institutions are still influential enough to become catalysts for positive change.

One target for change should, therefore, be the clergy. If the perspective of the clergy can be changed, we may then persuade them to help dissipate the conception of "homosexual as sinner" among the laity.

Some churches have taken steps in this direction. This is best exemplified in the Netherlands. In the United States, the Unitarian's National Assembly in 1970 rejected the "sickness theory" of homosexuality and endorsed homosexuals' civil rights. The Unitarians also called for a special effort on the part of their members to assist homosexuals and accept homosexuals in their ministry. National assemblies of the United Presbyterians and the Lutherans have also endorsed homosexual law reform, although they still define homosexuality as a sin (the United Presbyterians also seeing it as a sickness). While it is difficult to determine the influence of such endorsements, at the very least they deny religious legitimation to intolerance and can be of some consolation to religious homosexuals.

ATTITUDES

The preceding institutional areas seem to us to be major targets for change because of their support of a moral meaning of homosexuality that leads to grave injustices for a large minority. Our data suggest, however, that in the long run, the attitudes of rejection, fear, and contempt, and the latent hostility in everyday encounters must be changed as well. Informal attitudes may be difficult to change due to various factors about which we can only speculate, namely, the psychological function that prejudice has for some persons, the sociological role of minority groups for majority groups, the phobia about sex found especially in America, and so forth. Nonetheless, attempts should be made to combat antihomosexual attitudes directly. The following suggestions are offered to that end.

Sex Education.   Sex education courses usually restrict themselves to heterosexual behavior and reproduction. It would seem that accurate information on homosexuality, introduced in a *nonmoralistic* framework, and as a not uncommon form of sexual expression, would affect heterosexuals' attitudes in a positive way.[11] While research in other areas of prejudice suggests that its impact is limited, education may help to dispel falsehoods about a phenomenon that is too often presented as sick, alien, and bizarre.[12] In addition to lessening rejection by heterosexuals, such education would also alleviate many of the unnecessary identity problems of homosexually oriented people who will also be among the students in such classes.

Also, sex education should not be limited to young people. Such courses should be compulsory for people who have much to do with homosexuals, including police, physicians, and especially psychiatrists. These groups have, in the past, played a major role in perpetuating negative views of homosexuality.

The Mass Media.   The Task Force on Homosexuality noted the need to study the effects on the public of the portrayal of homosexuality in literature, drama, films, and so on. At present, the media seem to sustain prevailing stereotypes of the homosexual. The stereotype of the male homosexual as effeminate, flighty, and amusing often appears on television. Motion pictures have only begun to treat homosexuality in a more objective manner. Before the late 1960's, motion pictures used homosexuality, to quote one reviewer, "as a sensational third act revelation, after which the character discovered to be homosexual must obligingly commit suicide."[13] Whereas television has emphasized the effeminate aspect of the homosexual stereotype, movies have focused on homosexuals as sick and guilt-ridden.

How a more balanced picture of homosexuals might be gained through the media is difficult to determine. The greater openness that characterizes movies today may make for more representative films. For example, a character's homosexuality might be presented as secondary to his other attributes. A Western movie might explore the role of homosexuality in a society devoid of females. With regard to television, the presence of homosexuals on talk shows might counter-balance the stereotypes provided by comedy shows. The activities of ethnic minority groups against the dissemination of stereotypes in the media have provided a model that homosexual militants have copied; how successful they will be remains to be seen.

Research on the effectiveness of changing attitudes through the mass media is not encouraging.[14] Such research has shown that people avoid influence by perspectives contrary to their own by simply not exposing themselves to such perspectives or by misinterpreting them. By supporting more humane attitudes toward homosexuals, however, the changes we have suggested could make people more hesitant to act upon their negative attitudes.[15]

Other Public Support.   Research has found that the more credible, attractive, and powerful the person who is urging a change in attitudes, the greater the likelihood of change.[16] Thus, if persons who are credible, attractive, and powerful present more favorable attitudes toward homosexuals, then other people's attitudes may be modified.

In terms of credibility, professionals such as physicians, psychiatrists, and social scientists could be effective. As greater sex education in medical schools provides physicians with up-to-date knowledge on homosexuality, their attitudes may become less negative. Psychiatrists seem to be moving increasingly away from the "sickness" model of homosexuality. Social scientists, too, are moving away from seeing homosexuality as intrinsically a "social problem" to viewing the societal reaction toward homosexuals as the major problem. As members of these professions in increasing numbers view homosexuality as a non-pathological variant of sexual expression, efforts must be made to get them to communicate these views to the general public.[17]

Sources who are attractive to the general public might include professional entertainers and athletes. Consider, for example . . . the effect of entertainers' plugging homosexual civil rights on television, as many do for ethnic minorities.

Finally, the power of the source is an important element in changing attitudes. Politicians in Great Britain have championed the rights of homosexuals, despite widespread lack of public support. In America today, an important gesture would be for those in power to acknowledge and support the recommendations of the Task Force on Homosexuality.

HOMOSEXUALS AS A MINORITY GROUP

In addition to changing . . . [institutions and attitudes], a third strategy should be to obtain *positive* support for homosexuals from the larger society. For the time being, this would be facilitated, we feel, by a reconceptualization of homosexuals . . . and by accepting their life style as just one of many in a diversified society.[18] At the same time, it is our hope that ultimately homosexuals will not have to be differentiated. . .

Until tolerance is translated into acceptance, the harmful effects of rejection will remain. . . . Associated problems should be mitigated by providing special aid for homosexuals. Not only should opportunities for the integration of homosexuals into the wider society be available, but support should also be given to specifically homosexual institutions. The Netherlands can provide a model for such affirmative action in the governmental support given to homosexuals, for example, including homosexuals in the concerns of the Minorities Board.

Most important, however, we believe, will be the actions that homosexuals can take on their own behalf. . . . Homosexuals must . . . be willing to be more open about being homosexual.

. . . [H]omosexuals can pass easily, and in fact most do so. While we appreciate the unpleasant effects disclosure of one's homosexuality might have, we feel that in the *long run* the beneficial effects of greater openness would be substantial in bringing about societal change. But, as one "gay liberationist" notes, ". . . the fear of coming out is not paranoia; the stakes are high. . . . Each . . . must make the steps toward openness at . . . [his] own speed and on . . . [his] own impulses."[19]

Greater openness on the part of an increasing number of homosexuals, however, would have cumulative effects. Homosexually oriented young people would be more likely to have positive homosexual role models with which to identify. And as heterosexuals realize that people they know are homosexual, they are likely to recognize that their stereotypes are distortions and to rethink their views on homosexuality.

Notes

1. Earl Raab and Seymour Martin Lipset. "The Prejudiced Society," in Earl Raab (ed.), *American Race Relations Today* (New York: Anchor Books, 1962), p. 41. For other commentaries on the relationship between attitudes and behavior, see Frank R. Westie and Melvin DeFleur, "Verbal Attitudes and Overt Acts: An Experiment on the Salience of Attitudes," *American Sociological Review* 23 (December 1958), pp. 667–73; Irving Deutscher, "Words and Deeds: Social Science and Social Policy," *Social Problems* 13 (Winter 1966), pp. 235–54; Howard J. Ehrlich, "Attitudes, Behavior, and Intervening Variables," *American Sociologist* 4 (February 1969), pp. 29–34.

2. M.S.N.Y.'s legislative program for 1971 proposes that it be a misdemeanor for an employer to ask a job applicant if he has ever been arrested. They also propose the same for anyone divulging information about persons acquitted of any crime. They recommend sealing records to this end. Another proposal makes bonding companies which refuse to bond a homosexual guilty of a misdemeanor. *Mattachine Times,* November/December, 1970, p. 15.

3. See, for example, *Report of the Committee on Homosexual Offenses and Prostitution,* London: Her Majesty's Stationery Office, 1957 (The Wolfenden Report); Edwin M. Schur, *Crimes Without Victims* (Englewood Cliffs, New Jersey: Prentice-Hall, 1965); Gilbert M. Cantor, "The Need for Homosexual Law Reform," in Ralph W. Weltge (ed.), *The Same Sex* (Philadelphia: The Pilgrim Press, 1969), pp. 83–94; Sanford H. Kadish, "The Crisis of Overcriminalization," *Annals of the American Academy of Political and Social Science* (November 1967), pp. 157–70.

4. *Committee on Homosexual Offenses and Prostitution,* p. 24.

5. Cantor, "Need for Homosexual Law Reform." Nonetheless, it seems difficult to get sodomy laws repealed. In October 1971 the California legislature defeated a bill (the "Brown Bill") that would have legalized all forms of sexual behavior between consenting adults in private.

6. Some of the arguments for retaining laws against homosexuality are considered by the Wolfenden Committee, *Committee on Homosexual Offenses and Prostitution,* pp. 21ff; and Schur, *Crimes without Victims,* pp. 107ff.

7. U.S. Senate, Committee on Expenditures in the Executive Departments, Subcommittee on Investigations. Interim Report: "Employment of Homosexuals and Other Sex Perverts in Government," Senate Document No. 241, December 1950.

8. See, for example, a letter written by John W. Macy, Jr., former chairman of the Civil Service commission to the Mattachine Society of Washington, February 25, 1966, reprinted in Lewis I. Maddocks, "The Law and the Church vs. the Homosexual," in Ralph W. Weltge (ed.), *The Same Sex,* p. 101. These recommendations, however, have since been somewhat mitigated by the Federal Appellate Court, Washington, D.C., which stated that a homosexual cannot be dismissed from a government agency without proof that his homosexuality interfered with the agency's efficiency (Norton v. Macy, 417 Fed. 2d 1161 [D.C. Circ. 1969]). However, government officials still try to perpetuate such exclusionary practices; see "Government-Created Employment Disabilities of the Homosexual," *Harvard Law Review,* 82 (June 1969), pp. 1738–51, and Franklin Kameny, "Gays and the U.S. Civil Service," *Vector* (February 1973), pp. 8, 39–41.

9. For a convincing argument against federal employment policies, see William Parker, "Homosexuals and Employment," in *Essays on Homosexuality,* No. 4 (San Francisco: The Corinthian Foundation, 1970), pp. 13–19. Also note the similar recommendations of the National Institute of Mental Health Task Force on Homosexuality.

10. *Mattachine Times,* January 1971, p. 1.

11. We recognize that some people might object on the ground that this would encourage experimentation with homosexuality. First, there is no evidence that homosexual behavior would increase. Second, even if people did experiment more with homosexual behavior, we have no evidence that in a tolerant and nonmoralistic atmosphere this would be harmful. Third, to exclude homosexuality from sex education courses on such grounds would be to perpetuate for the sake of one moral stand an ignorance which is itself immoral in its consequences for a substantial number of persons.

12. For example, Stember reviewed a number of studies of the relationship between education and ethnic and racial prejudice and concluded that:

> Its chief effect is to reduce traditional provincialism—to counteract the notion that members of minorities are strange creatures with exotic ways, and to diminish fear of casual personal contact. But the limits of acceptance are sharply drawn; while legal equality is supported, full social participation is not.

Charles H. Stember, *Education and Attitude Change* (New York: Institute of Human Relations Press, 1961), p. 171.

13. Gene D. Phillips, "Homosexuality in the Movies," *Sexual Behavior* (May 1971), p. 21.

14. See, for example, Arthur R. Cohen, *Attitude Change and Social Influence* (New York: Basic Books, 1964).

15. Perhaps we have given less attention to the written media here than is warranted. We do agree, however, with the Wolfenden Committee's proposal that the press report homosexual offenses or homosexual conduct in such a way as to avoid the public labeling of those involved. *Committee on Homosexual Offenses and Prostitution,* p. 78.

16. See William J. McGuire, "The Nature of Attitudes and Attitude Change," in Gardner Lindzey and Elliot Aronson (eds.), *The Handbook of Social Psychology,* Second Edition (Reading, Massachusetts: Addison-Wesley, 1969), Vol. 3, especially pp. 177–200.

17. Unfortunately, "experts" and "professionals" in the area of sexual behavior are often self-appointed. This is problematic when their popularity is high but their knowledge is low. A case in point is the collage of misinformation and stereotyped thinking about homosexuality found in David Reuben's *Everything You Always Wanted to Know About Sex (But Were Afraid to Ask)* (New York: McKay Company, 1969).

18. See the essays by Frank Kameny and Helen Hacker in Edward Sagarin (ed.), *The Other Minorities* (Waltham, Massachusetts: Ginn & Co., 1971). Similar proposals are made by Anthony Grey and D. J. West in "Homosexuals: New Law But No New Deal," *New Society* (March 27, 1969).

19. Carl Whittman, *The Gay Manifesto* (New York: Red Butterfly, 1970), p.5.

DELINQUENCY NONINTERVENTION

Edwin M. Schur

*In this reading, a more radical labeling approach is considered. Ac-
cording to Schur, the worst thing we can do for delinquents is to single
them out and brand them "delinquent." Youthful misconduct, Schur
claims, is extremely common, but if left alone most youths simply
outgrow their mischievous ways. To single out some young persons
and call them "delinquent," Schur argues, is unfair and counterproductive. It is unfair in that so-called delinquents are labeled not because of
their actual deeds (which are shared by many) but because of other,
almost randomly related factors such as social class, race, or simply
bad luck. And such labeling is counterproductive because it merely
serves to "harden" the labeled ones, lowering their self-esteem and
denying them normal opportunities and social acceptance. All too
often, according to Schur, a vicious cycle is set into action and secondary
deviance results. Thus, Schur claims, teachers, law enforcement officers, and others should stringently avoid singling out some youths and
categorizing them delinquent. Moreover, any special programs set up
for young people with problems should be voluntary rather than compulsory. In the long run, Schur claims, problems of delinquency would
be lessened, benefiting not only young people but the rest of the
society as well.*

In radical nonintervention delinquents are seen not as having special
personal characteristics, nor even as being subject to socioeconomic
constraints, but rather as *suffering from contingencies.* Youthful "misconduct" . . . is extremely common; delinquents are those youths
who, for a variety of reasons, drift into disapproved forms of behavior
and are caught and "processed." *A great deal of the labeling of delinquents is socially unnecessary and counterproductive. Policies should*

be adopted, therefore, that accept a greater diversity in youth behavior;
special delinquency laws should be exceedingly narrow in scope or else
abolished completely, along with preventive efforts that single out
specific individuals and programs that employ "compulsory treat-
*ment."** For those serious offenses that cannot simply be defined away
through a greater tolerance of diversity, this reaction pattern may
paradoxically increase "criminalization"—uniformly applied punishment not disguised as treatment; increased formalization of whatever
juvenile court procedures remain, in order to limit sanctioning to cases
where actual antisocial acts have been committed and to provide
constitutional safeguards for those proceeded against. . . .

Much of the disenchantment with current delinquency policy arises
from the simple fact that it doesn't work. As we have seen, neither the
treatment reaction nor the reform response has provided any real basis
for confidence that our measures are effective in preventing delinquent
behavior or rehabilitating youthful offenders. Some programs do show
more promise than others, but the impact of the specific successes on
the overall problem of youthful misbehavior is minimal. A traditional
response to this situation has been to assume that the system merely
needs improvement. Hence the call for more and better facilities,
increasingly experimental rehabilitation schemes, further research—
including evaluation studies and elaborate "cost-benefit" and "systems"
analyses. Naturally, it is possible by these methods to increase efficiency
in juvenile justice and perhaps also to render the substance of the
system somewhat more meaningful. Yet the conviction is growing that
this kind of patching-up will not suffice. Many observers are coming to
believe that our present approaches to delinquency and juvenile justice
are *basically* unsound: that the underlying assumptions are all wrong,
and that present programs are not just ineffective but positively harmful. This belief arises not only out of direct experience and research in
the field of delinquency, but also from current thinking on the broader
topic of deviant behavior and social control. Social scientists, and
increasingly laymen as well, are reevaluating our society's response to
rule-violating behavior. . . .

LABELING ANALYSIS

One of the most influential strands of current sociological thought in
this area is alternatively designated the "labeling," "societal reactions,"
or "interactionist" approach.[1] According to this perspective, various
features of deviance situations are more directly attributable to the
impact of social reaction processes than to the personal characteristics

*Italics added.

or socioeconomic situations of individual offenders. Indeed, the very notion of deviance itself presupposes rules or norms against which the individual has offended. As a leading spokesman for this outlook puts it:

> . . . *social groups create deviance by making the rules whose infraction constitutes deviance,* and by applying these rules to particular people and labeling them as outsiders. From this point of view, deviance is *not* a quality of the act the person commits, but rather a consequence of the application by others of rules and sanctions to an "offender." The deviant is one to whom that label has successfully been applied; deviant behavior is behavior that people so label.[2]

This does not mean that the acts we label burglary, or assault, or car theft would never occur if there were not formal rules defining them. Rather, the argument is that the reactions to such behaviors will largely determine their social meaning and consequences. To that extent, the labeling position is extremely relativistic. Particular acts are not intrinsically "deviant"; their deviant character emerges out of the interaction between offending individuals and the informal and formal responses of reacting individuals and agencies—including official agencies of social control. This crucial definitional aspect of deviance becomes quite clear in the case of some of the more controversial elements in delinquency laws. Thus, if one were to remove from such laws categories like "incorrigibility" or "associating with bad companions," it is unlikely that youthful behavior would change very much. However, the social meanings and consequences of various kinds of behavior might be dramatically altered. "Incorrigibility" is in large measure a judgment that some people pass on other people; it is not an objective behavioral category on the meaning of which we would all agree. . . .

A societal reactions perspective, then, is more concerned with what is made of an act socially than with the factors that may have led particular individuals into the behavior in the first place. While these precipitating factors obviously have some importance, the labeling analysts believe they have been overemphasized. Many of the reaction processes that shape deviance situations remain crucial, they argue, *whatever* the precipitating factors in specific cases may be. In particular, the labeling approach stresses that the self-concepts and long-term behavior of rule-violators are vitally influenced by the interaction between them and agents of social control. The application of this notion to delinquency is far from new, a classic illustration being Tannenbaum's discussion of the "dramatization of evil" through which the early stigmatizing of a youngster as a trouble maker helps to propel him into a delinquent career:

> The process of making the criminal, therefore, is a process of tagging, defining, identifying, segregating, describing, emphasizing, making con-

scious and self-conscious; it becomes a way of stimulating, suggesting, emphasizing, and evoking the very traits that are complained of. . . .

The person becomes the thing he is described as being. Nor does it seem to matter whether the valuation is made by those who would punish or by those who would reform. . . . The harder they work to reform the evil, the greater the evil grows under their hands. The persistent suggestion, with whatever good intentions, works mischief, because it leads to bringing out the bad behavior that it would suppress. The way out is through a refusal to dramatize the evil.[3] . . .

As labeling theorists emphasize, once an individual has been branded as a wrongdoer, it becomes extremely difficult for him to shed that new identity. Tannenbaum expressed this most aptly when he wrote of the delinquent or criminal that, "the community expects him to live up to his reputation, and will not credit him if he does not live up to it."[4] . . . *Because the branding of an individual as a "delinquent" or "criminal" often will imply a broad recasting of identity, the person so stigmatized is hard put to convince others he is not really, or no longer, "like that."* And if anyone is unclear as to his real character, there is always the "record" testifying to his basic unworthiness. . . . In fact—and regardless of whether or not an official dossier is available to others for scrutiny—the taint from such a proceeding may often surround the individual for many years. Typically, these negative labeling processes snowball. A stigmatizing experience imposes new restrictions on legitimate opportunities and raises the probabilities of further deviation, which in turn will give rise to more serious negative reactions, and so on. And the public tendency to believe that "once a wrongdoer, always a wrongdoer," reinforces these vicious circles. . . .

We can now begin to see some of the meanings of the term "radical nonintervention." . . . Basically, radical nonintervention implies policies that accommodate society to the widest possible diversity of behaviors and attitudes, rather than forcing as many individuals as possible to "adjust" to supposedly common societal standards. This does not mean that anything goes, that all behavior is socially acceptable. But traditional delinquency policy has proscribed youthful behavior well beyond what is required to maintain a smooth-running society or to protect others from youthful depredations.

Thus, the basic injunction for public policy becomes: *leave kids alone wherever possible*. This effort partly involves mechanisms to divert children away from the courts but it goes further to include opposing various kinds of intervention by diverse social control and socializing agencies. . . . Subsidiary policies would favor collective action programs instead of those that single out specific individuals;

*Italics added.

and voluntary programs instead of compulsory ones. Finally, this approach is radical in asserting that major and intentional sociocultural change will help reduce our delinquency problems. Piecemeal socioeconomic reform will not greatly affect delinquency; there must be thoroughgoing changes in the structure and the values of our society. If the choice is between changing youth and changing the society (including some of its laws), the radical noninterventionist opts for changing the society. . . .

In his book *Delinquency and Drift,* Matza argues that the juvenile justice system promotes delinquency in a much broader sense than simply by selecting out individual offenders. As we saw earlier, he claims that the court hearing induces confusion and distrust among those exposed to it. Beyond that, he asserts, the juvenile court process creates an overpowering *sense of injustice* among youths who come before it or learn about it indirectly, and thus it strengthens rather than combats delinquency-generating attitudes. Matza states:

> The major meanings of fairness are captured, I believe in the following assertions: it is only fair that some steps be taken to ascertain whether I was really the wrongdoer (cognizance); it is only fair that I be treated according to the same principles as others of my status (consistency); it is only fair that you who pass judgment on me sustain the right to do so (competence); it is only fair that some relationship obtain between the magnitude of what I have done and what you propose to do to me (commensurability); it is only fair that differences between the treatment of my status and others be reasonable and tenable (comparison). Each of these statements poses an elementary component of justice.[5]

According to Matza, youths processed by the traditional juvenile court have good reason to feel that their treatment violates these basic criteria of fairness or justice. The proceeding is vague and inconsistent, and perhaps, in the eyes of some beholders, hypocritical and incompetent. It is hardly surprising then, Matza contends, if most youths judge those passing judgment in terms as harsh as those applied to themselves, and condemn the entire system of supposed "justice," which represents, in the youth's eyes, middle-class society.

While Matza's interpretation was based largely on general observation rather than on "hard" data, his argument makes sense in terms of what we do know about both youthful attitudes and the workings of the juvenile justice mechanisms. Findings from more recent empirical studies are inconclusive. In general, the argument that the court experience creates confusion seems to be valid. As we noted earlier, the organization of the juvenile justice system is very complex; it reflects a multiplicity of goals, conflicting interests, and the tensions between personnel with highly varying personal backgrounds and social and professional attitudes. The following statement is by a judge who is involved in juvenile work:

There has been a complete breakdown in communications between the personnel who work in juvenile court—breakdown between judges and social workers, between social workers and psychiatrists, between the probation officers and all these groups, and the juvenile officers . . . —a breakdown in communciation between the parties representing the various disciplines that appear in the juvenile courts.[6]

Interviews with children who actually have gone through the court procedure indicate that it is very difficult for them to understand what is going on. A recent research report quoted the following as typical of such reactions:

I couldn't understand anything he said. The only thing I understood was "you're committed." Everything else was a bunch of mumble-jumble. He went on and on a mile a minute and you sit there twiddling your thumbs and waiting for what he says . . . you're just listening for the main word, you're either committed or you're going home. You don't listen to that other stuff. They just said they didn't want to send me here [the Reception Center, where the interview occurred], that they didn't want to do it, that's all. I thought that was a bunch of baloney that they didn't want to send me here.[7]

In a related study, processed delinquents expressed extremely negative feelings about the entire court experience, although at the same time they did not claim that they had been unfairly treated.[8] These reactions probably vary a great deal from court to court, and from judge to judge. One investigation has indicated that the child's sense of participation in the proceedings (especially the extent to which he is allowed to speak) greatly influences his evaluation of the proceedings.[9]

. . . This double critique—focusing both on specific labeling processes and on broader questions of the entire system's legitimacy—has been aimed at another major agency of social control over youth, the schools. . . . The radical noninterventionist would point out the ways in which schools promote delinquency by early labeling of kids as troublemakers, and would question the legitimacy of the educational system's goals as well as its means.

Much of the labeling that occurs in schools varies according to the outlooks and practices adopted by individual teachers. The teacher is always in a crucial position to shape the student's course of development:

. . . what is made of an act depends almost entirely on how it is defined and evaluated by the teacher, including the issue of whether or not the act is a violation of the basic authority rule. The boy is using the teacher to define himself as autonomous, and, like his behavior on the streets, he often creates or provokes the situation in which he then defends his honor. Yet if a teacher is willing to concede the fact that school is meaningless to some boys and therefore that other activities besides "teaching and learning" will necessarily go on in class, and if he is willing to limit the scope of his jurisdiction to the activity of "teaching and learning" itself, then his authority is likely to remain intact, regardless of how much it may be "tested." Whether or not he wishes to persuade the boys to join the learning process is another matter. . . .[10]

All too often, unfortunately, an overriding concern with matters other than "teaching and learning" has meant that, "the balance has traditionally been on the side of debasement, exclusion, and locking out, rather than on the side of respect, reinvolvement, and recommitment of the misbehaving student."[11] Narrow conceptions regarding the potential learning capacities of large numbers of students, and individualistic and moralistic outlooks on disruptive behavior, abet this tendency.

Such processes, however, are not simply a result of the misguided efforts of individual teachers. Both the structure and the goals of the school system are heavily implicated. Unintended consequences of the so-called "tracking" or ability-grouping systems now employed so widely in our schools are particularly noteworthy. This procedure, by definition a labeling process, is almost bound to have undesirable social psychological side-effects. These dangers have been revealed by recent experimental research in which students' IQ scores and grades directly varied according to the nature of the information about their "prospects" provided to their teachers.[12] One analysis of tracking concludes that "if, as often claimed, American teachers underestimate the learning potential of low-track students and expect more negative attitudes and greater trouble from them, it may well be that they partially cause the very failure, alienation, lack of involvement, dropping out, and rebellion they are seeking to prevent."[13] Closely related to the tracking system are the activities of school counselors, recently subjected to an intensive sociological analysis. According to the authors of that study:

> In a bureaucratically organized school . . . the classification of students routinely initiates organizational actions that may progressively define and limit the development of such [student] careers. From this perspective, the criteria employed in the evaluation process, the information considered relevant and recorded, the interpretations made of such information, and the organizationally defined categories by which students are classified are important for an understanding of how the school produces senior students who are or are not qualified for college entrance, "highly recommended" or "poor prospects," "well-rounded personalities" or "maladjusted."[14] . . .

Increasingly, these selection and labeling processes begin very early in the school careers of children, and display a largely cumulative course. The self-fulfilling nature of such labeling is difficult for the child to reverse or overcome, and school records (both of academic work and of other behavior patterns) are, like hospital or court records, reinforced by the process of retrospective interpretation. These records follow the child throughout his school career and significantly affect the options open to him at various stages. In this sense, then, the schools—like the police and the courts—help produce "delinquents."

Basic goals of the school system also are being questioned in various analyses of youth problems. Beyond the enforced cultural assimilation to white middle-class values and norms that even the reformists might condemn, radical critics contend that the educational system must be challenged for socializing youngsters to live as members of what they see as a morally bankrupt way of life. The schools have become one more example (along with prisons and "training schools") of the self-alienating bureaucratic "total institutions" that dominate technocratic society. From all of these standpoints, it is questionable whether the schools—even when they are efficiently and fairly administered and staffed—are likely to meet the real needs of young people. An argument has long been made that schools may not be for everybody, that to some extent continued schooling represents an unwanted exclusion from adult responsibility, and that alternatives to compulsory schooling for older youths ought [to] be given more serious consideration.[15] Currently, radical educationists attribute many if not most of our social ills to compulsory schooling, and argue for a general "deschooling" of society. One of the major spokesmen for this position, Ivan Illich, asserts:

> If we do not challenge the assumption that valuable knowledge is a commodity which under certain circumstances may be forced into the consumer, society will be increasingly dominated by sinister pseudo-schools and totalitarian managers of information. Pedagogical therapists will drug their pupils more in order to teach them better, and students will drug themselves more to gain relief from the pressures of teachers and the race for certificates.[16]

This is well confirmed by developing tendencies in the treatment of, and reactions by, American youth.

TOWARD NEW PRIORITIES

. . . One point seems very clear: there is no single program that constitutes *the* solution to problems of youthful misconduct, nor can we realistically expect one to emerge suddenly. There is not even a readily identifiable combination of programs that would quickly and effectively reduce delinquency on a broad scale. However, there is a lesson to be learned from the process by which we reach that conclusion. Our energies and commitment ought no longer to be squandered in a futile search for simplistic answers, either in public policy or in "causal theory." There is no point in arguing endlessly about whether detached worker programs are better than guided group interaction schemes, just as there is only limited benefit to be derived from determining the exact social psychological mechanisms that lead individual children into delinquent behavior.

Furthermore, while it is apparent that many of the present programs do have some real but limited value, the processes by which particular programs are selected in the various jurisdictions reflect more than just rational assessment according to established criteria of effectiveness. Organizational need and vested interest, and the conflicting general perspectives on delinquency and juvenile justice necessarily influence policy-making in this field. Not that there is no room for rational planning. An enormous number of highly specific policies are now being chosen; obviously, the greatest possible wisdom should be brought to bear on these decisions. However, what is most needed at this juncture is a very broad perspective that can guide policy-making at all levels. Certain general conclusions and broad lines of priority immediately suggest themselves.

1. *There is need for a thorough reassessment of the dominant ways of thinking about youth "problems."* We can no longer afford the comforting illusion that these problems are completely attributable to identifiable individuals—whether we label them "bad," "sick," or "socially disadvantaged." The behavior patterns in question are part and parcel of our social and cultural system, and any efforts to change them must take that centrally into account. Youthful "misconduct," like misconduct generally, is inevitable under any form of social order. There is some leeway to influence the extent and forms of misconduct that prevail under a particular set of social conditions, but this influence can only operate as a consequence of efforts to shape the broader sociocultural and definitional contexts that the behavior reflects. From this standpoint the specific youth "problems" we now experience have to be recognized as one of the prices we pay for maintaining a particular kind of social structure and dominant value system. We have to consider whether it is worth paying the price. We may conclude on sober reflection that we have greatly and unnecessarily exaggerated the price; that we accept some of this behavior instead of considering it socially problematic and trying to "solve" it by legal methods. In some instances, we may feel that the price paid is so high and so alarming that major changes in our social and cultural systems are necessary.

2. *Some of the most valuable policies for dealing with delinquency are not necessarily those designated as delinquency policies.* This follows from the fact that delinquency reflects more general sociocultural conditions. Yet . . . we "compartmentalize" crime and delinquency phenomena. Somehow, when we try to remake our socioeconomic order and reshape our dominant cultural values, we do not feel that we are confronting the specifically disturbing behavior we call delinquency. The impact of such efforts must be indirect, and perhaps

incomplete, but we would do well to heed the following recent comment: "the construction of a just system of criminal justice in an unjust society is a contradiction in terms."[17] Since delinquency and juvenile justice are in some degree inherently political phenomena, major changes in this area necessarily require broad political decisions.

3. *We must take young people more seriously if we are to eradicate injustice to juveniles.* There is some evidence that the most potent deterrent to delinquency lies in bonds of attachment to conventional society. Perhaps we should concentrate more on strengthening those bonds than on combating "criminogenic" forces that supposedly have a hold on our children. This, in turn, implies not only the creation of a more just and egalitarian society, but also a legal system that young people can respect, and above all, a sense among young people that the society respects them. It is not necessary that we all join the counterculture. But our acceptance of cultural pluralism (as in racial and ethnic matters) must also govern our attitudes and policies toward youth. Our traditional reactions to youth and our definitions of youth problems have been very ambivalent—fear and envy mixed with admiration and fond concern.[18] Indeed, the fact that adults see youth as a "problem" reflects this outlook. Sane youth policies will have to be based on greater acceptance of young people on their own terms, a willingness to live with a variety of life styles, and a recognition of the fact that the young people of our society are not necessarily confused, troubled, sick, or vicious. These attitudes cannot emerge within the context of the present juvenile justice system, with its paternalistic, patronizing, even hostile philosophy.

4. *The juvenile justice system should concern itself less with the problems of so-called "delinquents," and more with dispensing justice.* A major first step in this direction would be to greatly narrow the present jurisdiction of the juvenile court. It is significant that even the President's Crime Commission, a far from "radical" body, has made such a recommendation: "in view of the serious stigma and the uncertain gain accompanying official action, serious consideration should be given complete elimination from the court's jurisdiction of conduct illegal only for a child."[19] But beyond this, the entire conception of "individualized justice" requires reassessment. In combination with the vagueness of delinquency statutes, the enormous amount of discretion vested in officials at the various stages of delinquency-processing invites uncertainty and confusion and sets the stage for discriminatory practices. Nor does the basic notion of "treating" the child's broad problems, rather than reacting to a specific law violation, appear to further the aim of "rehabilitation" in any meaningful way. In fact the sense of injustice to which this approach gives rise may, as we have

seen, actively reinforce attitudes that breed delinquency. The authors of *Struggle for Justice* are right when they insist:

> The whole person is not the concern of the law. Whenever the law considers a whole person, it is more likely that it considers factors irrelevant to the purpose of delivering punishment. The other factors, by and large, have been and will certainly continue to be characteristics related to influence, power, wealth, and class. They will not be factors related to the needs or the treatment potentialities of the defendant.[20]

Individualized justice must necessarily give way to a *return to the rule of law.* This means that while fewer types of youthful behavior will be considered legal offenses, in cases of really serious misconduct such traditional guidelines as *specificity, uniformity,* and *nonretroactivity* ought apply. Juvenile statutes should spell out very clearly just what kinds of behavior are legally proscribed, and should set explicit penalties for such violations (with perhaps some limited range of alternatives available to sentencing judges). This is quite consistent with what research has told us about the nature of delinquency causation and the efficacy of treatment, and carries the great advantage that it would increase clarity, ensure more equitable administration of justice, and would probably generate among young people greater respect for the legal system. Such measures would not constitute a "get tough" policy so much as a "deal evenly" one, and—it should again be emphasized—they would apply to a much narrower range of "offenses" than now exists. For those kinds of behavior that society is reluctant to simply "do nothing about," but for which a stern legal approach seems inappropriate, various "diversion" schemes . . . could be developed.

These policies would squarely face up to the euphemistic evasions that have characterized much of juvenile "justice" in the past, and they would state premises and goals candidly and decisively. It is not heartlessly conservative to recognize that there may be certain actions we wish to punish, provided the range of offenses is carefully circumscribed and the rules equitably administered. But most of the stern measures taken against young people have not been in their "best interests." Continuing to delude ourselves on that score can only impede the development of sane delinquency policy.

5. *As juvenile justice moves in new directions, a variety of approaches will continue to be useful.* Even if enough people with the power to effect legislative and judicial change become convinced that an entirely new approach along the lines I have indicated is needed, it will take time to reach that goal. While the system is moving in that direction (and I have tried to show that it already is), certain understandings that already are beginning to be part of the "conventional wisdom" in the delinquency field might well guide policy. With re-

spect to prevention programs, those with a collective or community focus should be preferred to those that single out and possibly stigmatize particular individuals. . . .

Notes

1. In this section I draw on ideas developed in my larger analysis of the labeling perspective. See Edwin M. Schur, *Labeling Deviant Behavior: Its Sociological Significance* (New York: Harper & Row, Publishers, 1971); for a collection of representative studies, see Earl Rubington and Martin Weinberg, eds., *Deviance: The Interactionist Perspective* (New York: The Macmillan Company, 1968).

2. Howard S. Becker, *Outsiders* (New York: Free Press, 1963), p. 9.

3. Frank Tannenbaum, *Crime and the Community* (Boston: Ginn & Company, 1938), pp. 19–20.

4. *Ibid.*, p. 477.

5. David Matza, *Delinquency and Drift*, (New York: Wiley and Sons, 1964), p. 106.

6. Quoted in Stanton Wheeler, Edna Bonacich, M. Richard Cramer, and Irving K. Zola, "Agents of Delinquency Control: A Comparative Analysis," in Stanton Wheeler, ed., *Controlling Delinquents* (New York: John Wiley & Sons, 1968), pp. 33–34.

7. Quoted in Martha Baum and Stanton Wheeler, "Becoming an Inmate," in Wheeler, ed., *Controlling Delinquents*, p. 166.

8. Brendan Maher, with Ellen Stein, "The Delinquent's Perception of the Law and the Community," *ibid.*

9. Paul D. Lipsitt, "The Juvenile Offender's Perceptions," *Crime and Delinquency*, 14 (January, 1968), 49–62.

10. Carl Werthman, "The Function of Social Definitions in the Development of Delinquent Careers," in President's Commission on Law Enforcement and Administration of Justice, *Task Force Report: Juvenile Delinquency and Youth Crime* (Washington, D.C.: United States Government Printing Office, 1967), p. 166.

11. Walter E. Schafer and Kenneth Polk, "Delinquency and the Schools," *ibid.*, p. 234.

12. Robert Rosenthal and Lenore Jacobson, *Pygmalion in the Classroom* (New York: Holt, Rinehart & Winston, Inc., 1968).

13. Walter E. Schafer, Carol Olexa, and Kenneth Polk, "Programmed for Social Class: Tracking in High School," in Polk and Schafer, *Schools and Delinquency*, pp. 46–47.

14. Aaron V. Cicourel and John I. Kitsuse, *The Educational Decision-Makers* (Indianapolis, Ind.: The Bobbs-Merrill Company, Inc., 1963), p. 75.

15. F. Musgrove, *Youth and the Social Order* (Bloomington: Indiana University Press, 1965).

16. Ivan Illich, *Deschooling Society,* Harrow Books (New York: Harper & Row, Publishers, 1972), p. 72.

17. American Friends Service Committee, Struggle for Justice: A Report on Crime and Punishment in America (New York: Hill and Wang, 1971), p. 16.

18. See Edgar Z. Friedenberg, *The Vanishing Adolescent,* Laurel Books (New York: Dell Publishing Company, 1962).

19. President's Commission on Law Enforcement and Administration of Justice, *Task Force Report,* p. 27.

20. *Struggle for Justice,* p. 147.

Selected References

Coleman, James William, "The Myth of Addiction," *Journal of Drug Issues* 6 (Spring 1976), pp. 135–41.
According to Coleman, drug users are influenced by the belief that they will develop a compulsive craving for narcotics, and much of their behavior stems from this belief. Thus, Coleman suggests, one way to tackle the problem of drug addiction and to lower the number of addicts is to get away from the stereotyped definition and image of drug addiction.

Friedson, Eliot, "Disability as Social Deviance," in Marvin B. Sussman (ed.), *Sociology and Rehabilitation,* Washington, D.C.: American Sociological Association, 1966, pp. 71–99.
With physical disability as a case in point, Friedson considers the role of official agencies in labeling deviants. Friedson shows how different official frameworks produce different estimates of the magnitude of the problem and hence influence the urgency and direction in which agencies try to solve the problem.

Green, Richard, "Homosexuality as a Mental Illness," *International Journal of Psychiatry* 10 (March 1972), pp. 77–128.
Green questions the practice of labeling homosexuality as a mental disturbance or abnormality. This article was published the year before the American Psychiatric Association moved in the direction urged by Green and voted to delete homosexuality from its list of disorders.

Grinspoon, Lester, *Marihuana Reconsidered,* Cambridge, Mass.: Harvard University Press, 1971.
Grinspoon urges the decriminalization of marihuana. Repressive laws, he argues, are more harmful to society than is marihuana use itself. Grinspoon is particularly concerned with the stigmatization of large numbers of young people and with the disrespect for the law that unnecessary criminalization brings.

Ohlin, Lloyd E., "The President's Commission on Law Enforcement and

Administration of Justice," in *Sociology and Public Policy: The Case of Presidential Commissions,* New York: Elsevier, 1975, pp. 93–115.
Ohlin considers the roles sociologists have played in helping to develop solutions to the crime problem. In particular, he calls attention to the great influence the labeling perspective has had in shaping many new programs.

Ryan, William, *Blaming the Victim,* New York: Pantheon Books, 1971.
Ryan critically examines the dynamics and consequences of teachers' labeling students according to academic potential and motivation and discusses the need for changes in the educational system.

Trice, Harrison M., and Paul M. Roman, "Delabeling, Relabeling, and Alcoholics Anonymous," *Social Problems* 17 (Spring 1970), pp. 538–46.
This article analyzes the factors involved in the success of Alcoholics Anonymous. Of central importance is the organization's effectiveness in getting the new member to accept the label "alcoholic." Thus, A. A. represents an interesting example of labeling as leading to rehabilitation, rather than merely to greater and greater secondary deviation.

Szasz, Thomas S., "The Ethics of Addiction," *International Journal of Psychiatry* 10 (March 1972), pp. 51–76.
Szasz's article (and replies from three experts in the field of drug addiction) focuses on what underlies the labels applied to drug use. The politics of drug prohibition and the need for changes in definition are also examined.

Questions for Discussion

1.   Do you agree with the arguments in favor of decriminalizing or reducing the penalties for marihuana use? Could the same arguments be applied to heroin? Why or why not?

2.   Do you agree with Schur's argument that the labeling of delinquents only reinforces their deviant tendencies? Can you think of other forms of deviance for which the same argument might be made? Do you think Schur is naive in thinking that boys will outgrow their delinquency if left alone?

3.   How do you think the readings in this chapter would be evaluated by someone employing the deviant behavior perspective? The social pathology perspective? How would a person using the labeling perspective describe the programs described in Chapter 5?

4.   How do you evaluate the labeling perspective and the type of solutions it suggests? What contemporary social problems do you believe are best dealt with by the labeling perspective? Can you think of any contemporary social problems to which the labeling perspective would not apply?

III / THE PROSPECTS

7 / THE MOSAIC OF SOLUTIONS

So far we have reviewed the five perspectives most commonly used by sociologists in analyzing and proposing solutions for social problems. Sometimes the use of a particular perspective is explicit, as when a sociologist devises a program for juvenile delinquents modeled along the lines suggested by the deviant behavior perspective. In other cases a particular perspective may be used only implicitly. For instance, activists may urge welfare recipients to unite and confront their opponents, without necessarily being aware that they are using what sociologists call the value conflict perspective. In either case, it is not always predictable which perspective will be applied to a particular problem, or whether the diagnosis and the proposed solution will even employ the same perspective. Indeed, the interrelationships between the five perspectives are often rather complex. Before considering these interrelationships, however, let us briefly review the major themes and characteristics of each perspective.

THE FIVE PERSPECTIVES: A RAPID REVIEW

Social Pathology. From this perspective, social problems are situations or conditions that offend one's moral sensibilities or, in the more recent version of this perspective, that are dehumanizing. They are produced by "sick" individuals or a "sick" society. How can social problems be solved? In the early version of social pathology, which blamed social problems on sick or inferior individuals, the answer was to teach such people a higher standard of morality and middle-class values. If they were uneducable (e.g., because of "bad blood"), the solution was thought to lie in segregation and sterilization, so that at least they could not spread their pathology to the rest of society.

The more recent version of the social pathology perspective sees social problems as manifestations of dehumanizing social conditions and institutions. Early social pathologists suggested that individuals be changed to better fit into society, while modern social pathologists suggest that individuals develop a heightened sensitivity to basic human needs and that society be changed to better fulfill those needs.

Social Disorganization.   Because of culture conflict, normlessness, or breakdown of rules, social institutions and relationships become uncoordinated, individuals become frustrated, social controls break down, and a variety of social problems ensue. For the most part, these situations come about as a result of rapid or uncontrolled social change that throws things into a state of disequilibrium.

In the social disorganization perspective, the key to solving social problems lies in developing a clear, consistent, and effective set of rules, slowing the pace of social change, and bringing the system back into synchrony. As situations become more predictable and more in tune with the rest of the social system, social problems will be reduced.

Value Conflict.   According to this perspective, different groups naturally have different values. When these values collide and one group begins to feel threatened, a social problem arises; and in these situations, it is usually the group with the most power that wins.

According to the value conflict perspective, group solidarity is the key to successfully resolving social problems. People with this approach usually advocate that groups address social problems by uniting, organizing, and actively confronting their opponents. Marx and Engels's famous slogan, "Workers of the world, unite!" illustrates this. The solution to a particular social problem may range all the way from arbitration and compromise to open rebellion or group domination.

Deviant Behavior.   Social problems, from this point of view, are caused by people breaching social norms—i.e., engaging in "deviant" behaviors. Such people may engage in illicit behaviors because they lack the opportunities for accomplishing their goals by accepted means. The presence of deviant opportunities (e.g., in a deviant subculture) may also play a key role in promoting deviant activities. And of course peer influences are important in determining whether one will utilize legitimate or illegitimate opportunities.

This perspective suggests three courses of action for solving social problems. First, so-called deviants should be given greater opportunities to succeed in more conventional ways—e.g., through education, a good job, social acceptance. Second, deviant opportunities should be curtailed—e.g., by cracking down on deviant subcultures and businesses. Third, persons who engage in deviant behaviors, such as convicted felons or known juvenile delinquents, should be placed in groups where their peers encourage them to behave in more conventional and acceptable ways and punish them for behaving in deviant ways.

Labeling. According to this perspective, social problems are situations that have been effectively *labeled* as bad or harmful. Until it is recognized and labeled, a situation is not, from this perspective, a social problem; once labeled, a situation is a social problem. Thus a social problem is defined by how people view it, rather than by how harmful it may be from an objective point of view.

Such labeling may be carried out by official agents of social control (e.g., police or legislators) or by moral crusaders who take it upon themselves to convince the public that their own values and views are the right ones (e.g., Right-to-Lifers). Labeling a particular situation or group as criminal, sinful, or otherwise bad, however, sometimes creates even greater problems than it solves. Labeling an individual, for instance, may simply reinforce whatever deviant tendencies s/he may have had to begin with. And passing laws against behavior that many people enjoy (e.g., drinking or gambling) is likely to produce a criminal subculture, profits for organized crime, and police corruption, as well as turning many ordinary citizens into "criminals" and breeding disrespect for the law.

From the labeling perspective, many social problems can be reduced by redefining the problematic situation. Get rid of the unnecessary laws, particularly those prohibiting activities that many people will continue to engage in anyway (e.g., prostitution, gambling, homosexuality). In addition, this approach suggests, agents of social control, as well as ordinary people, should be very cautious about applying deviant and stigmatizing labels to others (e.g., "delinquent," "mentally ill," "subversive").

Thus, each of the five perspectives has its own emphasis for diagnosing and solving social problems. The social pathology perspective suggests solving social problems primarily through *moral education*; the social disorganization perspective stresses the need for better *rules*; the value conflict perspective urges *group action*; the deviant behavior perspective concentrates on *resocialization*; and the labeling perspective recommends *changing definitions* and *caution in labeling*.

ALTERNATIVES AND INTERRELATIONS

From these five perspectives, a variety of solutions can be generated for any given social problem. The following are examples of *actual proposals suggested by citizens or government officials to address the problem of poverty in the United States and the massive welfare bureaucracy that has been created to deal with it.* From the proposals, it can be seen that the different perspectives can produce quite different proposals indeed.

Social Pathology.   According to the early social pathologists, the poor are shiftless and lazy; they lack the proper moral values and work ethic. The problem of poverty, it was assumed, could be solved by teaching the poor these values—e.g., in settlement houses. More recently it has been suggested that the welfare bureaucracy only reinforces poor work attitudes and thus produces further generations of poor people. Some have proposed that welfare mothers be forced to take jobs, and others have suggested that the government pay poor people to limit their family size or that welfare mothers be sterilized!

   Several contemporary sociologists using the modern social pathology approach make quite different recommendations. They see capitalism as the root problem and advocate some form of socialism as a healthier and more humane economic system. Poverty and welfare bureaucracy, they imply, would cease to be a problem in a socialist state.

Social Disorganization.   The New York City Welfare Department in the early 1970s had a budget of $2 billion and a staff of 27,000 employees. Yet the department faced massive problems because of its own social disorganization. It had a backlog of unprocessed forms involving nearly $20 million a year, long delays in catching recipients who cashed duplicate checks (after claiming that the originals had been lost), and a high rate of worker inefficiency. To reduce this disorganization, a new executive director instituted a quota system to improve worker efficiency, overtime to reduce the backlog of paperwork, and a new computer system to speed up the identification of duplicate check cashers.

Value Conflict. For too long welfare recipients have assumed that they are powerless, and so they have put up with an inefficient bureaucracy with little outward protest. To try to remedy this situation, in 1966 an activist named George Wiley (a Ph.D. in chemistry) helped welfare recipients form an organization called the National Welfare Rights Organization. The purpose of this organization was to publicize the conditions under which people are entitled to welfare assistance and to get recipients to band together to protest aspects of the system that they dislike.

Deviant Behavior. As part of President Lyndon Johnson's "War on Poverty," a number of programs were set up to provide poor people with expanded opportunities for education and job training. These included Headstart, the Job Corps, and various loan programs for post-secondary education. By providing greater opportunities for poor people, it was assumed, welfare rolls could be reduced.

Labeling. Part of the problem with current welfare systems, labeling theorists charge, is the stigma that goes along with being on welfare. This stigma is a blow to recipients' self-esteem and leads others to disrespect them as well. In recent years an increasing number of citizens and politicians have suggested a redefinition of public welfare. Rather than using the term welfare payments, for instance, they suggested calling it income maintenance. And rather than defining such payments as a substitute for earned income, they could be redefined as an income supplement. These changes are aimed at upholding poor people's self-image and sense of integrity while also encouraging them to earn what money they can without a cut-off of payments.

The different perspectives, then, are likely to suggest quite different solutions for a particular social problem. It is not always easy to say which of the alternative solutions is best. Each is likely to involve a different set of costs and rewards and to address a different facet of the problem. What one group regards as a minor aspect of the problem may be of paramount importance to another, and a terrific solution for one aspect (and one group) may leave another aspect untouched or even make it worse. One solution may hold real promise for long-term effectiveness, yet another may seem more desirable because it is easier to implement or meets less opposition. One solution may be very pragmatic, while another is more appealing morally or symbolically. Thus, evaluations of alternative proposals depend on the evaluator's own specific concerns and what trade-offs one is willing to make.

A variety of alternative solutions representing different perspectives is probably most likely to be found for social problems that are large-scale and complex and that involve many different groups, both lay and professional. While it can be confusing ("Even the experts can't agree!"), such a variety may provide fertile ground for forming a truly comprehensive program when different approaches are combined to attack different aspects of the problem.

The perspectives can be combined in other ways as well. Sometimes one perspective is used to diagnose a problem while another is used to formulate a solution. Both the deviant behavior and value conflict perspectives, for instance, are very fertile for suggesting concrete and manageable plans of action, and they are often used to generate solutions for social problems initially diagnosed or conceptualized from another perspective. Several observers, for instance, have denounced poverty from a social pathology perspective but then advocated a value conflict solution. In this view, poverty is a dehumanizing condition resulting from a "sick" economic order; to solve the problem poor people should band together and take action in their own behalf, including disruption and confrontation when necessary.

Another illustration is provided by the homosexual rights movement. Gay activists often combine a diagnosis from the labeling perspective with proposed solutions from the value conflict perspective. The problem, they claim, is that society has labeled homosexuality sick, sinful, and in many jurisdictions criminal. Homosexuality is simply a normal sexual variation, they argue, but because it is so stigmatized homosexual men and women suffer needless guilt, anxiety, and discrimination (e.g., in employment and housing). The solution they advocate is for homosexuals to unite, organize, and exert political power.

In various self-help organizations we see still another combination: a social pathology diagnosis and a deviant behavior solution. In Alcoholics Anonymous, for instance, the initial problem is seen as an individual weakness or sickness (alcoholism is viewed as an allergic reaction), while the cure is seen as coming from association with others in a supportive peer group.

Any number of combinations are possible. Yet we can make certain generalizations about the kind of combinations that are most likely to occur. There seems to be a natural affinity between the value conflict and labeling perspectives. The people who use one are likely to feel sympathetic toward or also use the other. Both of these seem to be especially applicable to problems arising from cultural diversity— i.e., from the fact that there are different groups in the society with different, and often conflicting, values and lifestyles. These two perspectives also seem especially applicable to problems that are controversial. They tend to be used in dealing with situations less serious than, say, murder or rape and are more likely to be invoked in dealing with such marginal problems as public smoking or vice laws. Finally, both of these approaches seem to be used by people with "underdog" sympathies.

There also seems to be a natural affinity between the social disorganization and deviant behavior perspectives. In a sense, one implies the other—social disorganization produces deviant behavior, and deviant behavior in turn is the basis for identifying states of social disorganization. Proponents of these views tend to hold rather conventional views of morality and conformity and to be more politically conservative than those using the value conflict or labeling perspectives. Social disorganization and deviant behavior are often applied to situations that are regarded as problems by most people, or at least by the dominant groups in the society— e.g., problems of juvenile delinquency and unemployment.

Finally, a number of different perspectives may be used in succession as attempted solutions in turn produce their own social problems. A classic example can be seen in the events surrounding Prohibition. During the late 1800s and early 1900s, opponents of liquor, who were for the most part rural Anglo-Saxon Protestants, banded together and fought for a law to prohibit the manufacture and sale of liquor—In short, they used a value conflict approach to enact their own values into law. In 1920, with the passage of the Eighteenth Amendment, they succeeded in attaining this goal. Soon, however, it became clear that this "solution" was generating a host of new problems. Illegal drinking became a popular pastime, and otherwise law-abiding citizens began to flout the law. A black market developed and organized crime flourished. Political and police corruption grew. In short, a "solution" from the value conflict perspective merely served to generate other problems from the labeling, social disorganization, and deviant behavior perspectives, and in a decade, the amendment was repealed. In the long run, we often see a sequence of perspectives being employed as people attempt to cope with problems, solutions, and the further problems that those solutions generate.

CONCLUDING NOTES

We have seen some of the ways that the five perspectives can be used, singly or in combination, for analyzing social problems and attempting to solve them. In the future, some new perspectives might arise as conditions change in sociology and in the society. Or there might be a resurgence and revision of one of the perspectives already established, as we have seen in recent years with the social pathology perspective. Whatever the case, we would venture to make a few predictions about the conditions under which different types of perspectives might have most appeal.

In so doing, it is relevant to consider two basic and interlocking themes in sociology: social order and social conflict. During some periods, sociologists tend to emphasize order and let conflict fall into the background; at other periods the reverse is true. This change in focus seems to parallel the fortunes of the larger society. During times of turmoil and strife, for instance, sociologists and lay people alike tend to emphasize conflict. The late 1960s is an example of one such time. Yet during times when social life seems to go smoothly, as in the 1950s, sociologists emphasize order and social integration. In the future, we would expect this pattern to continue. During periods of conflict people will probably gravitate toward the "new" social pathology, value conflict, and labeling perspectives, while the "old" social pathology, social disorganization, and deviant behavior perspectives will probably be most popular during periods of decreased social conflict. As society continues to become increasingly complex and as scholars and citizens become more aware of social problems, we would guess that an increasing number of problems will be approached using several perspectives at once. Readers should be on the alert for the perspectives that underlie proposed solutions and should recognize their implicit values, assumptions, and models of reality. And whether as a professional sociologist or an informed citizen, the reader should always view proposals with a critical eye and with an awareness that so-called solutions sometimes cause more problems than they solve.

Selected References

Etzioni, Amitai, *The Active Society: A Theory of Societal and Political Processes,* New York: The Free Press, 1968.
Etzioni believes that society can define and actively control and solve its own problems. In this book he sets forth the theoretical model by which this can be accomplished.

Freeman, Howard E., and Clarence, C. Sherwood, *Social Research and Social Policy,* Englewood Cliffs, N.J.: Prentice-Hall, 1970.
Freeman and Sherwood provide a brief statement of how to link problem-solving policies with systematic research on the consequences of such intervention.

Hastings, William M., *How to Think about Social Problems.* New York: Oxford, 1979.
The author wrote this book as a primer for citizens. His intention was to help people to think clearly and simply about social problems and how to solve them.

Lazarsfeld, Paul F., William H. Sewell, and Harold L. Wilensky (eds.), *The Uses of Sociology*, New York: Basic Books, 1967.
This collection assesses potential and actual applications of sociological knowledge to the solution of social problems and problems associated with such applications.

Lynd, Robert S., *Knowledge for What?* Princeton: Princeton University Press, 1939.
Lynd says that social scientists can maintain their ethics and objectivity, but only if they produce knowledge that helps in solving social problems.

Manis, Jerome G., *Analyzing Social Problems,* New York: Praeger, 1976.
Manis reviews several paradigms for viewing social problems and then presents his own objectivist definition of social problems: "Social problems are those social conditions identified by scientific inquiry and values as detrimental to human well-being." He discusses his own position and how people can identify, assess, and solve social problems.

Reynolds, Larry T., and Janice M. Reynolds (eds.), *The Sociology of Sociology: Analysis and Criticism of the Thought, Research, and Ethical Folkways of Sociology and Its Practitioners,* New York: David McKay, 1970.
This book presents a collection of papers demonstrating that the definition and solution of social problems by sociologists is actually a "social problem" within the field of sociology itself.

Shostak, Arthur B., *Modern Social Reforms: Solving Today's Social Problems.* New York: Macmillan, 1974.

The author presents a "cookbook of reform," a collection of "recipes" for solving many old as well as new social problems.

Shostak, Arthur B. (ed.), *Putting Sociology to Work: Case Studies in the Application of Sociology to Modern Social Problems.* New York: David McKay, 1974.

A collection of twenty-four essays documenting sociologists' experiences in trying to help people solve social problems.

Questions for Discussion

1.   Now that you are familiar with all five perspectives, which one(s) do you find most useful for devising possible solutions to contemporary social problems? Why? Does the usefulness of each perspective depend on which particular social problem you are trying to solve? If so, how? If not, why not?

2.   Consider several social problems currently discussed in the mass media or among your acquaintances. Delineate the various solutions you have heard proposed for these problems. Can you identify the perspective(s) underlying these proposed solutions? On the basis of what you have learned from this book, how would you evaluate the various proposed solutions?

3.   To what extent do the solutions suggested by these five perspectives overlap? What are the major conflicts between solutions suggested by the different perspectives?

4.   Using some social problem that interests you, analyze the problem from each of the five perspectives and outline a solution from each perspective. What are the major differences between your five solutions? Which do you prefer? Now provide an *eclectic* solution, using elements from a number of perspectives.